Operas & Plays

Operas & Plays
Gertrude Stein

Foreword by James R. Mellow

STATION HILL PRESS

Published by Station Hill Press, Inc., Barrytown, NY 12507, with grateful acknowledgment to the National Endowment for the Arts, a federal agency in Washington, DC, and the New York State Council on the Arts, for partial financial support of this project.

Distributed by The Talman Co., Inc., 150 Fifth Ave., New York, NY 10011.

Produced by the Institute for Publishing Arts, a not-for-profit, tax-exempt organization.

Designed by Susan Quasha and George Quasha.

Grateful acknowledgment is extended to the Collection of American Literature, the Beinecke Rare Book and Manuscript Library, Yale University, for permission to reproduce photographs from the collection used on the cover of this book. Back cover photograph was made by Alvin Langdon Coburn in 1913.

Library of Congress Cataloging-in-Publication Data

Stein, Gertrude, 1874-1946.
  Operas & plays.

  I. Title. II. Title: Operas and plays.
PS3537.T32306   1987   812'.52   87-1868
ISBN 0-88268-039-0

Manufactured in the United States of America.

CONTENTS

Foreword

THE WORD PLAYS OF
GERTRUDE STEIN

The theater of Gertrude Stein is as radical today as it was seventy or more years ago when, in the course of her early experiments, Stein started writing her odd word plays. These theatrical exercises—which began, she tells us, with "What Happened: A Play"; a play in which nothing happens—soon developed into a dramaturgy stripped bare of the essentials: plot, character development, scenery, stage directions. Even the dramatic structure, if it could be called that, did not clearly distinguish between scenes and acts. What was left was the actor (not always identifiable) and the written word.

The operas and plays of this volume (first published in 1932 by Stein herself in her privately printed Plain Edition) range over the unconventional and controversial specimens of her work from 1913 to 1931. They are literally—and literarily—"word plays," clear evidence of Stein's intention of making the word the prevailing element of her theatrical enterprise. It was also indicative of Stein's high spirits as a dramatist that she made extensive use of puns that are ingenious and/or banal: can tickle for canticle (in "Saints And Singing"), jonquils and a character named John Quilly (in "A Lyrical Opera").

There are plays in which a single act might consist of a single sentence and in which Act I may occur forty six times before the play progresses to Acts II and III—which are similarly repeated. There are gossipy, name-dropping plays in which famous friends and acquaintances—Picasso, Eugene Berman, Andre Masson, Virgil Thomson, for instance—arrive on the scene, much as they might have done at Stein's legendary studio on the rue de Fleurus. ("At Present: Nothing But Contemporaries Allowed.") In "Objects Lie On A Table," it appears, she attempted to make a play on the subject of a still life.

The actors' lines, in monologue or dialogue, may issue from some unidentified voice or consist of a random stage direction. Sometimes they are merely Stein's remarks about a character, "Therese. Has not arrived in her place" ("Civilization"); or her comments on her progress in writing the play; "It is going on nicely"—an abrupt convergence of the time in the play with the real time of the author. ("They Must. Be Wedded. To Their Wife.") And there are lines which, coming from out of the blue,

> Calm yourself Emil, you are not widowed yet. ("Saints And Singing")
> I am the daughter of enthusiasm. ("Reread Another")
> A blonde boy can be appointed and maltreated by West Point Cadets. ("A Bouquet. Their Wills.")

open up momentary glimpses of clear understanding in the general confusion. But in Stein plays, generally, characters declaim, ruminate, recite, reminisce and, much of the time, speak past one another. They seldom engage in the direct confrontation or physical action that we ordinarily expect in conventional drama. Well before Beckett or Pinter, Stein immobilized her characters in talk, talk, talk.

There was a method to her madness. Plot and action would have involved her in detailed scenarios and climactic denouements, imposing a conventional structure which she wanted to avoid. (Yet it is worth remembering that Stein could be contradictory in her intentions. Her play, "A Movie," included here, is pure Chaplinesque scenario.) In her 1935 lecture "Plays" (still the essential explication of her dramatic intentions), Stein explained her aims for the play "What Happened"—a play inspired by a dinner party she had attended. Stein maintained that she had wanted to make a play "without telling what happened, in short to make a play the essence of what happened." Therefore she dispensed with a story-line: "What is the use of telling a story since there are so many and everybody knows so many and tells so many." And without the story line, the divisions of acts and scenes became more or less arbitrary. By discarding the conventional beginning, middle and end, she hoped to create a state of continuous immediacy in which the audience would neither anticipate the future nor recall past action. To borrow a phrase from Picasso, for Stein, a play was "a sum of destructions."

Perversely, however, the most important of Stein's theater pieces included in *Operas and Plays*, the opera "Four Saints in Three Acts," written in collaboration with Virgil Thomson, succeeded because of its additions rather than its deletions. In the 1934 production, in addition to Thomson's vital and vibrant score, there was a scenario (provided by the painter Maurice Grosser); a ballet (choreographed by Frederick Ashton); and the customary scenery and decor (the famous cellophane set-design, created by Florine Stettheimer)—necessary amenities for a production that became one of the most talked-about theatrical ventures of the Depression years. Yet even those concessions testify to Stein's radical departure from the conventional theater.

The opera (especially in performance) strikes one as a *sacra conversazione* in the tradition of the Renaissance masters; saints in conversation, characters engaged in an uneventful moment out of time. (A moment that predicates an eternity of such pleasant moments). Appropriately enough, given its subject matter, "Four Saints" is pure joy as an operatic occasion—a rare phenomenon in the usual operatic repertoire of melodramatic plots and dire events.

It is true that many of Stein's hermetic texts resist complete explication. She remains an isolated and eccentric playwright. The plays, however, do respond to interpretations based on a knowledge of her life and her relationships. As in Picasso's Cubist paintings and collages, a bit of chair caning, the label from a bottle of *vieux marc*, a newspaper logo, amidst the chaos of disjunctive forms, reveal the subject as a still life, so in a Stein play, a name, a scrap of conversation, a flight of lyricism, yield up the parameters of a play. The irony is that, for all their avantgardism, Stein's plays, once the random clues have been detected, often turn out to be parlor dramas. She is a playwright with a penchant for domestic scenes. In "A Lyrical Opera Made By Two," for instance, the setting is suspiciously like the studio room at the rue de Fleurus with its rows of pictures and its chintz-covered armchairs. The "large medium sized pleasant handsome man" and "fair sized dark charming medium sized lady" are clearly stand-ins for Stein and her companion Alice B. Toklas, though translated into husband and wife. The references to Pussie (Alice's nickname), a birthday and April 30th (Alice's birthday) underscore such an interpretation, as do the terms of endearment. The line "Kiss my lips she did kiss my lips again she did kiss my lips over and over again she did," is a direct lift from one of Stein's earlier poems, "Lifting Belly," a poetic diary-account of her life and travels with Alice while they were distributing hospital supplies during World War I in France.

There is still much to be discovered in Stein's writing. Among the modernist writers, she still remains a last outpost for the industrious textual explication that has been devoted to her contemporary rival, James Joyce, and to the more celebrated playwrights like Beckett and Ionesco who came after her radical experiments in theatrical writing.

James R. Mellow
December 1, 1986

FOUR SAINTS

IN THREE ACTS

An Opera to be Sung

To know to know to love her so.

Four saints prepare for saints.

It makes it well fish.

Four saints it makes it well fish.

Four saints prepare for saints it makes it well well fish it makes it well fish prepare for saints.

In narrative prepare for saints.

Prepare for saints.

Two saints.

Four saints.

Two saints prepare for saints it two saints prepare for saints in prepare for saints.

A narrative of prepare for saints in narrative prepare for saints.

Remain to narrate to prepare two saints for saints.

At least.

In finally.

Very well if not to have and miner.

A saint is one to be for two when three and you make five and two and cover.

A at most.

Saint saint a saint.

Forgotten saint.

What happened to-day, a narrative.

We had intended if it were a pleasant day to go to the country it was a very beautiful day and we carried out our intention We went to places that we had been when we were equally pleased and we found very nearly what we could find and returning saw and heard that after all they were rewarded and likewise. This makes it necessary to go again.

He came and said he was hurrying hurrying and hurrying to remain he said he said finally to be and claim it he said he said feeling very nearly everything as it had been as if he could be precious be precious to like like it as it had been that if he was used it would always do it good and now this time that it was as if it had been just the same as longer when as before it made it be left to be more and soft softly then can be changed to theirs and speck a speck of it makes blue be often sooner which is shared when theirs is in polite and reply that in their be the same with diminish always in respect to not at all and farther farther might be known as counted with it gain to be in retain which it is not be because of most. This is how they do not like it.

Why while while in that way was it after this that to be seen made left it.

He could be hurt at that.

It is very easy to be land.

Imagine four benches separately.

One in the sun.

Two in the sun.

Three in the sun.

One not in the sun.

Not one not in the sun.

Not one.

Four benches used four benches used separately.

Four benches used separately.

That makes it be not be makes it not be at the time.

The time that it is as well as it could be leave it when when it was to be that it was to be when it was went away.

Four benches with leave it.

Might have as would be as would be as within within nearly as out. It is very close close and closed. Closed closed to let letting closed close close close chose in justice in join in joining. This is where to be at at water at snow snow show show one one sun and sun snow show and no water no water unless unless why unless. Why unless why unless they were loaning it here loaning intentionally. Believe two three. What could be sad beside beside very attentively intentionally and bright.

Begin suddenly not with sisters.

If a great many people were deceived who would be by the way.

To mount it up.

Up hill.

Four saints are never three.

Three saints are never four.
Four saints are never left altogether.
Three saints are never idle.
Four saints are leave it to me.
Three saints when this you see.
Begin three saints.
Begin four saints.
Two and two saints.
One and three saints.
In place.
One should it.
Easily saints.
Very well saints.
Have saints.
Said saints.
As said saints.
And not annoy.
Annoint.
Choice.
Four saints two at a time have to have to have to have to.
Have to have have to have to.
Two saints four at a time a time.
Have to have to at a time.
Four saints have to have to have at a time.
The difference between saints forget me nots and mountains have to have to have to at a time.
It is very easy in winter to remember winter spring and summer it is very easy in winter to remember spring and winter and summer it is very easy in winter to remember summer spring and winter it is very easy in winter to remember spring and summer and winter.
Does it show as if it could be that very successful that very successful that he was very successful that he was with them with them with them as it was not better than at worst that he could follow him to be taking it away away that way a way a way to go.
Some say some say some say so.
Why should every one be at home why should every one be at home why should every one be at home.
Why should every one be at home.
In idle acts.
Why should everybody be at home.
In idle acts.

He made very much more than he did he did make very much of it he did not only add to his part of it but and with it he was at and in a plight.

There is no parti parti-color in a house there is no parti parti parti color in a house. Reflections by the time that they were given the package that had been sent. Very much what they could would do as a decision.

Supposing she said that he had chosen all the miseries that he had observed in fifty of his years what had that to do with hats. They had made hats for her. Not really.

As she was.

Imagine imagine it imagine it in it. When she returned there was considerable rain.

In some on some evening it would be asked was there anything especial.

By and by plain plainly in making acutely a corner not at right angle but in individual in individual is it.

How can it have been have been held.

A narrative who do who does.

A narrative to plan an opera.

Four saints in three acts.

A croquet scene and when they made their habits. Habits not hourly habits habits not hourly at the time that they made their habits not hourly they made their habits.

When they made their habits.

To know when they made their habits.

Large pigeons in small trees.

Large pigeons in small trees.

Come panic come.

Come close.

Acts three acts.

Come close to croquet.

Four saints.

Rejoice saints rejoin saints recommence some reinvite.

Four saints have been sometime in that way that way all hall.

Four saints were not born at one time although they knew each other. One of them had a birthday before the mother of the other one the father. Four saints later to be if to be one to be to be one to be. Might tingle.

Tangle wood tanglewood.

Four saints born in separate places.

Saint saint saint saint.

Four saints an opera in three acts.

My country tis of thee sweet land of liberty of thee I sing.

Saint Therese something like that.

Saint Therese something like that.

Saint Therese would and would and would.

Saint Therese something like that.

Saint Therese.

Saint Therese half in doors and half out out of doors.

Saint Therese not knowing of other saints.

Saint Therese used to go not to to tell them so but to around so that Saint Therese did find that that that and there. If any came.

This is to say that four saints may may never have seen the day, like. Any day like.

Saint Ignatius. Meant and met.

This is to say that four saints many never have. Any day like.

Gradually wait.

Any one can see that any saint to be.

Saint Therese	Saint Ignatius
Saint Matyr	Saint Paul
Saint Settlement	Saint William
Saint Thomasine	Saint Gilbert
Saint Electra	Saint Settle
Saint Wilhelmina	Saint Arthur
Saint Evelyn	Saint Selmer
Saint Pilar	Saint Paul Seize
Saint Hillaire	Saint Cardinal
Saint Bernadine	Saint Plan
	Saint Giuseppe

Any one to tease a saint seriously.

Act One

Saint Therese in a storm at Avila there can be rain and warm snow and warm that is the water is warm the river is not warm the sun is not warm and if to stay to cry. If to stay to if to stay if having to stay to if having to stay if to cry to stay if to cry stay to cry to stay.

Saint Therese half in and half out of doors.

Saint Ignatius not there. Saint Ignatius staying where. Never heard them speak speak of it.

Saint Ignatius silent motive not hidden.

Saint Therese silent. They were never beset.

Come one come one.

No saint to remember to remember. No saint to remember. Saint Therese knowing young and told.

If it were possible to kill five thousand chinamen by pressing a button would it be done.

Saint Therese not interested.

Repeat First Act

A pleasure April fool's day a pleasure.
Saint Therese seated.
Not April fool's day a pleasure.
Saint Therese seated.
Not April fool's day a pleasure.
Saint Therese seated.
April fool's day April fool's day as not as pleasure as April fool's day not a pleasure.

Saint Therese seated and not surrounded. There are a great many persons and places near together. Saint Therese not seated there are a great many persons and places near together.

Saint Therese not seated.

There are a great many persons and places near together.

Saint Therese not seated at once. There are a great many places and persons near together.

Saint Therese once seated. There are a great many places and persons near together. Saint Therese seated and not surrounded. There are a great many places and persons near together.

Saint Therese visited by very many as well as the others really visited before she was seated. There are a great many persons and places close together.

Saint Therese not young and younger but visited like the others by some, who are frequently going there.

Saint Therese very nearly half inside and half outside outside the house and not surrounded.

How do you do. Very well I thank you. And when do you go. I am staying on quite continuously. When is it planned. Not more than as often.

The garden inside and outside of the wall.

Saint Therese about to be.

The garden inside and outside outside and inside of the wall.

Nobody visits more than they do visits them.

Saint Therese. Nobody visits more than they do visits them Saint Therese.

As loud as that as allowed as that.

Saint Therese. Nobody visits more than they do visits them.

Who settles a private life.

Saint Therese. Who settles a private life.
Saint Therese. Who settles a private life.
Saint Therese. Who settles a private life.
Saint Therese. Who settles a private life.

Enact end of an act

All of it to be not to be not to be left to be to him and standing.
Saint Therese seated.
Left to be not to be not to be left to be left to be and left to be not to be.
Saint Therese seated and if he could be standing and standing and saying and saying left to be.
Introducing Saint Ignatius.
Left to be.
Saint Therese seated seated and left to be if to be if left to be if left if to be Saint Ignatius standing.
She has no one to say so.
He said so actually.
She can have no one no one can have any one any one can have not any one can have not any one can have can have to say so.
Saint Therese seated and not standing half and half of it and not half and half of it seated and not standing surrounded and not seated and not seated and not standing and not surrounded and not surrounded and not not not seated not seated not seated not surrounded not seated and Saint Ignatius standing standing not seated Saint Therese not standing not standing and Saint Ignatius not standing standing surrounded as if in once yesterday. In place of situations. Saint Therese could be very much interested not only in settlement Saint Settlement and this not with with this wither wither they must be additional. Saint Therese having not commenced.
Did she want him dead if now.
Saint Therese could be photographed having been dressed like a lady and then they taking out her head changed it to a nun and a nun a saint and a saint so. Saint Therese seated and not surrounded might be very well inclined to be settled. Saint Therese actively.
Made to be coming to be here.
How many saints can sit around. A great many saints can sit around with one standing.
Saint Therese a great many saints seated.
They move through the country in winter in winter entirely.
Saint Therese in moving. Now three can be seated in front.
A saint is easily resisted. Saint Therese. Let it as land Saint Therese.

As land beside a house. Saint Therese. As land beside a house and at one time Saint Therese. Saint Therese. As land beside a house to be to this this which theirs beneath Saint Therese.

Saint Therese saints make sugar with a flavor. In different ways when it is practicable. Saint Therese in invitation.

Saint Therese. Could she know that that he was not not to be to be very to be dead not dead.

Saint Therese so much to be with it withheld with that.

Saint Therese. Nobody can do so.

Saint Therese Saint Therese must be must be chain left chain right chain chain is it. No one chain is it not chain is it, chained to not to life chained to not to snow chained to chained to go and and gone. Saint Therese might be come to be in this not indifferently.

Saint Therese. Not this not in this not with this.

Saint Therese must be theirs first.

Saint Therese as a young girl being widowed.

Saint Therese. Can she sing.

Saint Therese. Leave later gaily the troubadour plays his guitar.

Saint Therese might it be Martha.

Saint Louise and Saint Celestine and Saint Louis Paul and Saint Settlement Fernande and Ignatius.

Saint Therese. Can women have wishes.

Scene Two

Many saints seen and in between many saints seen.
Saint Therese and Saint Therese and Saint Therese.
Many saints as seen and in between as many saints as seen.
Seen as seen.
Many saints as seen.
Saint Therese and sound.
She is to meet her.
Can two saints be one.
Saint Therese and fastening.
Very many go out as they they do.
Saint Therese. And make him prominent.
Saint Therese. Could a negro be be with a beard to see and to be.
Saint Therese. Never have to have seen a negro there and with it so.
Saint Therese. To differ between go and so.
Saint Therese and three saints all one. Saint Settlement Saint Fernande Saint John Seize Saint Paul Six. Saint Therese with these saints.

Who separated saints at one time.

Saint Therese. In follow and saints.

Saint Therese. To be somewhere with or without saints.

Saint Therese can never mention the others.

Saint Therese to them. Saints not found. All four saints not more than all four saints.

Saint Therese come again to be absent.

Scene III

Saint Therese. To an occasion louder.

Saint Therese coming to be selfish.

Saint Therese allow.

All four saints remembering not to be with them. Could all four saints not only be in brief.

Saint Therese. Contumely.

Saint Therese advancing. Who can be shortly in their way.

Saint Therese having heard.

In this way as movement.

In having been in.

Does she want to be neglectful of hyacinths and find violets. Saint Therese should never change herbs for pansies and dry them.

They think there that it is their share.

And please.

Saint Therese makes as in this to be as stems.

And while.

Saint Therese settled and some come. Some come to be near not near her but the same.

Surround them with the thirds and that.

Saint Therese might be illustrated. Come to be in between.

Beginning earlier.

And anything.

Around.

Saint Therese seated with the name and choosing.

How many are there halving.

Scene III

Therese in Saint Ignatius and Saint Settlment to be sure.

Saint Therese having known that no snow in vain as snow is not vain. Saint Therese needed it as she was. Saint Therese made it be third. Snow third high third there third. Saint Therese in allowance.

How many saints can remember a house which was built before they can remember.

Ten saints can.

How many saints can be and land be and sand be and on a high plateau there is no sand there is snow and there is made to be so and very much can be what there is to see when there is a wind to have it dry and be what they can understand to undertake to let it be to send it well as much as none to be to be behind. None to be behind. Enclosure.

Saint Therese. None to be behind. Enclosure.

Saint Ignatius could be in porcelain actually.

Saint Ignatius could be in porcelain actually while he was young and standing.

Saint Therese could not be young and standing she could be sitting.

Saint Ignatius could be in porcelain actually actually in porcelain standing.

Saint Therese could be admittedly could be in moving seating. Saint Therese could be in moving sitting.

Saint Therese could be.

Saint Ignatius could be.

Saint Ignatius could be in porcelain actually in porcelain standing.

They might in at most not leave out an egg. An egg and add some. Some and sum. Add sum. Add some.

Let it in around.

With seas.

With knees.

With keys.

With pleases.

Go and know.

In clouded.

Included.

Saint Therese and attachment. With any one please.

No one to be behind and enclosure. Suddenly two see.

Two and ten.

Saint Two and Saint Ten.

Scene IV

Did wish did want did at most agree that it was not when they had met that they were separated longitudinally.

While it escapes it adds to it just as it did when it has and does with it in that to intend to intensity and sound. Is there a difference between a sound a hiss a kiss a as well.

Could they grow and tell it so if it was left to be to go to go to see to see to saw to saw to build to place to come to rest to hand to beam to couple to name to rectify to do.

Saint Ignatius Saint Settlement Saint Paul Seze Saint Anselmo made it be not only obligatory but very much as they did in little patches.

Saint Therese and Saint Therese and Saint Therese Seze and Saint Therese might be very much as she would if she very much as she would if she were to be wary.

They might be that much that far that with that widen never having seen and press, it was a land in one when altitude by this to which endowed.

Might it be in claim.

Saint Therese and conversation. In one.

Saint Therese in conversation. And one.

Saint Therese in and in and one and in and one.

Saint Therese left in complete.

Saint Therese and better bowed.

Saint Therese did she and leave bright.

Snow in snow sun in sun one in one out.

What is the difference between a picture of a volcano and that.

Watered and allowed makes a crown.

Oysters ham and rose tree rose he arose and he arose.

Saint Therese not questioned for this with this and because.

They can remain latin latin there and Virgil Virgil Virgil virgin virgin latin there. Saint Ignatius to twenty.

A scene and withers.

Scene three and scene two.

How can a sister see Saint Therese suitably.

Pear trees cherry blossoms pink blossoms and late apples and surrounded by Spain and lain.

Why when in lean fairly rejoin place dismiss calls.

Whether weather soil.

Saint Therese refuses to bestow.

Saint Therese with account. Saint Therese having felt it with it.

There can be no peace on earth with calm with calm. There can be no peace on earth with calm with calm. There can be no peace on earth with calm with calm and with whom whose with calm and with whom whose when they well they well they call it there made message especial and come.

This amounts to Saint Therese. Saint Therese has been and has been.

What is the difference between a picture and pictured.

All Saints make Sunday Monday Sunday Monday Sunday Monday set.

One two three Saints.

Scene III

Saint Therese has been prepared for there being summer.
Saint Therese has been prepared for there being summer.

Scene IV

To prepare.
One a window.
Two a shutter.
Three a palace.
Four a widow.
Five an adopted son.
Six a parlor.
Seven a shawl.
Eight an arbor.
Nine a seat.
Ten a retirement.
Saint Therese has been with him.
Saint Therese has been with him they show they show that summer summer makes a child happening at all to throw a ball too often to please.
Saint Therese in pain.
Saint Therese with blame.
Saint Therese having been following with them here.
In this way to begin to thin.
Those used to winter like winter and summer.
Those used to summer like winter and summer.
Those used to summer like winter and summer.
Those used to summer like winter and summer like winter and summer.
Those used to summer like winter and summer.
They make this an act One.

Act Two

All to you:

Scene One

Some and some.

Scene One

This is a scene where this is seen. Saint Therese has been a queen not as you might say royalty not as you might say worn not as you might say.

Saint Therese preparing in as you might say.

Act One

Saint Therese. Preparing in as you might say.

Saint Therese was pleasing. In as you might say.

Saint Therese Act One.

Saint Therese has begun to be in act one.

Saint Therese and begun.

Saint Therese as sung.

Saint Therese act one.

Saint Therese and begun.

Saint Therese and sing and sung.

Saint Therese in an act one. Saint Therese questions.

How many have been told twenty have been here as well. Saint Therese and with if it is as in a rest and well.

Saint Therese does not live around she is very well understood to have been with them then.

She is very intently with might have been seen rested and with it all. It never snows in Easter.

Saint Therese as if it were as they say they say so.

Saint Ignatius might not have been born.

Saint Therese can know the difference between singing and women. Saint Therese can know the difference between snow and thirds. Saint Therese can know the difference between when there is a day to-day to-day. To-day.

Saint Therese with the land and laid. Not observing.

Saint Therese coming to go.

Saint Therese coming and lots of which it is not as soon as if when it can left to change change theirs in glass and yellowish at most most of this can be when is it that it is very necessary not to plant it green. Planting it green means that it is protected from the wind and they never knew about it. They never knew about it green and they never knew about it she never knew about it they never knew about it they never knew about it she never knew about it. Planting it green it is necessary to protect it from the sun and from the wind and the sun and they never knew about it and she never knew about it and she never knew about it and they never knew about.

Scene once seen once seen once seen.

Scene V

Saint Therese unsurrounded by reason of it being so cold that they stayed away.

Scene VI

Saint Therese using a cart with oxen to go about and as well as if she were there.

Scene VII

One two three four five six seven all good children go to heaven some are good and some are bad one two three four five six seven. Saint Therese in a cart drawn by oxen moving around.

Scene VIII

Saint Therese in time.

Scene IX

Saint Therese meant to be complete completely.

Saint Therese and their having been it always was what they liked likened because it was moved.

Saint Therese in advance advances advantage advance advantages. Saint Therese when she had been let to come was left to come was left to right was right to left and there. There and not there by left and right. Saint Therese once and once. No one surrounded trees as there were none.

This meant Saint Ignatius Act II.

Act II

Saint Ignatius was very well known.

Scene II

Would it do if there was a Scene II.

Scene III and IV

Saint Ignatius and more.
Saint Ignatius with as well.
Saint Ignatius needs not be feared.
Saint Ignatius might be very well adapted to plans and a distance.
Barcelona in the distance. Was Saint Ignatius able to tell the difference between palms and Eucalyptus trees.
Saint Ignatius finally.
Saint Ignatius well bound.
Saint Ignatius with it just.
Saint Ignatius might be read.
Saint Ignatius with it Tuesday.
Saint Therese has very well added it.

Scene IV

Usefully.

Scene IV

How many nails are there in it.
Hard shoe nails and silver nails and silver does not sound valuable.
To be interested in Saint Therese fortunately.
Saint Therese. To be interested in Saint Therese fortunately.
Saint Ignatius to be interested fortunately.
Fortunately to be interested in Saint Therese.
To be interested fortunately in Saint Therese.
Interested fortunately in Saint Therese fortunately interested in Saint Therese Saint Ignatius and Saints who have been changed from the evening to the morning.
In the morning to be changed from the morning to the morning in the morning. A scene of changing from the morning to the morning.

Scene V

There are many saints.

Scene V

They can be left to many saints.

Scene V

Many Saints.

Scene V

Many many saints can be left to many many saints scene five left to
many many saints.

Scene V

Scene five left to many saints.

Scene V

They are left to many saints and those saints these saints these saints.
Saints four saints. They are left to many saints.

Scene V

Saint Therese does disgrace her by leaving it alone and shone.
Saint Ignatius might be five.
When three were together one woman sitting and seeing one man lending and choosing one young man saying and selling. This is just as if it was
a tribe.

Scene V

Closely.

Scene V

Scene five Saint Therese had a father photographically. Not a sister.
Saint Therese had no mother and no other appointed to be left at hand.
Saint Therese famously and mind. To mind. To have to have to have
have Helen. Saint Therese have to have Helen have to have Helen. Saint
Therese have to have to have to have Saint Therese to have to have Helen.
An excuse.
Saint Therese as well as that.
Saint Therese robin.
Saint Therese not attached to robin.
Saint Therese. Robin not attached to Robin.
Saint Therese. Attached not attached to Robin.
Saint Therese. Why they could.
Saint Therese. Why they could why they could.

Saint Therese Saint Therese Saint Therese Saint Therese Ignatius why they could Saint Therese.

Saint Ignatius why they could.

Scene VI

Away away away away a day it took three days and that day. Saint Therese was very well parted and apart apart from that. Harry marry saints in place saints and sainted distributed grace.

Saint Therese in place.

Saint Therese in place of Saint Therese in place.

Saint Therese. Can any one feel any one moving and in moving can any one feel any one and in moving.

Saint Therese. To be belied.

Saint Therese. Having happily married.

Saint Therese. Having happily beside.

Saint Therese. Having happily had with it a spoon.

Saint Therese. Having happily relied upon noon.

Saint Therese with Saint Therese.

Saint Therese. In place.

Saint Therese and Saint Therese Saint Therese to trace.

Saint Therese and place.

Saint Therese beside.

Saint Therese added ride.

Saint Therese with tied.

Saint Therese and might.

Saint Therese. Might with widow.

Saint Therese. Might.

Saint Therese very made her in.

Saint Therese. Settled settlement some so.

Saint Therese Saint Therese.

Saint Therese in in in Lynn.

Scene VII

One two three four five six seven scene seven.

Saint Therese scene seven.

Saint Therese scene scene seven.

Saint Therese could never be mistaken.

Saint Therese could never be mistaken.

Saint Therese scene seven.

Saint Therese. Scene seven.

Saint Settlement Saint Therese Saint Ignatius Saint Severine Saint William Saint John Saint Ignatius Saint Alexander Saint Lawrence Saint Pilar Saint Celestine Saint Parmenter Saint Lys Saint Eustace and Saint Plan.

Saint Therese. How many saints are there in it.

Saint Therese. There are very many many saints in it.

Saint Therese. There are as many saints as there are in it.

Saint Therese. How many saints are there in it.

Saint Therese. There are there are there are saints saints in it.

Saint Therese Saint Settlement Saint Ignatius Saint Lawrence Saint Pilar Saint Plan and Saint Cecilia.

Saint Therese. How many saints are there in it.

Saint Cecilia. How many saints are there in it.

Saint Therese. There are as many saints as there are in it.

Saint Cecilia. There are as many saints as there are saints in it.

Saint Cecilia. How many saints are there in it.

Saint Therese. There are many saints in it.

Saint Lawrence Saint Celestine. There are saints in it Saint Celestine Saint Lawrence there are as many saints there are as many saints as there are as many saints as there are in it.

Saint Therese. There are many saints there are many saints many saints in it.

Saint Therese. Thank you very much.

Saint Therese. There are as many saints there are many saints in it. A very long time but not while waiting.

Saint Ignatius. More needily of which more anon.

Saint Ignatius. Of more which more which more.

Saint Ignatius Loyola. A saint to be met by and by by and by continue reading reading read read readily.

Never to be lost again to-day.

To-day to stay.

Saint Ignatius Saint Ignatius Saint Ignatius temporarily.

Saint Jan. Who makes whose be his. I do.

Saint Therese scene seven one two three four five six seven.

Saint Therese. Let it have a place.

Saint Therese Saint Ignatius and Saint Genevieve·and Saint Thomas and Saint Chavez.

All four saints have settled it to be what they must know makes it be what it is when they are defended by attacks.

Saint Genevieve can be welcomed any day.

Saint Chavez can be with them then.

Saint Ignatius can be might it be with them and furl.

Saint Therese with them in with them alone.

Saint Plan. Can be seen to be any day any day from here to there.

Saint Settlement aroused by the recall of Amsterdam.

Saint Therese. Judging it as a place to be used negligently.

Saint Ignatius by the time that rain has come.

Saint Genevieve meant with it all.

Saint Plan. Might meant with it all.

Saint Paul. Might meant might with it all.

Saint Chavez. Select.

Saints. All Saints.

Scene Eight

All Saints. All Saints At All Saints.

All Saints. Any and all Saints. All Saints. All and all Saints. All Saints. All in all Saints. All Saints. All Saints. All Saints. Saints all in all Saints. All Saints. Settled in all Saints. All Saints. Settled all in all saints. Saints. Saints settled saints settled all in all saints. All saints. Saints in all saints. Saint Settlement. Saints all saints all saints. Saint Chavez. In all saints Saint Plan in saint in saint in all saints saints in all saints. Saint Ignatius. Settled passing this in having given in which is not two days when everything being ready it is no doubt not at all the following morning that it is very much later very much earlier with then to find it acceptable as about about which which as a river river helping it to be in doubt. Who do who does and does it about about to be as a river and the order of their advance. It is to-morrow on arriving at a place to pass before the last.

Scene eight. To Wait.

Scene one. And. begun.

Scene two. To and to.

Scene three. Happily be.

Scene Four. Attached or.

Scene Five. Sent to derive.

Scene Six. Let it mix.

Scene Seven. Attached eleven.

Scene Eight. To wait.

Saint Therese. Might be there.

Saint Therese. To be sure.

Saint Therese. With them and.

Saint Therese. And hand.

Saint Therese. And alight.

Saint Therese. With them then. Saint Therese Saint Therese. Nestle. Saint Therese. With them and a measure. It is easy to measure a settlement.

Scene IX

Saint Therese. To be asked how much of it is finished.

Saint Therese. To be asked how much of it is finished.

Saint Therese. To ask Saint Therese Saint Therese to be asked how much of it is finished.

Saint Therese. Ask Saint Therese how much of it is finished.

Saint Therese. To be asked Saint Therese to be asked Saint Therese to be asked ask Saint Therese ask Saint Therese how much of it is finished.

Saint Chavez. Ask how much of it is finished.

Saint Plan. Ask Saint Therese how much of it is finished.

Saint Therese. Ask asking asking Saint Therese how much of it is finished.

Saint Settlement

Saint Chavez   How much of it is finished.

Saint Plan

Saint Therese.

Saint Therese. Ask how much of it is finished.

Saint Chavez. Ask how much of it is finished.

Saint Therese. Ask how much of it is finished.

Saint Settlement

Saint Therese

Saint Paul

Saint Plan   Ask how much of it is finished.

Saint Anne

Saint Cecile

Saint Plan.

Once in a while.

Saint Therese. Once in a while.

Saint Plan. Once in a while.

Saint Chavez. Once in a while.

Saint Settlement. Once in a while.

Saint Therese. Once in a while.

Saint Chavez. Once in a while.

Saint Cecile. Once in a while.

Saint Genevieve. Once in a while.

Saint Anne. Once in a while.

Saint Settlement. Once in a while.
Saint Therese. Once in a while.
Saint Therese. Once in a while.
Saint Ignatius. Once in a while.
Saint Ignatius. Once in a while.
Saint Ignatius. Once in a while.
Saint Settlement. Once in a while.
Saint Therese Once in a while.
Saint Therese.
Saint Therese. Once in a while.
Saint Ignatius. Once in a while.
Saint Ignatius Once in a while.
Saint Therese.
Saint Therese. Once in a while.
Saint Therese. Once in a while.
Saint Therese. Once in a while.
Saint Plan. Once in a while.
Saint Ignatius Once in a while.
Saint Therese.

Scene X
Could Four Acts be Three.

Saint Therese. Could Four Acts be three.
Saint Therese Saint Therese Saint Therese Could Four Acts be three Saint Therese.

Scene X
When.

Saint Therese. Could Four Acts be when four acts could be ten Saint Therese. Saint Therese Saint Therese Four Acts could be four acts could be when when four acts could be ten.
Saint Therese. When.
Saint Settlement. Then.
Saint Genevieve. When.
Saint Cecile. Then.
Saint Ignatius. Then.
Saint Ignatius. Men.
Saint Ignatius. When.
Saint Ignatius. Ten.
Saint Ignatius. Then.
Saint Therese. When.

Saint Chavez. Ten.
Saint Plan. When then.
Saint Settlement. Then.
Saint Anne. Then.
Saint Genevieve. Ten.
Saint Cecile. Then.
Saint Answers. Ten.
Saint Cecile When then.
Saint Anne.
Saint Answers. Saints when.
Saint Chavez. Saints when ten.
Saint Cecile. Ten.
Saint Answers. Ten.
Saint Chavez. Ten.
Saint Settlement. Ten.
Saint Plan. Ten.
Saint Anne. Ten.
Saint Plan. Ten.
Saint Plan. Ten.
Saint Plan. Ten.

Scene XI

Saint Therese. With William.
Saint Therese. With Plan.
Saint Therese. With William willing and with Plan willing and with
Plan and with William willing and with William and with Plan.
Saint Therese. They might be staring.
Saint Therese. And with William.
Saint Therese. And with Plan.
Saint Therese. With   William.
Saint Therese. And with. Plan.
Saint Therese
Saint Plan
Saint Placide How many windows are there in it.
Saint Chavez
     and
Saint Settlement.
Saint Therese. How many windows and doors and floors are there in it.
Saint Therese. How many doors how many floors and how many windows
are there in it.

Saint Plan. How many windows are there in it how many doors are there in it.

Saint Chavez. How many doors are there in it how many floors are there in it how many doors are there in it how many windows are there in it how many floors are there in it how many windows are there in it how many doors are there in it.

Changing in between.

Saint Therese. In this and in this and in this and clarity.

Saint Therese. How many are there in this.

Saint Chavez. How many are there in this.

Saint Chavez. How many are there in this.

Saint Settlement. Singularly to be sure and with a Wednesday at noon.

Saint Chavez. In time and mine.

Saint Therese. Settlement and in in and in and all. All to come and go to stand up to kneel and to be around. Around and around and around and as round and as around and as around and as around.

One two three.

There is a distance in between.

There is a distance in between in between others others meet meet meet met wet yet. It is very tearful to be through. Through and through.

Saint Therese. Might be third.

Saint Therese. Might be heard.

Saint Therese. Might be invaded.

Saint Therese and three saints and there.

Commencing again yesterday.

Saint Therese. And principally, Saint Therese.

Scene X

Saint Ignatius. Withdrew with with withdrew.

Saint Ignatius. Occurred.

Saint Ignatius. Occurred withdrew.

Saint Ignatius. Withdrew Occurred.

Saint Ignatius. Withdrew occurred.

Saint Ignatius occurred Saint Ignatius withdrew occurred withdrew.

Saint Sarah. Having heard that they had gone she said how many eggs are there in it.

Saint Absalom. Having heard that they are gone he said how many had said how many had been where they had never been with them or with it.

Saint Absalom. Might be annointed.

Saint Therese. With responsibility.

Saint Therese. And an allowance.

Saint Settlement. In might have a change from this.

Saint Chavez. A winning.

Saint Cecile. In plenty.

Saint Eustace. Might it be mountains if it were not Barcelona.

Saint Plan. With wisdom.

Saint Chavez. In a minute.

Saint Therese. And circumstances.

Saint Therese. And as much.

Saint Chavez. With them.

An interval.

Abundance.

An interval.

Saint Chavez. Abundance.

Saint Chavez. And an interval.

Saint Sarah. With them near one.

Saint Michael. With them near one with them.

Saint Chavez. Tire.

Saint Cecile

Saint Chavez

Saint Therese One two and alike like liked.

    and

     themselves.

Saint Chavez. Windows and windows and ones.

Saint Cecile. Obligation.

Saint Sarah. Their wonder.

Saint Michael. And their wonder.

Saint Chavez. And whether.

Saint Michael. With windows as much as.

Saint Cecile. More to be considered.

Saint Michael

    and   Considerable.

Saint Sarah.

Saint Chavez. In consideration of everything and that it is done by them as it must be left to them with this as an arrangement. Night and day cannot be different.

Saint Therese. Completely forgetting.

Saint Therese. I will try.

Saint Therese. Theirs and by and by.

Saint Chavez. With noon.

Act III

With withdrawn.

There is very much announcement and by the time they leave they leave altogether one at a time they do not leave it left and right and in the middle they withdraw what they need when they might meet with what after all is why they are not only with them but in the midst of them and withdrawn and left meaning to be with this as their belonging to it and as it is what is it when they are in the middle of theirs around they might be very nearly alike as if it is understood. Once and one at a time.

Barcelona can be told.

How do you do.

Very well I thank you.

This is how young men and matter. How many nails are there in it.

Who can try.

They can be a little left behind.

Not at all.

As if they liked it very well to live alone.

With withdrawn.

What can they mean by well very well.

Scene One

And seen one. Very likely.

Saint Therese. It is not what is apprehended what is apprehended what is apprehended what is apprehended intended.

Scene One

Saint Chavez. It is very likely that there are many of them.

Saint Ignatius. Instantly and subsistently.

Saint Stephen. And leading at night.

Saint Plan. Within with went in.

Saint Stephen. In a little time gradually.

Saint Manuel. Would they refuse to sanction it if they were asked and there was no way to have them carry out anything.

Saint Stephen. With them instantly.

Saint Eustace. In place of lurking.

Saint Chavez. By means of it all.

Saint Plan. Within a season of deliberation.

Saint Stephen. And reasonably insisting.

Saint Chavez. At that time.

Saint Ignatius. And all. Then and not. Might it do. Do and doubling with it at once left and right.

Saint Chavez. Left left left right left with what is known.

Saint Chavez. In time.

Scene II

It is easy to resemble it at most.

Most and best.

It is easy to resemble it most and leave it to them with individuality.

Saint Ignatius. In seems.

Saint Ignatius. In seems.

Saint Ignatius. Within it within it within it as a wedding for them in half of the time.

Saint Ignatius. Particularly.

Saint Ignatius. Call it a day.

Saint Ignatius. With a wide water with within with drawn.

Saint Ignatius. As if a fourth class.

Scene II

Pigeons on the grass alas.

Pigeons on the grass alas.

Short longer grass short longer longer shorter yellow grass Pigeons large pigeons on the shorter longer yellow grass alas pigeons on the grass.

If they were not pigeons what were they.

If they were not pigeons on the grass alas what were they. He had heard of a third and he asked about it it was a magpie in the sky. If a magpie in the sky on the sky can not cry if the pigeon on the grass alas can alas and to pass the pigeon on the grass alas and the magpie in the sky on the sky and to try and to try alas on the grass alas the pigeon on the grass the pigeon on the grass and alas. They might be very well very well very well they might be they might be very well they might be very well very well they might be.

Let Lucy Lily Lily Lucy Lucy let Lucy Lucy Lily Lily Lily Lily Lily let Lily Lucy Lucy let Lily. Let Lucy Lily.

Scene One

Saint Ignatius prepared to have examples of windows of curtains of hanging of shawls of windows of curtains of windows of curtains of windows of curtains of hangings of shawls of windows of hangings of curtains of windows of hangings of curtains of shawls.

Saint Ignatius and please please please please.

Scene One

One and one.

Scene One

Might they be with they be with them might they be with them. Never to return to distinctions.

Might they be with them with they be with they be with them. Never to return to distinctions.

Saint Ignatius. In line and in in line please say it first in line and in line and please say it first please say it first say it with first in line and in line in line.

Saint Ignatius. Met to be to be to leave me be with him in partly left to find find with it call call with to them to them that have to be with it as when letting letting it announce announced complacently in change change having fallen two to one in restitution in their inability to leave. Leave left as lost. Might white. From the stand-point of white.

Saint Sulpice. A masterpiece.

Saint Ignatius and friends. When it is ordinarily thoughtful and making it be when they were wishing at one time insatiably and with renounced where where ware and wear wear with them with them and where where will it be as long as long as they might with it with it individually removing left to it when it very well way well and crossed crossed in articulately minding what you do.

The friends at once. What is it when it is perilously left to it where there are more than there were.

And all and as if there is a mound.

He asked for a distant magpie as if they made a difference.

He asked for a distant magpie as if he asked for a distant magpie as if that made a difference.

He asked as if that made a difference.

He asked for a distant magpie.

He asked for a distant magpie.

As if that made a difference he asked for a distant magpie as if that made a difference. He asked as if that made a difference. A distant magpie. He asked for a distant magpie. He asked for a distant magpie.

Saint Ignatius. Might be admired for himself alone.

Saint Chavez. Saint Ignatius might be admired for himself alone and because of that it might be as much as any one could desire.

Saint Chavez. Because of that it might be as much as any one could desire.

Saint Chavez. Because of that because it might be as much as any one could desire it might be that it could be done as easily as because it might very much as if precisely why they were carried.

Saint Ignatius. Left when there was precious little to be asked by the ones who were overwhelmingly particular about what they were adding to themselves by means of their arrangements which might be why they went away and came again.

It is every once in a while very much what they pleased.

Saint Ignatius. With them and with them and uniformly.

Saint Chavez. To make it and why they were with them just as soon.

Saint Chavez. And roses very well. Very well and roses very well roses smell roses smell and very well and very well as roses smell roses smell very well. If hedge roses are moss roses larger. If moss roses are larger are there questions of how very well there are strangers who have to be known by their walk.

In a minute.

Saint Ignatius. In a minute by the time that it is graciously gratification and might it be with them to be with them to be with them to be to be windowed.

Saint Ignatius. As seen as seen.

Saint Ignatius surrounded by them.

Saint Ignatius and one of two.

Saint Ignatius. And one of two.

Saint Ignatius. And one of two literally.

Saint Ignatius. And one of two and one of two.

Saint Ignatius. And one of two literally.

Saint Ignatius. And one of two and one of two. One of two.

Saint Ignatius. Might when when is exchangeable.

Saint Ignatius. Might when.

Saint Chavez. In change.

Saint Chavez might be with them at that time. All of them. Might be with them at that time.

All of them might be with them all of them at that time.

Might be with them at that time all of them might be with them at that time.

Scene II

It is very easy to love alone. Too much too much. There are very sweetly very sweetly Henry very sweetly Rene very sweetly many very sweetly. They are very sweetly many very sweetly Rene very sweetly there are many very sweetly.

Scene III

There is a difference between Barcelona and Avila. What difference.

Scene

There is a difference between Barcelona and Avila.

There is a difference between Barcelona. There is a difference between Barcelona and Avila. There is a difference between Barcelona and Avila.

Scene IV

And no more.

Scene V

Saint Ignatius. Left to left left to left left to left. Left right left left right left left to left.

Saint Pellen. There is every reason why industriously there should be resolution and intermittence and furnishing of their delight.

By this time with them in intermingling and objection with them and with them and intermediately and allowance and left and more and benignly and acceptably accepting in their and by mischance with them indeterminately finally as change.

When they do change to.

Saint Vincent. Authority for it.

Saint Gallo. By this clock o'clock. By this clock by this clock by this clock o'clock.

Saint Pilar. In the middle of their pleasurable resolution resolving in their adequate announcing left to it by this by this means.

And out.

Saint Chavez. With a plan.

Saint Pellen. In sound.

Saint Gallo. Around.

Saint Pellen. In particular.

Saint Chavez. Innumerably.

Saint Ignatius might be what is underestimately theirs in plain and plan

and for which is left to because in this with it as much as is in connecting
undividedly theirs at that time. In this. Coming to be thrown.

They might use having it as high.

Left it to right.

Having used might it be with it as with it as mentioning when.

Having it as having it used usually to actually to additionally to integrally to to the owned to the owning owning out.

Might it be two at one time time and mine mine and time.

Saint Ignatius returns to come when.

Saint Plan. Without it with them.

Saint Chavez
     and   Without it with them with them without it.
Saint Pilar.

Saint Chavez. Without it with them without it.

With them with out it.

Saint Ignatius. Might be memorized.

Saint Chavez

Saint Pilar   With them with it.

and with them.

Saint Pilar. With them with with with with out with them.

Saint Chavez. Uniting it one at a time individually.

Saint Pilar. Need it in liking what is a choice between floating and adding.
Floating and adding makes smiles.

Saint Hilyar. With them and to to to add to add to it.

Might having it we do.

Saint Ignatius. Foundationally marvellously aboundingly illimitably with
it as a circumstance. Fundamentally and saints fundamentally and saints
and fundamentally and saints.

Saint Chavez. Found round about.

Saint Pilar
     and   Additionally in currents.
Saint Chavez.

Saint Chavez. Found round about without.

Saint Chavez.

Saint Pilar   With what and when it is universally leaving it ad-
     and   ditionally to them as windowed windowed windowed
Saint Fernande.   windowed where.

Answerably.

Scene VI

They might have heard about them altogether.

Scene VII

Saint Chavez. It is very well known that that which has been noticed as needing violence and veils may be what they meant when they said it.

Saint Chavez. By that time.

Saint Chavez. What they meant by it when they said it. By that time.

Saint Chavez. There has been an incredible reason for their planning what is not by any manner of means their allowance in having let it be theirs by negligence.

Saint Andrew
        and   Letting it be third at all.
Saint John Seize.

Saint Sarah
        and   By it a chance.
Saint Leonard.

Saint Ferdinand
        and   With this one at at time.
Saint Plan.

Saint Plan
        and   With them and must.
Saint Arthur.

Saint Agnes.   Letting it alone.

Saint Henry. With me by and by.

Saint Sylvester. Leaning and letting it be what to wish.

Saint Plan. Leaning and letting it be what to wish.

One Saint. Whose has whose has whose has ordered needing white and green as much as orange and with grey and how much and as much and as much and as a circumstance.

Saint Ignatius. Windowing shortly which makes what have they joined to parks and palaces. Undoubtedly.

One and two might be through.

Through certainly.

Saint Therese. With them and for instance.

Saint Therese. Like and it might be as likely it might be very likely that it would be amounting to once in a while as in a way it could be what was meant by that at once. There is a difference between at most at once.

In at the time.

Saint Therese. Intending to be intending to intending to to to to. To do it for me.

Saint Ignatius. Went to.

Saint Ignatius. Two and two.

Saint Chavez. Might be what was when after all a petal two and water three.

Scene V

Alive.

Scene VI

With Seven.

Scene VII

With eight.

Scene VIII

Ordinary pigeons and trees.

If a generation all the same between forty and fifty as as. As they were and met. Was it tenderness and seem. Might it be as well as mean with in.

Ordinary pigeons and trees. This is a setting which is as soon which is as soon which is as soon ordinary setting which is as soon which is as soon and noon.

Ordinary pigeons and trees.

Scene IX

Saint Therese. Face and face face about. Face to face face and face face out.

Saint Therese. Add to additional.

Saint Chavez. Might make milk sung.

Saint Chavez. Might make. In place. Saint Therese.

Saint Therese. In face of in face of might make milk sung sung face to face face in face place in place in place of face to face. Milk sung.

Saint Ignatius. Once in a while and where and where around around is a sound and around is a sound and around is a sound and around. Around is a sound around is a sound around is a sound and around. Around differing from annointed now. Now differing from annointed now. Now differing differing. Now differing from annointed now. Now when there is left and with it integrally with it integrally withstood within without with out with drawn and in as much as if it could be withstanding what in might might be so.

Saint Chavez. In in time.

Many might be comfortabler. This is very well known now. When this you see remember me. It was very well known to every one. They were very careful of everything. They were whatever it was necessary to have to alter. They might be as thankful as they were that they were not perfectly predispossessed to deny when they were able to be very soon there. There one at a time. Having arranged magpies so only one showed and also having arranged magpies so that more than one showed. If magpies are so arranged that only one shows it is not more noticeable than if they are so arranged that more than one is showing against the horizon in such a way that they are placed directly not only where they were but where they are. Adding coming forward again.

A great deal of the afternoon is used by this as an advantage. It is meritorious that we do not care to share. It is meritorious by them with them able and ably.

Saint Ignatius. Forty to fifty with fifty and all and a wall and as all and as called called rather.

Saint Therese. A widow weeded way laid way laying and as spelled.

Saint Chavez. Might and right very well to do. It is all colored by a straw straw laden.

Saint Ignatius. Very nearly with it with it soon soon as said.

Saint Ignatius. Windowing clearly.

Saint Chavez. Having asked additionally theirs instead.

Saint Therese. Once in a minute.

Saint Therese. In a minute.

Saint Ignatius. One two three as are are and are are are to be are with them are with them are with them with are with are with with it.

Scene IX

Letting pin in letting let in let in in in in in let in let in wet in wed in dead in dead wed led in led wed dead in dead in led in wed in said in said led wed dead wed dead said led led said wed dead wed dead led in led in wed in wed in said in wed in led in said in dead in dead wed said led led said wed dead in. That makes they have might kind find fined when this arbitrarily makes it be what is it might they can it fairly well to be added to in this at the time that they can candied leaving as with with it by the left of it with with in in the funniest in union.

Across across across coupled across crept a cross crept crept crept crept across. They crept across.

If they are between thirty and thirty five and alive who made them see Saturday.

If they are between thirty-five and forty and they are thought to be who made them see Saturday with having it come in and out in and three thirty.

Between thirty-five and forty-five between forty five and three five as then when when they were forty-five and thirty five when then they were forty five and thirty five when they were then forty five and thirty five and thirty two and to achieve leave relieve and receive their astonishment. Were they to be left to do to do as well as they do mean I mean I mean. Next best to having heading him.

Might it be left after all where they left left right left. Might it be left where they might have having it left after all left right left after all.

When they have heard it mine.

Left to their in their to their to be their to be there all their to be there all their all their time to be there to be there all their to be all their time there.

With wed led said with led dead said with dead led said with said dead led wed said wed dead led dead led said wed.

With be there all their all their time there be there vine there be vine time there be there time there all their time there.

Needed indented.

Can they and chest, choice, choice of a chest.

It is better and best and just as good as if they needed to have and wanted to have and did want to have and did want to have to have had it had it with them when they might just as easily endeavor in every way to have paraphanelia leave it as their habitual reference to when they are not by the time that they have been very likely to needlessly believe that they went to come to come handily as a desperately arranged charm. Might it be why they were not only but also went as well.

Let it be why if they were adding adding comes cunningly to be additionally cunningly in the sense of attracting attracting in the sense of adding adding in the sense of windowing and windowing and frames and pigeons and ordinary trees and while while away.

ACT III

Did he did we did we and did he did he did he did did he did did did he did did he did be categorically and did he did he did he did he did he did he in interruption interruption interruptedly leave letting let it be be all to me to me out and outer and this and this with in indeed deed and drawn and drawn work.

Saint Ferdinand singing soulfully.

Saint Chavez. Singing singing is singing is singing is singing is singing between between singing is singing is between singing is.

Saint Plan. Theirs and sign. Saint Cecile. Singing theirs and signing mine.

Saint Philip. Will it be less at first that they are there and be left by the time that it is carried as far as further.

Saint Philip. Let it be gone as it has to be gone in plenty of time.

Saint Sarah. She might be coming to have to have infancy.

Saint Michael. With a stand and would it be the same as yet awhile and glance a glance of be very nearly left to be alone.

Saint Therese. One at at time makes two at a time makes one at a time and be there where where there there where where there. Very well as if to say.

Saint Cecile. With it and as if as if it were a left to them and feel. I feel very well.

Saint Chavez. By the time that they were left perfect.

Saint Ignatius. Might be why they were after all after all who came. One hundred and fifty one and a half and a half and after and after and after and all. With it all.

Saint Chavez. A ball might be less than one.

All together one and one.

ACT IV

How many acts are there in it. Acts are there in it.

Supposing a wheel had been added to three wheels how many acts how many how many acts are there in it.

Any Saint at all.

How many acts are there in it.

How many saints in all.

How many acts are there in it.

Ring around a rosey.

How many acts are there in it.

Wedded and weeded.

Please be coming to see me.

When this you see you are all to me.

Me which is you you who are true true to be you.

How many how many saints are there in it.

One two three all out but me.

One two three four all out but four.

One two all about but you.

How many saints are there in it.

How many saints are there in it.

How many acts are there in it.

One two three four and there is no door. Or more. Or nor. Or door. Or floor or door. One two three all out but me. How many saints are there in it.

Saints and see all out but me.

How many saints are there in it.

How many saints are there in it. One two three four all out but four one two three four four four or four or more.

More or four.

How many Acts are there in it.

Four Acts.

Act four.

Saint Therese deliberately. Encouraged by this then when they might be by thirds words eglantine and by this to mean feeling it as most when they do too to be nearly lost to sight in time in time and mind mind it for them. Let us come to this brink.

The sisters and saints assembling and reenacting why they went away to stay.

One at a time regularly regularly by the time that they are in and and in one at at time regularly very fairly better than they came as they came there and where where will they be wishing to stay here here where they are they are here here where they are they are they are here.

Saint Therese. It is very necessary to have arithmetic inestimably and left by this in the manner in which they are not at all as patient as they were patiently were. One at a time in rhyme.

Saint Chavez. The envelopes are on all the fruit of the fruit trees.

Scene II

Saint Chavez. Remembered as knew.

Saint Ignatius. Meant to send, and meant to send and meant meant to differ between send and went and end and mend and very nearly one to two.

Saint Cecile. With this and now.

Saint Plan. Made it with with in with withdrawn.

Scene III

Let all act as if they went away.

Scene IV

Saint Therese. Who mentioned that one followed another laterally.

All Saints. One at a time.

Saint Chavez. One at a time.

Saint Settlement

      and   There can be two Saint Annes if you like.

Saint Anne.

Saint Philip. With them and still.

Saint Cecile. They will they will.

Saint Therese. Begin to trace begin to race begin to place begin and in in that that is why this is what is left as may may follows June and June follows moon and moon follows soon and it is very nearly ended with bread.

Saint Chavez. Who can think that they can leave it here to me.

When this you see remember me.

They have to be.

They have to be.

They have to be to see.

To see to say.

Laterally they may.

Scene V

Who makes who makes it do.

Saint Therese and Saint Therese too.

Who does and who does care.

Saint Chavez to care.

Saint Chavez to care.

Who may be what is it when it is instead.

Saint Plan Saint Plan to may to say to say two may and inclined.

Who makes it be what they had as porcelain.

Saint Ignatius and left and right laterally be lined.

All Saints.

    To Saints.

Four Saints.

    And Saints.

Five Saints.

    To Saints.

Last Act.

Which is a fact.

A LYRICAL
OPERA MADE BY TWO
To Be Sung

Scene

A large and lofty room cut by rows of pictures and in the middle corner a work-table round with drawers in the shape of a Maltese cross and on it a seal red small medium sized bull a tortoise shell lamp and a glass of tiny hyacinths fresh flowers and on either side one side a small arm chair with a large medium sized pleasant handsome man and on the other side a large arm chair chintz covered with a fair sized dark charming medium sized lady.

L.M.S.J.H.M. My wife is my life is my life is my wife is my wife is my life is my life is my wife is my life.

F.s.d.c.m.s.l. Nods once in agreement.

A lyric.   Come fire fly and light up baby's nose.

Scene changes they are once more seated.

Come fire fly and light up baby's nose. Come fire fly and light up baby's nose. Come fire fly and light up baby's nose.

In the villa Bardi at Florence a tall proprietor calling to his workman Paolo.

Seated L.M.S.J.H.M. also seated F.s.d.c.m.s.l.

A cuckoo bird is sitting on a cuckoo tree singing to me oh singing to me.

A cuckoo bird is sitting on a cuckoo tree singing to me oh singing to me.

A rocky undulating road side small orchids growing not abundantly and some lavender. Two walking.

John Quilly John Quilly my babe baby is sweeter than even John Quillies are.

Hesitation in memory does not make it difficultly to be disturbed.

John Quilly John Quilly my babe baby is sweeter than even John Quillies are.

Before this it is a preparation to make a fountain.

Beginning afterward.

Uno due tre quattro cinque se uno due tre quattro.

The palace of Louis XIV known as Versailles.

To have a guide will you have a guide no guide inside inside no guide.

Back to back in the presence of a fact.

Very nice and quiet I thank you.

A lyric when they have met.

He stopped to stoop and say Nellie and Lillie Lillie and Nellie Nellie and Lillie not Lillie not Lillie and Nellie not Nellie not Lillie not any Lillie not any Nellie very well and very bell what is a door just shut is a door more and more. Two sing. This my country has been enslaved. And we are free to see to see how sweet is she my sweet pretty prettily.

To go on with a favorite song.

She there.

Having a care

Careful

To be sure

To give

To she

With a melody

A renown

For a crown

Of a cow

Which

Will

Come out now.

When this

You see

Remember

Me to she

And she will say

Sing softly Caramel. A cow will be a large and loose Caramel. A cow will be a large a large and loose Caramel. And will be well. And will be well.

A Caramel.

A cow it will be how a large a loose a cow let it let it pet it get it set it. A cow how large and loose Caramel just as well Caramel.

A scene.

She sitting.

A cow coming.

He welcoming a cow coming.

A scene

A cow has come he is pleased and she is content as a cow came and went. He and she and sent. So nicely. To mean to mean that they advertise an odorless jasmine.

And now a little scene with a queen contented by the cow which has come and been sent and been seen. A dear dearest queen.

Scene

Quietly installed and not used to wishing. Husband is so simply sleepy he does love his wife alway Husband is so simply sleepy what does he what does he say.

An interval of not seeing anybody.

Meaning in a voice baby has a choice. Of me.

She can see tenderly shining out of me for she. And so, tenderly if it is me for she it is me for she tenderly in a cow coming out now tenderly me for she tenderly as a cow coming out come out now by she for me tenderly as a she coming out of a cow out of from she for me tenderly.

Another acting as she can makes it have come and fan the air with the sound of a poise from the end not a bend just come out out of a little she is a little not a very little tenderly out of she a cow comes out. My sweet dear hear.

My sweet dear does hear her dear here saying little and big coming and true discern and firmly coming out softly shoving out singly coming out all of the cow that has been registered as around now. The cow can come out and it does and the cow is now now that it has come out is was.

Navigation sub-marine of the cow come out of queen my queen. That is what the cow does it sinks and a little it sinks so sweetly, my own cow out of my own queen is now seen.

My own queen, has a cow seen by my own queen and it is now a sub-marine.

Kiss my lips she did kiss my lips again she did kiss my lips over and over again she did.

Mrs. misses kisses Mrs. kisses most Mrs. misses kisses misses kisses most. Which is what ever. Nearly never.

Expedite expeditions.

Very truly more.

One two

Before

Just exactly four
The most
Beautiful
Garment
Made for him
By her.

A little enough just a little and puff he does she does very well does he does she does she does he does was is pussy darling just at nine. A little fog many at a time he does she was she is she does he was he is he he is he does. Does do. Two two true true just do. In a minute.

Very likely.

One and two be.

And now solemnly prepare a cow for to-morrow just as now. Solemnly prepare a cow now for to-morrow some and how.

Solemnly prepare a cow.

Scene changes.

She is there.

Very well I thank you.

That means that I thank you because she is very well.   Very well I thank you the little belle very well very well I thank you very well.

The scene which changes is that she is there nicely and having been cold with the help of two fairly warm hot water bottles she is warm very well I thank you.

In the meantime very much to be hoped is that it is to be accomplished which it is by means of their having with fishes a cow a cow with fishes fishes fishes a cow with fishes wishes fishes a cow with fishes a cow with fishes fishes fishes fishes wishes. A scene changes commodiously it is the proper seating for a cow for a cow for wishes for fishes admirably.

It seems to be
A note to she
The sweet sweetie
But actually.
It is April Fool
To tender she
My   sweetie
She is all me
My sweetie
April full of fool which is me for my sweetie
Dear April
Which made she
To be

All
To he
April fool
To his sweetie
Which is she
Tenderly
Excessively
Sweetily
My April fool baby.

May June and Jew lie we love to be by little love who sees by does it have to decide now what knife to cut the soap with while little wifey is so sweetly by by her little hair so nicely greasy which is to please he who has to squeeze she in a particular and careful way as you may see on every day as well as to obey and never gather fray in suddeness politely knowing which is what. A plot. A complot a compot a restaurant and a fine time to say how do you do wifey.

Shouting this will be heard and so they sat down.

A scene at a dinner. Two of them sitting next to each other. They are very satisfied with the pudding except that it is cooling.

Are there many more.

Days in April.

Yes.

And why.

Because

One of them

Is very important.

Once every where everything is accumulating and then with allowance naturally reestablishing it contains when within seen melodiously a cow a cow in circumference and conferring. It is an intensified ministration which does determine. Here at her now. Make a large cow. Say fairer than now heavy heavy cow heave out now cattle cattle cow cup of bestow ladies hear once a lady always a lady.

Sectional a cow in sections all at once constitutional a constitutional cow how ever strong. This is balm to have it come and be left odorously. Thank you for this. What is a cake a cow cake what is at stake a cow cake. Thank you out loud. One two one two all out of you three four three four open the door open the door five six five six not a stick just gently ooze choose dear darling that you are. Sweety you will have it be sure.

Seated busily.

On her birthday.

I say it in flowers I do I do

I say it in flowers to you to you
I say it in pansies and roses and pinks
I say it in daisies and heavenly drinks
Of the flower of our love which is you and me. When this you see you are all to me and I am all to thee completely and continually.

On her birthday

Done a little in lilies mauve peas and roses. Done a little in tea roses pinery and poses. Done a little in catches catch as catch can stubbornly if it is expensive then who does it belong to. It belongs to an elegance which is fair. To introduce a chair.

Daisy comes to be expressive.

Round the center which is all seen through.

This side it hangs.

So does it there.

When they change it from there to there.

Where.

In the air.

Faithfully care.

To make it hang there.

It is a particular occasion.

When it rains.

Thank you so much for mid winter.

It can be sufficiently said that head to head ahead.

It need be sent along with a mixture of mid winter charm.

It can be indicated by nearly having it attended to in an instance of uniquely through, she would not go downstairs to see it but she did and she said thank you instead and so uniquely seated at once beside with a collection.

Collected addresses.

To address yes.

Tennessee and tenderness

Yes.

Sing questions.

Question one, who has whom.

Sing questions sing who has whom soon

Sing questions sing questions soon who has whom.

Sing questions soon sing questions who has whom.

Singing questions.

What is there to ask if they are here. Singing questions about how soon they can come to stay.

Come to stay may make it best to have it may be I will but I doubt it singing questions just as well as they may after April thirtieth there is may and after that there is the second of May. They sing questions about once a day.

She is very necessary to me.

Have help hare.

She is very necessary to me.

Leaving it out.

She is very necessary to be to me.

There is no hurry about washing hair.

Is there.

There is no hurry about washing hair is there.

She is very necessary about there is no hurry about have help hare.

Jack-rabbit made among a singling of a song sang with a women fairly well to lope and settle in a clattering to mingle settle petal with amount of mingle it should have arise as well as surprise.

Days of dainties.

How many hopes have lops of lopped off threes. Two and so much.

Changed to a scene of the two of them picking wild hyacinths of a helio-trope color.

Is it better to have a pink house inside and out and so get rid of the question of yellow.

Two of them crediting them with this.

If it is whatever they have had it for for it to be where they have it to have chestnut trees as trees very nicely as soon. Creditably.

She and he see.

Pinkily.

Sing a hymn of him of him of her of her of that of that of what is the make of a cover. Cover to cover he never did shove her.

Sing a hymn of singing sing a hymn of singing sing a hymn of singing singing is more than very much more than often often and soften sing a hymn of often often very often soft as a better kind of making it be whatever is very likely to soften.

Soft and a little while while determine the difference between a metre and feet and so architecture flourishes. Sing singing will willingly sing singingly singing. The singing bird is singing on a Pologna tree singing to me oh singing to me.

Settle about settling.

Singing about singing.

Willing about willingly

So often soften.

Singing a singing bird is singing on a Pologna tree singing to me oh singing to me. A Pologna tree has mauve blossoms and they come out before leaves on a spreading Pologna tree. A chestnut tree has blossoms and leaves at the same time so has a Pologna tree. A singing bird is singing on a Pologna tree singing to me oh singing to me. After singing a very much more than a decision. He decided she decided they decided that the house is not to be divided but to face out both ways without a difference of their being a difference as a difference to be a difference not to be a difference to be a difference to be made. The sun and shade a shade in the sun and the sun in the shade and the sun in the sun shade. She made the sun in the sun shade which makes it be the time after before they ask what is the matter with it, very well have it as it is after it is by the time that it is with more than whether it is often soften. A singing bird is singing in a Pologna tree singing to me oh singing to me. The scene changes they have decided that it has not been what has been thought. They think. A scene of whether or no they are to be very satisfied. Sentences of deliberation.

They like to bow like an albatross only there isn't time. When they think and shrink that they can be there and where is it that they like they look alike. With this. Kiss.

An albatross when it is a penguin may make it charitable to be able splendid in isolation and depended on destination and loving with plenty of sensible investigation of principally adding when in as Mont Blanc a pencil stencil is not the same as free hand betaken.

We undertake the overthrow they understand this above all why they must. Must and just just is exactly forbidden.

Partly in having ever sharp a mixture.

They sat together he resting and she knitting.

Can they decide that a house is a home, home with a department.

Little letter kiss me.

A house a spouse.

Little letter kiss me does a house have a spouse.

Little letter kiss me does a little letter house have a spouse little letter kiss me a house have a spouse.

Scene One

Having a hand full of whatever it is. Does she believe that cradles are much.

Hand in hand they sit and settle to hear if it is called aloud that there is a little following.

Say may say may may has three saints which are freezing and will he million or three to be a incandescent does make with whim with a bead which was found was an a malachite when it was lost and was gold when it was found all round.

Neighbors are better better and better whenever they have pansies there. Pansies are my favorite flower.

Convince convinced behave better with a meaning that there is in rose a color.

Rose a color means more than each other.

Blue a color means that they have after next as better.

Green a color means it be to behave in a chance.

Violet a color means mauve and scarlet and lavender or in another.

Yet a color means that which consideration in emigration.

This makes singing in a minute.

She may or may not be a bathing beauty. She may have had a month in which to say how do you do when it is all true.

She makes hymns do. Do may be thorough better aware cumbersome in declare may marry.

How many little wings in cumbersome. How many little wings in wedding. How many little wings in weigh way way away weighed in the balance and not found wanting. Fatty fair weather is the same announcement as fatty do well. When she says come I do not come but when she says come come I come. I come and a little makes it be fairly very much indeed.

Weed is a place where they sing just as well as ever.

Next to a blessing kept quite as well funnily much just as when as dwell upon which made it settle some which for as especial in mentioned be wise for the change of prediction. To predict darling, darling pussy darling.

Sing mention.

A pliable certainty.

As they came they sat she with a sheet and he with a sheet she with a sheet of linen and he with a sheet of paper embroider as well. She sat with a sheet of linen he sat with a sheet of paper sat with an embroider as well.

What is the difference between silk and linen. Both admirable.

She sat sated he sat dated, she sat stated he sat waited an edible as well. She sat mated he sat belated as indicated and as well. Sing securely.

It is might which made a flattery with account because mining prodigiously leave rest with by made nearly have inculpated come mean with following final be fortune to be never by the increase with variable in the conclusion that peonies have odors. Come climb with have in place of preciously few. Few or or dew. Spelled like an inter rail and much be widen couple in continent become with weed wending might in shuttle. If he could knit if he could sit who would ask wood of them who would.

One two three come to eat prettily and thank you for everything.

Two at a meal.

Hello darling hello dear hello wife hello here chanticleer.

They will be overrun with museums and wonder if they will have pretty things in it.

Scene two

Capture rose resemble grows. Capture decisive. Capture displaces. Capture dismay display. Why is it made up to be whenever after after chose. Water grass is finer than rhododendrons.

Two have been seated at lunch and are disturbed.

A lyrical opera not an announcement. Fairly well. Half begun is well done.

Shaven and shorn and not forlorn because he was there when she was born she was born regularly and sweetly as it is to be lengthened neatly an academy to smell completely as they can do. She was born as one may say neatly to accomplish as one may say sweetly what is to be known as one may say completely in measuring it not to do any harm. It is very nearly mellow that she can love and predict that it is to be nicely in coloring it in a minute without a follow and it is not only known as a cow but now. Yes yes the address, dress dress in a press press press and caress caress caress in express express express with a stress a stress of an aptness to kindle and confess that she will be a progress from which it is called farm in waving it alight. Alight which is it. She makes it do. Do do be my own one do do do do do do.

Rose is a rose and a pansy he chose.

Rose is a rose and he chose a pansy.

Pansy is short for Pussie.

When a brooch has been lost and found who is half of all around and makes mainly tell which half plan caucases conferences can dwell we dwell in our home uninterruptedly, uninterrupted may maggie can well well happen tell she is content that it is found. I see the moon and the moon sees she god bless the moon and god bless she which is me.

Once sewing always sewing, this is a scene at noon.

Who has a stork who eats pork who has lurked here where they may have pleasure.

Who can couple amaze and place who can ridicule extra and before who can make it do whatever it does in ran before made as assay to produce with apply in coupling can placate repercussion in indite when bright.

She can sing reason.

That is my sight.

We make repeal retell remain readily well as a peignoir. Have a door but when is it a pleasure to leave well enough alone.

A marriage and a wedding makes a tender ten to one. Ten to one is all at present present present when he was right about it. It is very obliging that a pencil when it is round is light and when it is black is perfect and when it is white on the end is Mont Blanc.

Tender present tend to her.

A pencil yet and she is my pet her hair is washed and she is all known her half is met and this is a dress and she knows and she sews one two three she is is meant just as yet when it is best and let let it alone and do not make propositions to her as to what to do for her as to when to ask it of her and this is what is meant by establishment when it is made around with about and a sound and it is all just as it was thanks to this which is meant to be inaccurate. A scene in which it is better to have made as much in a way of it in a way as when very likely in their making it be a little different they can have advantages to be renewed. Let us hum. If we hum we mean that we are tired at noon. So let us not hum let us hum so that we mean that we are tired at noon so let us not hum let us hum and we can mean that we can be leaving it as having it soon at noon let us not hum very much as we can think differently about their night and morning being once in a while in summer. The scene which they manage is this they are as polite as they are in the making of it do.

A scene in singing singing is singing humming is humming and wedding is a wedding morning and an afternoon. Can a pigeon have its neck on one side.

Here is a song among the ten tender.

When lent lender.

When sent sender.

When ten tender

And you muse about.

Here is a song about with chances.

He chances to be easily put into the use of when it is undoubtedly that peonies are fragrant.

Come singing of how it is better to have it be this way all day.

If it is a change of dress how much are there to be thought accrue.

One one one.

Like makes it be that she that she.

Like makes it be that makes it be that she that she.

One of the band of hope, hope like that.

A scene of upstairs where there is a second floor from door to door.

Here where there is no second floor and no door to door.

Find out what she wants.

Find out what she wants.

Find out what she wants.

That is amusing music.

Find out what she wants.

How are daisies found every where. By public parks.

Three at a time. In before the making it have not hidden but pocketed. It is portably a pleasure pleasure trove.

With ways.

Sewing is what she has to do.

I have liked to have what it is they like do like to like to have a help an ever present help in here in here why do they do why do they do it in a hurry too.

One one she is my little son of a gun.

As seen in chapters.

Chapters when they need a monk, monkey see monkey do I do what I see her do need to do. Monkey see and monkey do and to see to it that I do what she sees me says she needs to have me see to. Monkey see monkey sees monkey does monkey does monkey sees monkey sees monkey does does do what monkey sees monkey does do and do do. Monkey see monkey does monkey sees monkey does monkey sees monkey does monkey does monkey sees. Adding sees to sees. Does do.

Just to finish it to-day with a little of the way to be way lay which is amusing.

Made in spite of four and nine representative in finally be next to having a chance of it in mean and while it is coupled with and about where they may have fancies. One of which is to be like like whichever she chose and owes and owes it to them. Which is why there is a half of a polite in polite. One two three when this you see have half in better come cover it with a breathing just the same. She is my delight one of it have to be as bright. Brightly in her with her to her may her for her call her leave it to her let her with her can she way lay way lay is all wrong way lay is a song sing song of be. Be polite. Give with all your might. Have her delight you which is fortunately for her to be for me to be for her to be for me to be for me for her for her to be me for me for her and she for me and come.

CAPITAL CAPITALS

Capitally be.

Capitally see.

It would appear that capital is adapted to this and that. Capitals are capitals here.

Capital very good.

Capital Place where those go when they go.

Capital. He has capital.

We have often been interested in the use of the word capital. A state has a capital a country has a capital. An island has a capital. A main land has a capital. And a portion of France has four capitals and each one of them is necessarily on a river or on a mountain. We were mistaken about one of them.

This is to be distressing.

We now return to ourselves and tell how nearly the world is populated.

First a capital.

Excitement.

Sisters.

First capital.

When we were on an island it was said that there was a capital there. And also that there was a capital on the mainland.

Did he and his wife and his sister expect to eat little birds.

Little birds least of all.

All the capitals that begin with A.

Aix Arles and Avignon.

Those that begin with be Beaux.

That makes four.

These that begin with B.
Barcelona.
Those that begin with m.
Marseilles and Mallorca.
You mean Palma.
Yes P.
Palma de Mallorca.
Do this in painting.
Will you have a strawberry.
Outcropping of the central mountain foundation.
Mountain formation and capitals.
Strawberries and capitals.
Letters a b and m and capitals.

Capitals.

First Capital   Capital C.
Second Capital   Capital D.
Third Capital   Capital Y.
Fourth Capital   Capital J.
Fourth Capital.
They said that they were safely there.
Third Capital.   Safer there than anywhere.
Second Capital.   They came there safely.
First Capital.   They were said to be safely here and there.
First Capital.   Capital wool.
   When we say capital wool we mean that all wool pleases us.
Capitally for wool
First Capital.   Egypt.
Second Capital.   Rabbit.
Third Capital.   Fingering.
Fourth Capital.   Ardently silk.
Fourth Capital.   Spontaneously married.
Third Capital.   Camel's hair.
Second Capital.   Eider Down.
First Capital.   Chenille.
First Capital.   It comes from the caterpillar I think.
Second Capital.   If travellers come and a rug comes, if a rug comes and
travellers have come everything has come and travellers have come.
Third Capital.   The third capital, they have read about the third capital.
It has in it many distinguished inventors of electrical conveniences.

Fourth Capital.   In how many days can every one display their satisfaction with this and their satisfaction.

Fourth Capital.   Let us count the fourth capital. Rome Constantinople Thebes and Authorisation.

Third Capital.   There are a great many third capitals.

Second Capital.   Surrounding second capitals are third capitals and first capitals.

First Capital.   The first capital remind me of derision.

First Capital.   Decide.

Second Capital.   To reside.

Third Capital.   And what beside.

Fourth Capital.   My side.

Fourth Capital.   At my side.

Third Capital.   And when can they say that there is no room there.

Second Capital.   When a great many people filter.

First Capital.   In.

First Capital.   They play ring around a rosey.

Second Capital.   They play London bridges.

Third Capital.   They play High Spy.

Fourth Capital.   They play horses.

Fourth Capital.   We have all forgotten what horses are.

Third Capital.   We have all forgotten what horses there are.

Second Capital.   We have all forgotten where there are horses.

First Capital.   We have all forgotten about horses.

Capital this and capital that. This is capital and that is capital.

First Capital.   Capital One.

Second Capital.   Capital Two.

Third Capital.   Capital Three.

Fourth Capital.   Capital Four.

Capital Four.

Fourth Capital.   The fourth capital is the one where we do dream of peppers. It is astonishing how a regular curtain can be made of red peppers. A long curtain and not too high.

Third Capital.   The third capital is one in which thousands of apples are red in color and being so they make us in no way angry.

Second Capital.   The second capital is one in which butter is sold. Can butter be sold very well.

First Capital.   The first capital is the one in which there are many more earrings. Are there many more earrings there than elsewhere.

Capital One.   Acclimated. We are acclimated to the climate of the first capital.

Capital Two.   We are acclimated to the climate of the second capital.
Capital Three.   If in regard to climates if we regard the climate, if we are
acclimated to the climate of the third capital.
Capital Four.   The climate of capital four is the climate which is not so
strange but that we can be acclimated to it. We can be acclimated to the
climate of the fourth capital.
Fourth Capital.   If every capital has three or four who lock their door and
indeed if we mean to care for their home for them we can complain of lack of
water. Water can be bought.
Third Capital.   If in any capital there are three or four who mean to present
themselves tenderly then indeed can we silence ourselves by thanking. We can
thank then.
Second Capital.   If in any capital they are more seldom seen more and
more seldom, if they are more and more seldomly seen what then what of
them.
First Capital.   If in every capital there are more than there were before
how may a capital continue this preparation. They prepare themselves to say
that they will stay.
First Capital.   In the first place the first capital is very well placed.
Second Capital.   In the second place the second capital has more sugared
melon.
Third Capital.   In the third place the third capital is aroused.
Fourth Capital.   In the fourth place all four capitals have many shovels.
Fourth Capital.   Except me.
Third Capital.   Accept me.
Second Capital.   Expect me.
First Capital.   Except me.
First Capital.   I do I will.
First Capital.   Very still.
Second Capital.   Catalogue.
Third Capital.   A station.
Fourth Capital.   It is Sunday and beside it is raining.
Fourth Capital.   Spoken.
Third Capital.   Outspoken.
Second Capital.   Presses.
First Capital.   Addresses.
First Capital.   Counting.
Second Capital.   Recounting.
Third Capital.   Extra meals.
Fourth Capital.   Spaces.
Fourth Capital.   Indeed.

Third Capital.   Hearty Kisses.

Second Capital.   In a minute.

First Capital.   Shut the door.

First Capital.   In this way in as they say this way, in this way they say they are as they may say this way. In this way things matter.

First Capital.   Cannot express can express tenderness.

First Capital.   In this way as they say in this way as they say they cannot express tenderness. As they say in the way they say they can express in this way tenderness, they can express tenderness in this way.

Second Capital.   If they are good if they are good to me if I can see that they are good if I can see that they are good to me, if I would if I could I could say that they are good if I would say that they are good to me, if I could if I would, if they could be good if they would be good if they are good, are they good are they good to me do you hear me say that they could be good did they hear me say that they could be good, that they are good that I say that they are good to me.

Third Capital.   If they belong to being more than strong, do they care to be strong do they care to belong do they belong to being strong. If they hear a second day do they say a second day comes before a first day any way. Capitally strong do they belong does it belong to them to be capitally strong. I will say so to-day. They do not answer me in syllables.

Fourth Capital.   To settle and to settle well, to settle very well to settle. Do they settle do we settle do I settle do they settle very well do they settle well do we settle, well do we. Do I settle. Do I settle very well. Very well I do settle. I do settle very well. They do settle very well.

Fourth Capital.   Resemble it.

Third Capital.   To resemble it.

Second Capital.   They resemble it.

First Capital.   They resemble.

First Capital.   I state that the first capital is the one that has been won to see it settle on itself denial. I deny we deny they deny. I deny what that they are safely there and no one comforted him.

Second Capital.   Do not annoy any one needing to feel strongly that if wishes were horses beggers would ride and why are ridden horses still used, why are they still used why are ridden horses still used.

Third Capital.   Reasonable wishes do not color reasonable wishes, reasonable wishes are not colored by reasonable wishes, reasonable wishes are rarely colored to be reasonable wishes.

Fourth Capital.   Mountains are not merely out croppings they are usefully employed in reasonable association. We resonably associate with one another and are elaborately aware of waiting. Wait again for me.

Fourth Capital.   Capitals are plenty there are plenty of capitals.

Third Capital.   Why do they enjoy capitals and why are capitals places rapidly united. We unite ourselves together.

Second Capital.   The capital seems to be the capital.

First Capital.   A capital is not easily undertaken nor is it easily aroused nor indeed is it impervious.

First Capital.   Thoroughly.

Second Capital.   And very pleasantly.

Third Capital.   Nearer to it than that.

Fourth Capital.   Eagerly accepted.

Fourth Capital.   They are.

Third Capital.   They do.

Second Capital.   They will.

First Capital.   They are to-night.

First Capital.   Paul.

Second Capital.   Not Paul.

Third Capital.   Paul Cook.

Fourth Capital.   Three Capitals in all.

Fourth Capital.   I intend to learn to stay away.

Third Capital.   I intend to endeavor consolation.

Second Capital.   Many win.

First Capital.   Many many times in the way.

First Capital.   Happily a little calling and covering.

Second Capital.   Happily a very little changing and repeating.

Third Capital.   Very happily properly placed as a castle.

Fourth Capital.   We were very content with the inroad.

Fourth Capital.   Inlay.

Third Capital.   He mentions me.

Second Capital.   Am I in it.

First Capital.   He leaves the kitchen as well.

First Capital.   In sight of the first capital because of this capital beside this as a capital because of this as their capital and becoming this becoming their possession by way of this and their having the possession, permit to credit you with an excellent reason for remaining here. Permit me to do this and also permit me to assure you that coming again is not as pleasant as coming again and again and coming again and again is very nearly the best way of establishing where there is the most pleasure the most reasonableness the most plenty the most activity, the most sculpture the most liberty the most meditation the most calamity and the most separation. If rose trees are cut down again and again he can be busily engaged and if he is busily engaged can he nourish hope and if he nourishes hope can he converse and if he converses can he say he hopes that some day he will supply the same that he did supply when the sun heated and the sun heated. When the mountains are near by and not high little mountains made at the right angle are not high and yet we can imply that they are neither near by nor high and they are near by and they are near high. The capital was nearly eight hundred miles away. This gives me no idea of its distance of the distance from here to there.

Second Capital. For capitals.

If a second capital has pleased them all if a second capital is second only in such a way that there is no reason to arouse me, to arouse me, a second capital in all a second capital, does know that he found it to be so, does he know that he has told us that in walking that in walking he has been more than sufficiently clearly seeing that if a park is green that if a park is green may he be sure of his path may he and may he in association may he in his place may he in such a place may he indeed might he have been employed in such a place and in what way was he employed was it in relation to meat to vegetables to bread to cake to fruit to ices or indeed was it in relation to the homes where all who are religious find themselves crowded. Did he crowd in. No indeed, he meditated in this way, every noon as soon as he was responsible and he was he was responsible to no one, to wife and child and all and he came at their call. Call again.

I often mention what has been seen no no one can say more no one can say any more than that it has been seen that a king has been seen not a king not has been seen not that a king has been seen, not that there has been seen, not that there has been seen not a king not that there has been seen, and when did he wish to waver, waver and waver, and when did he wish to wave it away, wave it away and he will say to-day and January for a day.

Third Capital. I see, say that I see. I see that I say that I see.

Fourth Capital. He went to stay and had his father and his mother been there long. Had his father and his mother been there long and was there no reason for that. Was there no reason for this and he was not found to be splendid. Who was really the manager of the distribution of light. He was not prepared to receive them here and there. Here and there, here and there. Read it again. Here and there.

Fourth Capital. Has a reason.

Third Capital. For this.

Second Capital. More than all.

First Capital. The rest.

First Capital. Did they clear themselves of men and women and did they seem to be able to be especially related.

Second Capital. Did they seem to be especially related and did they fasten their bamboos as hedges every two years.

Third Capital.   Did they fasten their bamboos as hedges every two years and did they have any objection to their rejection.

Fourth Capital.   Were they really rejected and did they object as it would seem that they did.

The fourth Capital. If they have to do this and they have to do this, if they have to do this can they attend to their daisies.

The third Capital. And if they attend to their stones and stones are in a way useful can they attend to baggage.

The second Capital. In attending to baggage a great many are caught in the rain.

The first Capital.   It is Sunday and beside it is raining.

The first Capital.   It is too cold to rain.

First Capital.   In the meantime do you see. Yes I see. In the meantime do you see me. Yes I do see you.

Second Capital.   If you went and if you came if they came if you went and came, indeed spring does come before winter that is to say even here. Now understand what I mean. One may say that winter is as winter. They meant to winter.

Third Capital.   Met again or not met.

Fourth Capital.   I see you see he sees me, he can see you can see they can see me.

Fourth Capital.   I meant to say that.

Third Capital.   They meant that beside.

Second Capital.   Ignorant negroes.

First Capital.   Not as ignorant as negroes.

First Capital.   Capital for capital and who knows better than that that capital is mine.

    Capital for capital.

    Crowd for crowd.

    Out loud for out loud.

    Crowd for crowd.

    Capital for capital.

Second Capital.   Capitally.

    Capital for capital.

    Question for question.

    A caress for a caress.

    A river for a river and a spring for a spring. Spring comes very early here, it comes before the days are longer.

    Capital for capital.

    Candy for candy.

    Curtains for curtains and crowds for crowds.

Crowds for crowds.

Curtains for curtains.

Candy for candy and capital for capital.

Third Capital.   Capitals for capitals.

Plants for plants.

Bridges for bridges and beds for beds.

Beds for beds.

Bridges for bridges.

Plants for plants and capitals for capitals.

Fourth Capital.   Capital capitals.

Capitally.

Capitally Capable.

Articles for articles.

Buds for buds.

Combs for combs and lilies for lilies.

Lilies for lilies.

Combs for combs.

Buds for buds.

Articles for articles.

And capitals for capitals.

We know how to remove harness and grass.

Capitals for capitals.

Fourth Capital.   And capitals for capital.

Third Capital.   And capital and capital.

Second Capital.   And more than capital.

First Capital.   For their capital.

First Capital.   Yes yes.

First Capital.   Able to able to able to go able to go and come able to come and go able to come and go able to do so.

In this way we may date to-day.

What is the date to-day.

What is the date to-day.

I wish to tell all I know about Capitals.

Capitals are the places where every one exactly deprecates the necessity of going away, where every one deprecates the necessity there is to stay where every one utters a welcome that is sufficiently stirring and where every one does know what makes them so, so what so very nearly wider.

Now let me see why capitals are steadily repeated.

I repeat the first Capital.

I repeat I repeat.

I repeat the second Capital.

You repeat you repeat I repeat the third Capital.

We repeat we repeat I repeat the fourth Capital.

They repeat they repeat.

I repeat that a capital is a treat.

I repeat that they retreat from the capital and that they retreat.

I repeat that they compete for a capital.

I repeat that they compete.

Do they compete.

I repeat that they defeat that they defeat that they defeat that they deplete that they complete that they seat a great many people in there and it is it is there that they are seated. I know why I say what I do say. I say it because I feel a great deal of pleasure of satisfaction of repetition of indication of separation of direction of preparation of declaration of stability of precaution of accentuation and of attraction. And why do you spare little silver mats. Little silver mats are very useful and silver is very pretty as to color.

SAINTS AND SINGING

A Play

Saints and singing. I have mentioned them before. Saints and singing need no door they come before, saints and singing, they adore, saints and singing, or, saints and singing, and this play is about a choice of sentiment. I choose you. And what do you choose. I choose you. We have been baffled by harmony.

Act One. Scene One.

Prelude

And how do you dispose of me.

I dispose of you by being intimate and impersonal. And how do you dispose of me. I don't dispose of you at all.

So many people pray that you will furnish them ribbons and sashes. And do you. No. I furnish them with cakes and little houses. And Christmas trees. We have abandoned Christmas trees.

Not for Christmas.

No for Thanksgiving.

To-morrow is Thanksgiving and what am I giving.

Act One Scene One

I have felt called to call all a revision and I revise Helen Wise, and Beatrice Wise and Henry Wise. I have felt called to call for a decision, and I have decided to abide by religion and all the splendid acts of ministration and administration executed by you and others.

This is so gay.

Herbert.   Can you guess why I admire what I admire.

James.   For my liberty I am willing to be addicted to ripening.

Arnold.   Guess at prayers.

William.   I am William.

And what does he say.

He says how readily I can see the day, the day and the night and the protection of his mother. We recall sisters. And a countryman said. When are we up.

End of Scene I

Scene II

A field full of berries and a body if well known and calculating cousins. In America we do not allow for their cousins. In America we do not allow for that, for this, that cousins can wish and do we mean to be allowed very much. We make allowances to those to whom we give it.

Scene II

Feel me.

I feel very well now.

Do you feel very well now. I feel very well now and I feel that I will feel for you, I feel so very well.

All for Hannah.

Hannah is not welcome.

All for Henry.

Henry smiles and when he smiles he feels the need of a recital.

Can we recite with a song.

I sing.

You sing.

We sing.

And now mention me.

I mention you to him and to her.

I mention her.

I mention him. I mention him. I do mention, how frequently we wonder, how often does Jessie how often does Jessie employ, employ those she can mention.

She can mention to me when this you see you are all to me.

It was almost it was mostly thought out by records and moist houses, it was mostly thought out by moist houses that bed-rooms should be heated.

Arnold. How are you Arnold.

How are you Benjamin Arnold and Cora Couperous. How do you do Benjamin and when are you willing to be ready too late. When are you willing to be ready too late. When am I willing to be ready too late.

And Cora what do you think about the loyalty of a section. What do you think about loyalty. What claims have you on Benjamin, and how often do you languish.

How can we be feeble very feeble so feeble, how can we be so feeble now.

I have had every excuse, I have made every excuse, I have given every excuse for men for women and for children. Men women and children make the population.

I do believe in calling. Call me, call me back call me back again, call me by a name. I wonder I do wonder about saints and singing. They sing the same name. Could they sing the same name just the same.

Edward would be a better name. George has the name just the same. So then.

Coming, I am coming. Yes I am coming. He called me by my name.

And I.

I make a new name, and yet every name is the same, it is always in the name.

It is said that the name is the same name.

Are you coming. Hope is coming. Henry Hope is coming.

Henry Hope is married and Henry Hope is married and he is coming.

Henry Hope mentioned me to him.

Do please please please please me.

I have often thought of swimming in water.

Scene III

If there is in between if there is in between the tradition, if there is between that tradition the tradition of laying of laying across the pieces of translations. Translate everybody.

Jennie Charles.

How do you do how do you resume mentioning religion.

Jennie Charles. I am so very well.

I am so very well, and he is my most admiring and startling selection.

And then easily.

And then so easily.

Jennie French.

How have you met Jennie Nightingale.

And please be another Jessie.

When I say Jessie what do I mean.

And now altogether I esteem I esteem the best and the very best and the very best of all of them.

I flatter myself that extra thought, that I give extra thought that I give them, I give to them my extra thinking.

In this way a lesson, in this way they lessen Egyptian and Arabian thinking.

And now do you remember recognition.

A play.

I play.

You play.

Mistinguett can play.

What can we play.

We can play that to-day letters say, Mistinguett have a day.

Oh that way.

I say.

Mistinguett does not get away.

When I wish, veal, when I wish hare when I wish radishes there. When I wish that Paul, Constance, and religion have their place, have their places. I say I play in between their care.

Comes the scene.

In between their, in between their necklaces, in their way of wishes. Can you be rowdier.

I have no wishes.

Gather I gather I gather that you are not teased.

Excite I do excite, excite we excite, how do we excite.

We gather we would rather we would rather gather that we, what can religion sing.

I sing.

You sing.

I sing to you.

You sing.

Now be a flower in May. Now be a flower anyway.

Make names.

Make their names.

Make their names say.

Make their names make sense when they say.

What do they say.

They say speeches.

What do they say.

They say count to day, at count to-day.

They say they rapidly say, they say very rapidly just what they say.

How can you be Robert, Robert himself. How can you be so readily filled with the interest of my thoughts.

I have.

You have.

I have my willingness.

And wind sounds like rain, wind when it is turning. How a little nature makes religion, and how a little religion makes creation makes a saint in singing and now rush and hush. We are not going to meeting.

An Interlude

Can tickle can tickle.

Why can he can tickle her.

Can tickle can tickle.

He can tickle her.

Can tickle.

Can tickle.

He can tickle her.

Can tickle.

Can tickle.

He can make her purr.

Where where over there. I do I do love her hair.

Where Where over there I do do make a pair.

What what I forgot. I do not forget my dot.

One two Three, One Two Three, One Two One Two Holy Holy Gee.

What.

What.

I forgot.

What What.

What What.

A succession of addresses.

Act II

Scene I

How do you do.

I do not neglect you.

I feel very readily that in these circumstances, Dolly is wild, that in these circumstances, believe me that in these circumstances I see you.

I see you again.

I will see you again.

Come and see me.

I love the moon or dawn.

Jenny. Yes of course certainly and I believe you and as for my husband you know very well that he is not the father of my child. You have known it all. You know he has a child. You know that prayers her prayers, not the child's prayers, but the friend's prayers, she who is sixty nine and capable of praying capable of praying for nine mornings and not singing not even singing not even singing. Prayers do not mix us.

Donald and Dorothy and a collision.

Donald and Dorothy and Antwerp. How many are killed every day by accidents.

Dorothy I say, I say to you Dorothy that you have only stayed a day.

A Scene between a Woman an Egyptian and an Australian.

Hear me speak.

I hear you when you say that you are a wife that you have been worried and that you have placed a cream where it belongs.

A cream.

And not a quarrel.

A cream and not a quarrel.

Forgive me, a cream and not a quarrel.

She can address him. He can address them. She can dress him. He can dress them. She can dress him. He can he can, She can address him, He can.

He can address them.

Exercise me I say, I say exercise me. Exercise me I say you may you may exercise with me to-day. Exercise me I say and I say exercise with me and I exercise with her to-day, I say, exercise with me I say exercise with me.

I master pieces of it. Exercise in mastering pieces of it. Exercise in master-pieces. Exercise in her mastering her pieces. I am exercising I am exercised, I am exercised in mastering pieces, I am exercised in masterpieces. Capital. He capitally said, there is the basket of wood and of bread. Capital he said. Capitally he said. I am glad she is able to bring it. And now, wood is gay and bread is gaily and butter is gaily said to be eaten. Mrs. Eaton and Waldemar George, Mrs. Eaton Miss Eaton, Miss Eaton and Waldemar and George.

Miss Eaton and Miss Beaton. Mary why do you remember Mary.

I remember you remember can you remember Carry.

Carry and tea can she carry me.

Carry and tea, Carry the tea, Carry the tea for me and for Mildred and for radium and for X ray. Carry the tea away. Thank you.

Lipschitz Lipschitz Lipschitz and his friend. Lipschitz Lipschitz do you love to blend, Lipschitz Lipschitz how many are there here.

Lipschitz Lispchitz, you can guess it without fear.

They are here.

Thank you.

And interlude in music is an interlude indeed. And interlude in mockery. I do not admit mockery.

On the first day of the new year he writes.

And I write too and I say, standard, the standard of yellow and crimson. So historic.

And now please.

Wishes.

I wish for a kiss. I wish for the rest of the day.

And I wish I was a fish. And I wish the most.

Plenty of irritation.

Why do you wash older weddings.

Why do you wash older weddings.

One two three four five six seven. Come again and talk of heaven.

One two three four five six seven.

I come to you so noisily that you astonish me.

Scene II

Why do we stamp.

Don't walk too hard walk gently and continuously and persistently but don't walk too hard.

A compliment. I am a complement to you. You compliment me. I arrange to compliment you. So next to nothing. Why do flashes of older women. Why do flashes of older women compliment him and them.

Why do flashes of older women how can he hear the same name. Dolly. I stretch to Dolly. Nelly I dare to tell her, Nelly is your name. Nelly, a million or three are three or four, and you, you love the remainder of their door.

Nelly why do you wish me.

Nelly why do you wish for me. Nelly why do you wish for me there, Nelly why do you wish me to be there, Nelly.

How realisable are apples and butter. She says apples and potatoes. And we say apples and butter and rapidly diminishing. Who diminishes rapidly.

Sound.

How does it sound.

How do you sound. How do you season. How do you read the reason. How do you How do you How very nearly do you, How do you very nearly breathe.

Books that is paper that is the paper, the paper in books is useful in any army, can be useful in any army, and where can religion tear, where can religion tear away, where can religion tear away from there.

Shout to a man. Men, shout to a man. I shout. Saints who are singing, Saints and singing, I shall keep him from fur. I shall keep fur away from him. I shall not let him. I shall not let her, I shall not let him, I shall not let her use fur. Fur and splendidly willing. Come to the window and sing there.

Saints and singing. Everywhere.

Have you my knife.

He is very sweet to see that he has money readily. And accidentally witness. He can accidentally witness what he can mean.

I mean and you mean.

Remember that I know what I want and I know how to get it. Also remember finishing touches. Also remember me to Emily.

Scene III

I hear that he was rapidly seen.

Rapidly seen to be what.

I hear that he was rapidly seen to be there at all. I hear that he was most subtle most subtly spread with what he was not worthy, not worthy of regulation.

How can chances How can there be chances how can there be chances for him. Oh my dear, cannot you stay, cannot you stay there and feel that yesterday, and to-day are full of all the measure of repetition. Repeat what.

In repeating all in repeating, in repeating all is awaited. They wait they might wait.

A parlor.

A parlor in where nuns are.

Scene IV

Center and enter. I enter to go there.

Five o'clock and nearly all well.

Please press across. Please press across what.

And where.

Nearly everywhere. In an entanglement. How can they spare her to be in an ecstacy. I feel the exact recollection.

Constance Street.

Do come in.

Do come in.

Do come in.

Constance and Elisabeth have not the same name. One is Constance Street and the other is Elisabeth Elkus. It is easy to be three and there they are more often recognized as three.

Thank you for your edition. Thank you very much. And now all walk together and play that silence is restless. I rest so blankly. And you did ask her to send it and did she.

Golden Gate is the second one.

I plan and you plan to meet me. He plans he does not plan at all and he does not call.

A hymn for a whim.

And coffee needs to be wretched and honey needs to be wretched and glasses need to be there.

Come and bear with me.

And now how to be sacred.

Flashlight and bird line and new dollars. If you receive a legacy is the money there. If you receive more do you have to be widowed. Does a widower stare.

I can be here there and everywhere. Does a widower repeat his adjective. Does he say can I harden.

And now something is relatively separate. I separate her from them. And was she aside from this firm and an apple.

Sing to me.

Able to sing to me. Able to sing to them. Able to sing to them of me.

Able to sing to them of me and of them. Able to sing to me. And to them of me and of them.

I sing to them when I sing a second song.

How can I measure threads.

Come together.

They came there and we said I have heard more voices and you have heard more of their voices and we have heard of their voices.

How can you remember that one out of ten. How can you remember that one out of every ten. How can you remember when they were found. Are you bound to remember that they abound.

Are you bound to be a second winter. Can you argue with me. May you live long and prosper.

Scene V

Can you step backward and step on a wooden arrangement of a carving. Can you step backward and step on a round piece of wood which is a part of the arrangement of a wooden carving. Did you. And then he said I hope that you understood me.

He said that he would not be credited with carefulness.

Can you believe in a variety in marbles. I like marble painted. And I like marble imitated.

And I like marble revered.

And as for me I worship reproduction of marble.

And as for me I believe that the coloring the doubling of coloring looks like avarice. Please him by revealing by what has been said and done.

I carefully interrupt and I say Constance go away.

Do be careful of me and do not say again what do I measure again. You measure as a treasure.

Dolly is clearly here. You mean she is clearly not here.

Trouble me please to say if you love a woman you give her money.

And you also say how can I believe in water berries.

I know black currants have religious faces I know that very well and I know that religious faces are very apt to be very well related to corals and fairly acknowledged rounds.

I am around.

Can you mingle vegetable roots with precious herds. Herds of cold cows and herds of good dogs and herds and herds, have you heard of a bird that repeats me.

I can easily follow the cloud about. And about there. Yes about there we stare and we say Harden why do you take offence at the reason you give for everything. Why do you not take offence at the reason that you give for everything. Why do you read lists.

Follow me latterly. That is what I say. Latterly. Follow me.

He is not so expectant, he is not so very splendid, he is not so well intentioned as she is and yet what does she do she annoys every Jew.

How do you know that language I know that language very well. I have faith beside.

And the instant obedience.

And the instant obedience.

When.

Calm yourself Emil, you are not widowed yet. You know very well that you are wedded to your running. You never run away and you never satisfy your librarian.

You never satisfy decidedly you never satisfy, very decidedly do you ever satisfy weddings. Do you ever satisfy their weddings, do you ever satisfy, life and riches. Do you ever satisfy riches. And please do not please her.

Christmas kisses.

Sing to the satisfaction of Monday Wednesday and candlesticks. Can you remember candlesticks. I can remember when the change occurred, I can remember relieving Chinese masterpieces relieving mingled Chinese and European wideness and really asking blessings on San Francisco. Saint Francis, Saint Nicholas Saint Chrysostom and Saint Bartholomew. Saint Bartholomew is nearest to raised eyelashes, eyebrows and columns, and trees begin with a trunk and mountains with meadows. I merrily read I merrily lead I merrily sing to crosses. I believe in respect I believe in relief I believe in actual plenty. I believe in actual plenty in plenty of time. Harden. How are you.

I am very well. Harden what do you think of measuring heat. I feel the cold equally. Harden what are mildewed grapes.

They are to be found in certain seasons.

And what benefit is there in raised pearls.

Raised pearls are beautiful to the eye, and I I like the waiting here. You mean you want the waiting to be here that is to say you wish that the waiting should take place here.

Yes I mean exactly that. I mean to be very exact. I mean to call you, I mean to come, I mean to be especially seen and very nearly established. I mean to cloud the rain and to articulate to articulate very clearly I mean to articulate very clearly and to pronounce myself as aroused. Are you aroused by them or for them. Neither the one nor the other.

Continuation of Scene V

Aunt Louise had once broken her leg as a girl and it was a little sensitive and twenty years later when for the first time she skated again she broke her leg all over again but it did not cause the slightest excitement.

This time a great many people found investigation to be a necessity. Come again Harden. Come again.

I ask questions and he said I have a feeling that he has not been able to answer me.

And what do you ask him.

I ask him about representation. Politically. No neither politically nor numerically but actually. Actually how readily are you how readily do you promise ringing. How readily do you promise to suggest saints and singing saints and then singing. How readily do you promise Harden. Harden, how readily do you promise this threatening this to be threatening. How readily do you vary your caress. How very readily.

How very readily.

Deliberately inclusive.

Pardonably debilitated.

Reserved for them.

Reserved toward them.

And silk for noon. Never silk neither for noon or for morning.

Never any of their silk. Never any of that silk for them neither for them nor before them. Never any mailing never any of silk covering of a silk covering before them in front of them nor behind them. How do you use silk.

Care to go.

Do you care to go.

Do you care to go there.

Feel it restlessly and do not deface stories.

Two stories or three stories.

Six stories are higher. And very much higher. Oh so very much higher.

Harden are you willowy. Are you very famous. Are you famous for these embellishments. Are these embellishments in your occupancy of round ones. Are these recognised embellishments. Are there meagre cuts. Are there very meagre rounds.

How round are rare flowers. How very round are very rare flowers.

How very round are they there. How very rare are they around there.

Not there.

Not where you are when you are privately there.

How famous are the meeting places of religion and law.

How famous are the meeting places of religion and towns. How famous are the meeting places of cousins and exhibitions. How famous are they always, how very famous are they always. How very famous are they always when they are there.

Who can answer and a pardon. Who can answer and pardon faith and reproduction. Who can answer swinging women. Who can answer him there I glance, you glance, you glance at them when they are there.

You recognize that the collection that the collection that the collecting of them that their collecting of them causes them to be there.

Where.

There.

ACT III

Scene I

I have every confidence in their religion and I say nuns every day and I say girls at play and I say she is working all day. She is sixty nine and she has nothing to say except that she will receive her pay. And does she stay.

Harden come in.

Harden come in to tea.

Harden come in to see me.

Harden come in Harden he does not spin nor is he that twin, he is has the right to win he must come in.

Come in again it is always a pleasure to see you.

Scene II

I rapidly read printed matter and I find that nothing at all has been left behind.

Can you believe that he is not there.

Can you believe that he is not here.

Can you believe that brown is one color, that chocolate color and eider down color matter. Oil cloth matters. Can we replace it.

We have replaced and very cheaply and we have not received their good wishes for a pleasant winter. We have received their good wishes.

Converse with me. In a play you converse with me.

They play they partly play this play on the day. On their day.

Scene III

Now read louder. Prayers are not read aloud to be louder, they are louder but not read aloud and saying what are you saying to me Harden can you see.

Say it to me.

Say to me, can you see.

Say can you see to this for me. I can easily see to this and I will see to this and you will see what the result will be.

Harden can you plunge yourself across.

Fight presents, you guess.

You guess that you can fight and read their address. How can you smile bewilderdly. How can you speak to yourself and make of that a principle in repetition.

Reading flowers. How do you read flowers. I read flowers by languages and muttering. How can you resemble that which is heard. How can you. Speak to me Harden.

Speak to me and tell me what is the cause of the principal relief of retribution. Religion let us. Let us spring. In the spring we make golden butter.

And modesty, modesty ate prettily, modestly he ate very prettily. And what chance have we of meeting again.

What are the chances of our meeting again.

Establish records. He says that he won that before. Thank you.

Thank you for winning.

And now saints and singing and what a scene.

This is the scene.

Scene Four

Open the door.

Scene IV

Before I had begun I was very well arranged for. I had arranged everything very well.

He was not as precious as he had roused himself to be and necessarily very necessarily Roger hums.

To be obliging can he be rapidly be called Harden. Can he be rapidly called by those who love sending saints to do their singing.

Please me.

I please you as a dilatory victory I please you. Do please me. He pleases me connectedly. He pleases me connectedly and usefully regularly. Please me for planting pleasingly the signs of the thing I have here what have you here.

Harden how can you ask. I have here a great many different signs of saintly singing. Saintly singing analysed to me.

Rub it.

When you have a silver lamp rub it.

When you have a silver lamp and you rub it you clean it.

This is equally true of other silver.

When you have other silver and you rub it you clean it. This is true of all the silver.

Now once more Harden, what are your passages. How often have you crossed the ocean. How many people have you met in crossing, toward how many have you incurred the obligation of rejoining them and how very many are you willing to moisten rapid repetition with angular vibration. You are not angular, you do not vibrate nor do you caution men and women as to war and liberation. Run to war and liberation, run to saints and education, run to gardens and elimination run to singing and division, do divide beside do divide beside, do divide saints and singing, do divide beside saints and singing, do divide singing and beside can you ring beside can you ring beside the use and air of elaboration and a vision. Be a vision of the outstanding and nearly impassable religion. Do you read religion. Do you adore singing. Do you blunder to that saint and say I do not pray to-day. What happens next.

He recharges the ship, the steamer, the boat and the color. He recharges the color the meadow the ceiling and the voice. He recharges the words the music and the opera. He recharges the choice.

I choose you, and what do you choose.

I choose the rest.

And what do you depend upon. I depend upon what I need and what I have, and I will undertake to establish a dynasty in this way. A dynasty does not stay. No indeed but neither does it go away. And what are the ample expenditures. They are these. Instruments, pears, hats, and oleanders. How easily oleanders please us. Do not they. Harden do you go away. No not to-day. Read to me while you stay.

Scene V

Everybody sees a saint and yesterday.

Repeat to me about yesterday.

Everybody sees a saint and yesterday, everybody sees a saint.

They serve three years seven months and twelve days.

They considered that the day they were benefited by everything was equal to the willingness those who were willing showed in beatitude in gratitude.

He is acquainted with the recognition that is predicted.

I read of a saint there.

Where.

Reading matters.

I read of a saint having been there.

Where.

In China.

In Savoy.

In despair.

I read of a saint having been where.

Everywhere.

I read of a saint. He read of the reason that the saint became a saint there.

He reads of the reason that the saints take care. They take care of them there. Saints take care of them everywhere.

And where are saints taken when they are taken away from prayer. They are taken to be made saints to take care of those who love them and who love prayer. Saints are the saints who are the saints who take care of those who take care of prayer and who beware of accrediting to themselves a large share. So then saints and singing seem there, seem to be there, seem to be and are there.

Saints and singing save themselves from the wear and tear of sound in there and they declare, they love to be their indentation there.

Saints and singing and I do care.

How do you care, I care for their care.

Do that nicely, I do that nicely, I do very nicely do that.

And leave me the I leave to you all the rest of the revelation.

The amount of the creation and the question of memory enters into this question readily. I read about calculation recognition and inexperience.

Now cloud the issue. Cloud the issue so that words cause you to tease me. You are a frightful tease.

You tease me frightfully just as you please. And it pleases you to blunder and when you blunder why do you repeat precious you are so precious. Why do you repeat, treasure treasure I love you without measure. Why do you repeat, I repeat what you repeat.

I do not neglect florid graces. I do not neglect torrid races, I do not neglect plenty of places. I do not neglect exaggerated spaces, I do not neglect original traces nor do I neglect absences. Who is absent. Shall I mention Nelly and Harden. Shall I mention Harden again. No I will not mention what I have no intention of corroborating. Witnesses corroborate. I do not have to deny that the reason why I do not deny witnesses witnessing is because the origin the real origin of exhibiting acting is this. Mountains of saints singing. Mountains and mountains of saints singing and singing. Saints witnessing and corroborating. Mountains of saints witnessing and singing. Do sing please.

The origin of mentioning saints singing were nuns praying. The origin of nuns praying was splendid rehearsing. And the origin of repetition is the Harden admission. I admit that he that they that it is not a pause.

Who pauses.

I believe that notwithstanding all of the repetition, all of that repetition makes more imperative what I have just indicated.

What have you indicated.

I have indicated good fortune.

This is the end of the play.

Saints and singing which had a good beginning and now has a very good ending.

Saints and their singing.

Saints and singing do not come to this as an ending. Saints and singing. Read me by repetition. Saints and singing and a mission and an addition.

Saints and singing and the petition. The petition for a repetition.

Saints and singing and their singing.

Saints and singing and winning and.

Do not repeat yourself.

A LIST

Martha.	not interesting.
Maryas.	Precluded.
Martha.	Not interesting.
Marius.	challenged.
Martha and Maryas.	Included.
Maryas.	If we take Marius.
Mabel.	And an old window and still.
Mabel Martha and Maryas.	Various re-agents make me see victoriously.
Maryas.	In as we thrust them trust them trust them thrust them in. In as we brush them, we do not brush them in. In as we trust them in.
Mabel Martha and Mabel and Martha.	Susan Mabel Martha and Susan, Mabel and Martha and a father. There was no sinking there, there where there was no placid carrier.
Martha.	not interesting.
Maryas.	Not included.
Mabel.	And an old window and still.
Marius.	Exchange challenges.

Maryas. If added to this speeches are made are speeches played, speeches are included and thrust in and they trust in and they trust in speeches and they brush them in.

Martha. Smiles.

Mabel. And still she did mean to sing-song. We know how to very nearly please her.

Marius. Exchange challenges for challenges and by and by defy, and define by and by Battling Siki and so high. He is higher than they say. You know why beads are broader, in order to be in order to be an order to be strung together.

Maryas
and Yes indeed.
Martha.

Maryas. Can intend to seize her objects seize the objects place the objects, place the objects.

Martha. A list.

Maryas. A list.

Marius. A list.

Martha

Maryas. A list.

Martha

Maryas. A list lost.

Martha. A list lost reminds her of a fire lost. Smoke is not black nor if you turn your back is a fire burned if you are near woods which abundantly supply wood.

Maryas. A list lost does not account for the list which has been lost nor for the inequality of cushions shawls and awls. Nowadays we rarely mention awls and shawls and yet an awl is still used commercially and a shawl is still used is still used and also used commercially. Shawls it may be mentioned depend upon their variety. There is a great variety in calculation and in earning.

Marius. A list.

Mabel. A list.

Martha. A list.

Martha. There is a great variety in the settlement of claims. We claim and you claim and I claim the same.

Martha. A list.

Maryas. And a list.

Mabel. I have also had great pleasure from a capital letter.

Martha. And forget her.

Maryas. And respect him.

Marius.   And neglect them.

Mabel.   And they collect them as lilies of the valley in this country.

Martha.   A list.

Maryas.   Sixteen if sixteen carry four, four more, if five more carry four for more if four more carry four, if four carry fifty more, if four more five hundred and four and for more than that, and four more than eighty four. Four more can carry sixteen if you please if it is acceptable.

Martha.   She knows very well that if five are sitting at a table and one leaning upon it, that it makes no difference.

Maryas
and
Martha.   Nearly all of it has made nearly all of it. Nearly all of it has made nearly all of it.

Maryas
and
Martha.   Nearly all of it has made nearly all of it has made nearly all of it has made nearly all of it.

Martha
and
Maryas.   Nearly all of it has made nearly all of it.

Martha.   Plenty of time as the pansy is a bird as well as a flower rice is a bird as well as a plant, cuckoo is a flower as well as a bird.

Martha
and
Marius.   A single instance of able to pay any day and as you say we exchange ribbons for ribbons and pictures for pictures successfully.

Marius.   Is spelled in this way.

Maryas.   They saved it why did they save it they saved it as wire. In this way did you hear me say did they save it in this way, did they save it and will they use it in this way.

Maryas
and
Martha.   Maryas and Martha.

Maryas
and
Martha.   Did you hear me say cloudlessly.

Maryas.   Yes,

Maryas
and
Martha.   Yes.

Maryas.   May be I do but I doubt it.

Martha.   I do but I do doubt it.

Martha and Maryas.	May be I do but I doubt. I do but I do doubt it.
Marius and Mabel.	Please to please. Pleasure to give pleasure.
Marius.	To please and to give pleasure.
Marius and Mabel.	To please and please and to give pleasure and to give pleasure.
Marius.	To please and to give pleasure.
Marius and Mabel.	If you please if you please and if you give pleasure.
Marius.	If you give pleasure and if you please.
Marius and Mabel.	Please please and pleasure.
Marius.	I am very pleased I am indeed very pleased that it is a great pleasure.
Martha.	If four are sitting at a table and one of them is lying upon it it does not make any difference. If bread and pomegranates are on a table and four are sitting at the table and one of them is leaning upon it it does not make any difference.
Martha.	It does not make any difference if four are seated at a table and one is leaning upon it.
Maryas.	If five are seated at a table and there is bread on it and there are pomegranates on it and one of the five is leaning on the table it does not make any difference.
Martha.	If on a day that comes again and if we consider a day a week day it does come again if on a day that comes again and we consider every day to be a day that comes again it comes again then when accidentally when very accidentally every other day and every other day every other day and every other day that comes again and every day comes again when accidentally every other day comes again, every other day comes again and every other and every day comes again and accidentally and every day and it comes again, a day comes again and a day in that way comes again.
Maryas.	Accidentally in the morning and after that every evening and accidentally every evening and after that every morning and after that accidentally every morning and after that accidentally and after that every morning.

Maryas.	After that accidentally. Accidentally after that.
Maryas.	Accidentally after that. After that accidentally.
Maryas and Martha.	More Maryas and more Martha.
Maryas and Martha.	More Martha and more Maryas.
Martha and Maryas.	More and more and more Martha and more Maryas.
Marius.	It is spoken of in that way.
Mabel.	It is spoken of in that way.
Marius and Mabel.	It is spoken in that way and it is spoken of in that way.
Marius and Mabel.	It is spoken of in that way.
Mabel.	I speak of it in that way.
Marius.	I have spoken of it in that way and I speak it in that way. I have spoken of it in that way.
Mabel.	I speak of it in that way.
Mabel.	Spelled in this way.
Marius.	Spelled in that way.
Mabel.	Spelled in this way and spelled in that way and spoken of in this way and spoken of in that way and spoken in this way.
Martha.	In this way. If in a family where some member is devoutly religious another member of the family is ill, other members are not at home and other members have been killed in war, a ball is given for whose benefit is the ball given. For the benefit of the three young ladies who have not as yet left their home.
Martha and Maryas.	It was unexpected but intended, it was intended and expected, it was intended.
Maryas.	It was intended and in a reasonable degree and not unreasonably she valued it as she was intended to value it as she was expected to value as she expected to value as she intended to value. She did intend to remain. Remember she did intend to remain. She did intend to remain.
Martha.	Not too merrily for me. She had thirty three thirds. Safely. In

	this way she has a standard, she keeps to it and although she may be although she may be although she will be changed, she will change.
Maryas.	Not too long.
Maryas and Martha.	Not too long.
Maryas.	To long and to long.
Martha.	To long.
Maryas.	Able to long able to be and to be safely to be safely able to be safely to be safely to be seen to be seen able to long to be safely to safely be here and there to be there. Able to be there. To long. Who is longing now.
Martha.	Change songs for safety, change their songs for their safety. Safely change their songs.
Maryas.	Change songs and change singing and change singing songs and change singing songs for singing songs.
Martha.	Not how do you do.
Maryas.	Not yet.
Maryas and Martha.	And not yet and not who are you and how are you not how are you.
Martha and Maryas.	And not yet not how are you and where are you and how are you and not yet how and where are you and we are here.
Maryas and Martha.	Where are you.
Maryas and Martha.	How are you.
Martha and Maryas.	How do you do and how are you.
Marius.	As a change from this.
Marius.	In a way to change in that way to change this.
Marius.	In this way.
Marius.	To change in this way.
Marius.	And if they were in various ways differently decided, and if they were delighted, no not delighted, and if they were accidentally relieved and repeatedly received and reservedly deceived, if they were separately announced and deposed and respectfully recalled

and regularly preceeded, indeed they were there indeed they were there and in the way of it all and why did they ask what do they mean when they say that hay is no more fruitful than fruit and birds no more plentiful than battles. Battles are arranged here and there. Battles are arranged for here and there. Streets have been named so they have, a street might be named Battle Street.

Mabel. And if they were to be here and there and they are very often here, will I be pleased.

Marius
and
Mabel. If they are very often here and there and they are very often here and they are very often here.

Mabel
and
Marius. They are here very often.

Martha. Yes and know.

Maryas. Yes.

Martha. Every day by the by every day has a connection between what happened when she kneeled and what she left when she came back to kneel.

Maryas. Every day has a connection by the by every day has a connection between when she went and when she was separately sent.

Martha. Every day has a connection between six and seven in the morning and the disturbances of certainly causing and the disturbance of certainly calling and the disturbance of certainly returning and the disturbance of certainly telling that no address was given. That is a strange story of the address that was found and turned out to be given by her and it was her habit to give her address. Written down to be written down. We do not color her for that, this does not color her, this does not make lilacs white, they mostly are when they are made in winter.

Maryas. Made in winter, when they are made in winter.

Maryas
and
Martha. This is not an instance of being polite and perfect.

Maryas. Eighty and eighty pages.

Martha. Eight and eight pages.

Martha
and
Maryas. Eight pages and eighty pages.

Martha. An instance and for instance, for instance did she leave her key and for instance were we pleased to see that she came to be

carefully pleased to be that she came to be carefully that she came
to be careful.

Maryas.   Contents and intend. I intend to be careful of ashes Tuesdays
kneeling and prizes. I intend to be careful of kneeling Tuesdays
ashes and prizes.

Martha.   We have allowed for it.

Maryas.   You do prepare it for me.

Martha
and   We do we will and not forever.
Maryas.

Marius.   How do you spell Marius.

Mabel.   How do you spell Mabel.

Mabel
and   We spell them both correctly.
Marius.

LIST A

Maryas Martha Marius Mabel.

Maryas
Martha   A list may be taken care of.
Marius
Mabel.

Maryas   If a list is taken care of by five, if five are sitting at a table if four
Martha   are seated at a table and one is leaning upon it it does not make
Marius   any difference.
Mabel.

Marius   If five are seated at a table and one is leaning upon it it does not
Martha   make any difference.
Maryas
Mabel.

Marius   And if there are four seated at a table and one is leaning upon it
Martha   it does not make any difference.
Maryas.

Maryas.   An instance of this is when we have all meant to be well dressed.

Maryas.   An instance of this is when we have all meant to be well dressed.

Maryas.   Dress well.

Martha.   I know.

Maryas and Martha.	We know how.
Maryas Mabel Martha and Maryas.	We know how now.
Martha and Maryas.	A sector is a piece cut out, a fragment is a piece broken off and an article is all of one piece.
Maryas.	Stems and pleasantness.
Maryas.	I see I see how creditably and when they stand and she stands and there are stands.
Martha.	And how creditably they prepare and she prepares and there are there as there are.
Maryas.	And how creditably if they care.
Martha.	Very creditable as who can share their thanks for that. Yes that is it and we are not excited.
Martha and Maryas.	If you can only tell him so.
Martha and Maryas.	If they do and plenty of them would.
Martha.	If we do.
Maryas.	Can you procure a place for a pillar.
Martha.	And he thought of it and saw it.
Martha and Maryas.	He thought of it and saw to it.
Martha.	That which is lost becomes first comes first to be sent.
Maryas.	And might it be predicted by me.
Martha.	Extravagantly very extravagantly.
Martha and Maryas.	We translate this into that and Mary is so gracious and Mary.
Martha.	A second list makes one day, a second list makes some day, a second list makes Monday, a second list makes Sunday, a second list makes more than one day a second list makes one day and makes one day.
Maryas.	We never kissed, we have never kissed.

Martha.	A second list.
Martha and Maryas.	A second list makes a second list.
Marius.	If you do prepare to carry olives away from olive trees and rain away from rain and you are necessarily in that case pleased with me are you in earnest when you say that there are plenty of pleasures left.
Mabel.	One hundred and one make a second list as naturally one hundred finishes one, probably the first one.
Marius and Mabel.	We could be married.
Maryas.	One authority.
Martha.	No monotony is necessary since I do visit. You do visit, yes I do wisely to visit where my visits are appreciated.
Maryas.	Is wisdom perfect.
Martha.	And festive.
Marius and Mabel.	A Sunday is marked as a Sunday.
Maryas.	In this way perfectly.
Martha.	In this way not so carefully.
Marius and Mabel.	In this way they are allowed to retaliate.

THIRD LIST

Maryas.	Texas.
Martha.	Mary.
Maryas and Martha.	Texas berry.
Maryas.	To meet to meet me here.
Martha.	To meet me here.
Martha and Maryas.	To meet me here.
Maryas.	Examples of wool. Samples of wool. Samples of silk and wool. Sheep and wool.

Lions and wool.
Lions and sheep and wool. Lions and sheep and wool and silk.
Silk and sheep and wool and silk. Silk and sheep, silk and wool,
silk and sheep and silk and wool and silk. Sheep and silk and wool
and silk and sheep.

Martha. If a feather meant a feather and if a feather meant a feather, we
would gather together and it would not matter. What would not
matter. My dear it would not matter.

Martha. In a minute.
Marius
Maryas And a third.
Mabel.
Mary. A third of it.
A fourth.
A fourth of it.
A fourth.
A fourth of it.

Martha. In a minute and a third a third of it.
Marius. A third of it and in a minute a fourth of it.
Mabel. In a minute and a fourth of it in a minute and a fourth of it.
Mary. In a minute and a fourth of it, a third of it and in a minute and a
third and a fourth of it.

Maryas. We calm.
Martha. We can call silver silver.
Marius. We can mix silver with silver.
Mabel. We can mix more silver with silver.
Mary. We can mix more than silver with more than silver.

Maryas
Martha
Marius If there are four seated at a table and one of them is leaning upon
Mabel it it does not makes any difference.
and
Mary.

FOURTH LIST

Martha. If I am displeased.
Martha. One may say that one may say that a brother tardily marries.
Maryas. In this way.
Maryas
and Make it selected.
Martha.

Maryas.	We were not confused by separation.
Martha and Marius.	If you confuse if you are separated by confusion, if you exchange standing for standing, I often think about exchanging standing for standing.
Martha.	Anybody can anybody settle it for me.
Martha.	We have met, to be safely arrived. To exchange kneeling for kneeling.
Martha and Maryas.	And thoughtful.
Martha.	In no great merriment.
Martha and Maryas.	I have exactly they have exactly they have called them all in.
Martha.	Equally so.
Maryas.	It is very well to know this.
Martha.	I have no longer any actual reason for this as well.
Maryas.	Very evenly.
Martha and Maryas.	Can we say we do not.
Martha and Maryas.	Fourteen and more are inconsistent.
Martha.	Fourteen and more and they are one may believe, they are one may believe liable to abuse.
Martha.	Indeed for them and differently preserved pears.
Martha and Maryas.	Indeed for them.
Martha and Maryas.	In a minute or very nervously or very nervously or in a minute.
Martha.	Next to their end.
Martha and Maryas.	They left it a half an hour later.
Martha and Maryas.	Return it to me.
Martha and	Two at half past one.

Maryas.	Three at half past two.
Martha and Maryas.	Three at half past three.
Martha.	I present well.
Maryas.	I represent well.
Martha and Maryas.	We are pleased to be represented by them for them.
Martha.	What was it that was said.
Maryas.	No secrets.
Martha and Maryas.	No secrets and no secrecy.
Martha Marius Maryas and Mabel.	To see and to see.
Martha Marius Maryas Mabel and Mary.	To see and to see and to see.
Martha.	We are not to see.
Maryas.	I am to see where I am to go and what I am to do.
Martha.	You do and I do.
Maryas.	You do too.
Martha and Maryas.	They do believe that no secrets and not secretly will make investigation easy.

LIST FIVE

Martha.	This is the way a play fades away.
Martha.	You praise me as you say.
Maryas.	Ordinarily in this way.
Martha and Maryas.	Ordinarily you praise me as you say you say you praise me.

Martha.	And a measure. To measure exactly how often six and one, how very often six and one how often is there to be reasonable certainty. How often are they reasonably certain. Six and one and not another more than one.
Maryas.	I smile for certainty.
Martha.	Martin too was certain to be known.
Maryas	
Mabel	How are you known you are known by your name and your share.
and	Share and share alike.
Martin.	
Mabel	
Martha	Rain mingles with water and a tree can be sweet and can you mingle
and	water with rain and suck at a tree.
Maryas.	
Martha.	Mentions the place.
Maryas.	Yields abundant resemblance.
Mabel.	Needs only adequate calls.
Marius.	Needs only division of birth.
Martin.	Only needs mentioning here.
Mary.	Only needs mentioning here.
Martha	If they ask me to leave them and they ask them to leave me if they
and	ask me to leave them and they ask them to leave if they ask them to
Maryas.	leave and they ask me if they ask me and if they ask them, if they ask them and if they ask them and if they ask them and if they ask me if they ask I say yes that is it.
Maryas.	They said he said, he said, two centers, two centers, two surroundings, two surroundings, two centers, and two centers, and they centre, and their center, they centre, they do not centre here.
Mabel.	Mabel little Mabel with her face against the pane and it may as can say wistfulness may no wistfulness may, they come again to-day and to-morrow they go to America.
Martin.	Exactly Martin, and may useful and preliminary offshoots.
Marius.	Recognise it by the name in the way of deliberation and baskets. A great many baskets are made here and there and with some care, that is to say one may give an order to them and indeed they may fulfill. They may even learn to weave and braid officially and not fancifully and in this way they have many certainties and many mountains and a cow, I doubt if they will have a cow. I say they advisedly and speaking entirely in a different sense. You do understand me.

Mary.   Mary may no I may say may Mary. So that season is anonymous
           and indeed easily as they own land in town and country.

A LAST LIST

Marius.   Choose to choose you cannot expect me to choose you.
Martha.   Carrots and artichokes marguerites and roses. If you can repeat it
           and somebody chose it, somebody shows it, somebody knows it. If
           you can repeat and somebody knows it.
Maryas.   Half of the marriages, valentines and half of the marriages. I did
           the valentines and half of the marriages.
Mabel.   A little girl is very nearly the same size as she was she was very
           nearly the same prize and we may say excited.
May.   And Mary.
Martha
Mabel
Maryas   We may marry.
 and
Mary.

OBJECTS LIE ON A TABLE

A Play

Nuns ask for them for recreation.

First a nun. Have you meant to have fun and funny things. Do you like to see funny things for fun.

Objects lie on a table.

We live beside them and look at them and then they are on the table then.

Objects on a table and the explanation.

Who says glasses.

Who says salt in Savoy.

Who does say pots of porcelain.

And who does say that earthen ware is richer than copper, glass, enamel, or cooking. We have the very best celery salad and selection. Now then read for me to me what you can and will see. I see what there is to see.

You want to show more effort than that.

And now how do you do.

I have done very well.

The objects on the table have been equal to the occasion. We can decorate walls with pots and pans and flowers. I question the flowers. And bananas. Card board colored as bananas are colored. And cabbages. Cabbages are green and if one should not happen to be there what would happen, the green would unhappily unhappily result in hardness and we could only regret that the result was unfortunate and so we astonish no one nor did we regret riches. Riches are not begun. They have a welcome in oceans. Oceans can not spread to the shore. They began description and so we relish seas. Over seas objects are on the table that is a wooden table and has not a marble top necessarily. So thank every one and let us begin faintly.

As to houses certainly houses have not the same restfulness as objects on the table which mean to us an arrangement. You do not arrange houses nor do you fancy them very much. I have a fancy for a house.

When I appeal I appeal to their relation. What is a relation. A British Dominion. And will there ever be no memory will there even not be a memory. I remember you. And you. Yes you remember you remember me. And I say to you you do remember do not you and you you feel as I do. I remember you, and you are certainly aroused by the apple the descent from the cross and the dog and the squirrel. You do please when you please.

Combining everything with everything.

This is their flour.

I find that milk salt flour and apples and the pleasant respective places of each one in the picture make a picture.

Esther.

I prefer a merry go round.

And I a street.

And I nothing at all says Rose as she decides to stay away. But she comes again repeatedly.

Have you hesitated about singing.

Have you hesitated about singing.

He said he had met her there.

And now we have explained the interest a cellist can show in a sculptor. She does not play the cello any more but she does continue to cover the wood the stone and the wood and color the wood. She does not color the wood.

And now houses and buildings and houses and the buildings containing houses. I live in a house here and there is a house there. Do not bother to remember about the other place of worship. See to it that you have an equal respect for all who are all together.

And then when you mean to see me.

Call to me.

Come to me readily and prepare in that way.

What do you know about fields and table-cloths.

Objects are on the table when I am there. And when you are not there.

Let me explain this to you.

About ten pages.

And what are their ages.

Their ages are you know, you know what their ages are and their weights and their measures.

And you know how very soon we can be up before noon.

Yes. To-morrow and then we will buy we will buy we will not buy, yes we will not buy all that we need to buy because we will not be able to agree about them. You agree with me.

And so we will see just what we need to gladden their Christmas tree.

Objects on the table do not imitate a house and we do not mean Esther.

How does Esther be named Esther and not take cognisance of Ahasuerus but only of Olga she is a Russian how dare she.

Does he shine when he means to whine. Of course he does and now speak connectedly.

He said that he respected the expression of opinion and she said, I believe in looking facts in the face. And he said and what do you see when you do as you say you do and she said I see but you and he said the same to you. And then they said they greatly appreciate the painting of houses and objects on a table.

Come up out of there is very well said when the instinct which has lead to the introduction of words and music not pictures and music, not pictures and words not pictures and music and words, not pictures not music not words when the instinct which has lead to the spread of rubbing has been shed then we will invite each one to sign himself Yours sincerely Herman G. Read and very quickly I include everything in that new name.

We will now consider an ancient quadrille we will.

Ladies change.

How can you neglect admissions.

And she was seated and she said I am not pledged to much retribution.

Come again.

Forward and back.

Look right and not left.

And lend a hand.

The lend a hand society.

Calming.

Pocket the watch.

Can soldiers surround a chinaman.

Pray then.

Pray then why do you wish for this thing.

Providing.

Providing you need strengthening why do you reiterate that you are coming.

Going and coming.

Was he willing.

Has he been willing.

When is he willing to vary everything.

He says he invents nothing and then I say do not invent a table cloth to-day do not let the table table that you invented stay. And he says I am very willing but I have had to invent something to fill in and I say to him you had better really have it and he said I am not able to get it and I say to him I am sorry I have not one to lend you and he says oh that is quite alright I will realize that I can replace it and I say I am willing to address you and he replied, I do not doubt that you will be of great assistance to me and as for the result that is still in question.

What is the difference between houses and a table. What is the difference between objects on a table and furniture in houses. Had you ever thought of that. Objects on a table make a standpoint of recompense and result, furniture in houses do decide matters.

Very well let us come to that decision.

No they come together.

Scotchmen, frenchman chinaman negro and the black races. When will you adopt. You or me, when this you see remember me.

Chinamen are cautious with negroes with frenchmen with scotchmen and with candles. They are cautious with oil and impoverishment.

No one is easily impoverished then.

And now compare them with these.

They have instincts they cook and turn and apples and salt. These have their way, they are not wretched with wood and gold nor are they eager with riots. And so many people appeal. They appeal to flushing. They flush when they have no rapid silence there. And they do not despise arrangements. Who can be merciless to the best armament. And do they like poise. I like the noise. I do not like the noise. How can you forget riches. Riches can mean prejudice. Can riches mean that. Yes in a crew. How can you cut a fish. Babies look, boys look and we look.

We look there.

Believe the future that he tells her.

Really though she told him. He was not disappointed because I had warned him. Objects have been recognised as a knife, a pot, a pan, a cover, a ladle, carrots, apples and a salt cellar. These all have been recognised which really is not so astonishing as his aunt is a farmer and cultivates her own ground and has cows and sheep and a sheep dog. His mother is an exceedingly capable manager and his father has been connected with the government. He is now over age and has been retired on a pension. His sister and brother-in-law have a hard ware store and do a successful business although in their part of the country it is exceedingly difficult to get payment. You can see that it is not astonishing that the objects are easily recognised. They are a chair, table, tea cup, tea pot, a pot, a ladle, a bottle a pan, a cover carrots, salt-cellar with salt in it, apples and a pitcher.

It would appear that she is near, it would appear that he is near he is nearly he is merely delayed.

And so he will come.

And so he will come.

And so he will come.

And so he will come.

He will be welcome.

He will come when he has time.

And what will he do then.

He will say that objects are to-day recognised as something with which to play. And we will reply this is not why we like them here but the real reason is that we have not displaced them for a violin simply because of this reasoning. We have displaced them because we have replaced them.

Thank you so very much for this explanation.

Please tell Mr. Edmund Holt that if he will understand I will be delighted.

And houses with their hooks upon which in the country they still do need to hoist furniture and water and other hooks that support the lights. It is very interesting that a light or a house is sometimes on the side and sometimes at a corner and in either case it compares very nicely with the house even in the day time when the light is not lit and the house is not necessarily ready to be recognised. A house readily recognised is no longer necessary and yet can we deny recognition can we deny that yesterday we were certainly not displeased with our residence.

How lovelily the wall how lovelily all of the wall and we do not necessarily hesitate he did not, he found it thin. The wall is thick and not heavy and has a support and when you look at it again they have not changed anything and yet it is to be painted red and a lemon yellow and pretty soon every ten years they will again oblige every one to do something, to paint the houses and arrange a wall which is crumbling. This is the law that they are reinforcing. And where did his mother get her ration. She did not she had copper and earthen ware pots and so she found then when he went away she had nothing to say. How neatly a man and a woman who go away every day come home to stay. They are very neat in their washing and ironing and in their eating and drinking and in their sleeping and waking. Can you believe that he uses their room all day. Can you believe this I say to you and he has said to me that he was under no obligation to them for anything. He was not satiated with eating how could he be in choosing bananas or a persimmon. How can he be violently radiating when ordinarily he was visiting and when visiting they had said to him, listen while we are talking. He talked readily while he was listening. Objects on a table are hazardous.

Imitate a cheese if you please. We are very well pleased with gold coin and ribbons.

Imitate a cheese very well if you please, and readily reflect how can you be credulous of more than the assumption of imitating ham. We were not pleased with the imitation of the lamb.

I have a special taste in feeling. I can feel very well. I can feel that some resemblances the resemblance between a sausage made of sugar and a sausage made of meat is not as great as the resemblance between an object made of almonds and an object made of wood. How often do we see what we have not readily recognised. I readily recognise the object that has the most perfect quality of imitation. Then can you be astonished by a meal. How easily you had rather blame him and blame them and how easily she had rather fly than swim. We have discouraged her together we have discouraged her altogether. Dogs are good for photography and recoil. Do please at the rate that you do please how can you be so anxious.

She was told to be measured and she said assuredly I shall be there. How often do you mean to remain. Remain to me the culminating tender tree. And how can a woodbine twine.

And now how do you feel what you hear.

I come back to expecting a house and a farm and not a farmhouse and a southern climate in the north. We do not go very far north. Mountains are just the same, very nearly the same. I have had a special taste in rivers. And now remember to see me.

Objects on a table are all there and I do not care to say that they have been studied. Study again and again and leave me to my wishes I wish that they could copy all of it as well as they do copy it. No one can say yes again· Have I forgotten that fruits do not remember flowers, that flowers contain what they contain and that together with fruit they do not possibly force me to be round and innocent. I am prepared to share fruits and at the same time know that I have wished to be queen. How can she stay there very easily. She gets up and she says very well this is quite what I mean.

So we consider flowers masculine. We have not mentioned the resemblance between trees and streets and all of the things that have not been constructed. How can you prejudice him.

We are not only patient but satisfied, we are not only satisfied but more than satisfied. Do we suppose that a rose is a rose. Do we suppose that all she knows is that a rose is a rose is a rose is a rose. He knows and she knows that a rose is a rose and when she can make a song as to which can belong as to what can belong to a song. Now let us pray that a table may that a table may very well stay, that a table may that a table very well may stay to be settled for in that way. And when the objects may be disposed in this way upon the table upon which they will not permanently be put away. We had a wish and the wish was that when rose colored ribbons and no roses because of course after all roses are supposed to be of the color of imitation trees. How can you imitate trees so prettily. I find I have changed my meaning, I find I have changed my meaning in changing my meaning from the meaning I had to this meaning. I mean to do right. I do not mean to settle the clamor by reiterating have you met one another and do you care to ask a question. I ask the question I say have you succeeded, you succeed. Can you succeed and do you succeed. I succeed in recalling this to their mind. I do not fall behind.

AM I TO GO

or

I'LL SAY SO

A curious example of how it is not only with foreigners but with their countrymen that they succeed, indeed they even more successfully succeed with their own countrymen, his own countrymen.

A Play In Places

Near Annecy, Paris, Vence, Tahors, Some more.

In the first place.
Objects on a table and a survey of bridges and roads.
Interlude. In general, The general likes his coffee cold.
Interlude. The War.
Interlude. Not the War.
In the second place.
Paris. How do they occupy their room. In a way. They say that some time in the day, a whole day. A whole day every day. Twice a day, Two days, At least two days a week. At least two. Not as might be expected an incident, any such incident. And a use and a use for it.
In the third place.
Vence. Correctly on the road to Vence and once there, are we to admit that Shakespeare was as it were immodest, immodestly acquired. Are we to admit, that there is no drop and drop again drop it again. He'll say so.
In the fourth place.
Tahors, and very much more, in between alone, he alone seeks to avoid

not to avoid, to desert not to desert, to contract not to contract, to indicate not to indicate, to claim not to claim, to share not to share to estrange and to change, to change many to more and at las and very fast to change many more, not to exchange and across to expect to expect to neglect indications. In this result all participate and does he give up his room.

In the fifth place.

A senator, a senator is received concretely he is obliged to withdraw from the city of his heart and of his dreams and he is compelled to assist in the support of a pledge, he does not pledge himself but he is the sole support and there is no obligation, he has no satisfaction no portrait and no initiative, he has had he has been kindness itself in his own interest and in the interest he feels. Indeed he will say so and does and does want to be spared, does want to be spared and can not help himself exactly.

In the meantime and if it were a different season of the year there would be sunshine.

The curtain goes up on the beginning of Sunday. It is as if it were ordinary weather.

In the first place.

Objects on a table and a survey of bridges and roads.

A whole scene in a question.   Was he or was he and his brother and was he and messages and was he was his aunt was his mother was he and were he and his brother, were they, was he, was he a wonder was he, did he not arrive with the train whenever he had been away. Had he been away all this time. Was he ineradicably, was he and will he have mountains decline. Mountains begin to decline, will he eradicably will mountains decline, will he and will he and moutains and decline them.

A conversation with the family.

He and his brother and his sister and her husband and his father and if he has and his mother and her sister and they have and her children and they mean more.

When this you see remember me.

Conversations not hastily mounted.

It amounted to this.

Conversations.

The sister. Plumbing.

The father. Posting.

The brother. Winning.

The mother. No self abnegation.

The brother-in-law. Was not successful when as they may say, he may say so.

Actually as he will be he will be actually no menace to secrecy.

Conversations almost all the time and he is nearly there.

The first interlude.

Scene. Scarcely spoiled.

Why does he all the while why does he as it were fairly stare.

It is not commodious and to argue does not furnish insistence. Insistence is to be furnished. In this way changes are extemporary.

A conversation between them.

Actively rapidly.

Response.

Rapidly and actively.

Nor when.

Response.

Now and then.

Actively and more rapidly.

Response.

And when not more rapidly.

Now and then more actively.

Response.

Now and then not more than actively and rapidly.

Change.

Change of administration.

In general.

After that the use of mimeographs were introduced.

Everything went very well either or.

Or more.

Conversations with a general.

If they left to them.

Not in that case.

He asked him directly.

And chosen.

He chose to leave with his hat and cane as if it were on a Sunday.

Regularly speaking he spoke for himself.

In response.

And this is what they said.

If I had not come.
If you had not come.
And come.
I come.
No general meets.
In a general.
This in a general.
That in a general.
For a general.
Before the general.
In this case not in general.
Not to enjoy.
Not to annoy.
No general.
And in meeting.
If he had met.
Politely.
Engineering and copying and ink and accepting and every day has its had
a day.
Had you a day.
Have you had a day.
If you believe me I went away.
In this way better and better in this way and better and better.
Not to mean two years except to-day.
I accept to-day.
Not to be outdone in generosity.
Did he ever write again.
Not again.
And not again.
Then came or then came or then and then and as to then.
No division can know that to divide is to do division.
The general likes.
If he likes.
If he likes to be told.
And if he likes it to be told.
And if he likes it as well.
And if he tells as well.
And if to tell.
And as if to tell.
Very well.
This evening if necessary.

And so administration was in the recital.
To recount.
Not to recount as men and places.
He was of very great importance and in the future it might have been in
the future.
And now to present arms.
Cheers.
Not chairs.
Not not cherries.
Why does this why how do you do.
Or.
To the door.
Commence now.
To commence now.
This is what they did say.
The other day.

Interlude.

The war.
Why is paper scarce.
Paper is not very scarce.

Interlude.

Not the war.
Or not the war.
Indeed or not the war.
Or indeed or not the war.
Drawing paper is not scarce.
Or in drawing paper drawing paper is not scarce.
Nor is drawing paper scarce.
Or in or not in the war.
Either or.
Or the war.
Or not the war.
Or drawing paper.
Or scarce paper.
Or paper is not scarce.
Or drawing paper.
Or in that case.
Reasonably even angles.
Or even as reasonably as to angles.

Or to be as to be.
As it is to be as an aptitude.
As an aptitude to July.

In the second.

It is befalling him it has befallen him, it is rapidly becoming in origin an origin, it has rapidly befallen him, it is rapidly befalling him and it is rapidly becoming as in origin.
Not in conversation.
A frame.
To frame.
As a frame.
As if in a frame.
To blame.
There was no check upon which to put the blame. There was the check and there was a frame and it was not to blame. It was not shame shame fie for shame nobody nobody will know the name. And all the same he was to blame and blame as to circumstance shame as to circumstance resemble as to the same. The same. All the same. All the same as to this circunstance it was not to blame nor as to the mention of a frame. Nor a change of mind. Mind, do you mind, do you mind. Yes do you mind.
          All the change.
All the change there was was that objects were not on the table but in the hall and then conversations in the room were transferred to be as if in a square. A square may be a painting, a door or not at all. Not at all mildewed.
Mildewed is a foreign word.
Introduction to reach. Reach and rich tell me which.
In this way commencements begin.
Begin how.
To begin.
Begin and begun.
In the south there is no sun and in the mountains no gun. No gun.

Begun.

Begin again.
In the third place.
Varieties are as to oils and shoes. Varieties as to choose as to choose variety, as to vary more, more summers, more as to summers and more and more as to and as to more summers.
Winters as to winters as to more and more, more and more as to winters.

As to summers and as to winters more and more as to summers and more and more as to winters.

As to fairly well, very well, as to very well, very well and very very well, as to very well, as to very very well. As to as to tell as if as to tell to and very well as if as to tell very well. As if as to and very much more. As if as to. Not a commitment.

In the fourth place.

In between.

In between no matter what Nelly has had.

One. Enthrone.

Two. To throne.

Three. Palace.

Four. ministers.

Four. Hour glass.

Six. Plates.

Seven. Tickets.

And eighth. An eighth.

In between.

Dethrone.

Two. Hour glass.

Three. Fastidious.

Five. Expel him.

Four. No more.

Two. Touchingly.

One. An example.

In between.

Measuring.

Two. Not measuring.

Three. Call for it anyway.

Four. Stretches.

Four stretches of canvas and not ribbon.

Not ribbon.

Not in between.

No screen.

No no.

And no.

No not at all.

A question. What is the difference between Waldemar and George.

Answer. There isn't any.

Not in their meantime.

He met with he was met with and by.

Buy.

By and by.

Buy and not by and by.

Not by and by.

Not to buy and buy.

Not to buy and buy.

Not by and by.

By and by.

Who said.

He said.

Theme with variations.

And in the fourth Place.

Tahors and climax.

No climax.

Not as to a climax.

In the fourth place and Tahors and more.

More and Tahors.

More.

In the fourth place.

And more.

Was a greeting as it was as a greeting, was it as it was to be as to be greeting, in the fourth place. A greeting in the fourth place.

To favor in the fourth place.

As a favor in the fourth and as the fourth place as to the fourth place.

Four places.

In all of the four places.

As to all the four places.

In the fourth place.

As to the fourth place.

It was as to the fourth place.

A place and not in place.

And not as not to place.

In the fourth Place.

Not in the fourth place.

In the fourth place.

So soon, every one his or her as soon, so soon.
In a place.
Can place.
They have a place.
He can place.
And can place.
No place.
A place.
Place.
To place.
In a place.
In the fifth place.
No fifth place.
Fourth place.
A fourth place.
In the fourth place.
In place.
In that place.
Place to place a place my place, my place you place we place I place,
I place you place, we place, my place, my place, why place, you place my place.
I place my place, they place a place, for a place as for a place, to and as for the
place, in their place in my place. I and my, to place and my place.
In the fourth place.
Why.
Why in the fifth place.
And why in the fourth place.
And I and my place.
And I.
And my place.
And my place.
And I.
In the fourth and fifth place.
To-morrow and not to-morrow, to sorrow and not to sorrow, to borrow and
not to borrow, oh dear me no. And so.
To-morrow and not to-morrow to sorrow and not to sorrow to borrow and
not to borrow, oh dear me no.
And so bread known as sausages, cauliflower known as egg, butter known
as orange and so salad known as salad. Salad grown and known and eggs laid
and weighed and artichokes chosen and frozen and barley sown and grown and
wheat ground and found and cherries begged and thanked for, not to be thanked for not to be thanked for and returned and as a gift. And as a gift. To bow

and smile a while, to smile and bow and now all very well and now, to intend to not to pretend to and for for this and before before this and beside beside more, and more not any more and a chance not as a chance, to meet not in or on the street not on the street, do you compete, do you, and do you and do you feed do you feed at all do you at all feed on it at all. Do you eat much. Do you eat very much. And always as one might say eider down. To suddenly save so much and very much. Very much and so much and so there. Alright and so there.

Do you happen to know the address of any one of any one and any one.
Mr. Mansard is not contemptible.

REREAD ANOTHER

A Play

To be played indoors or out

I wish to be a school.

When wings, when teeth and wings, when birds and shots, shot tower, how easily we describe mellow.

Don't think a shot tower means war, it only means shot guns, or shooting.

Now we breed.

First Mountain.   You're a chinaman.

Second Mountain.   Please yourself.

Third Mountain.   I like warm weather.

Then there are no schools. No nothing but birds nests. What a happy May.

I have followed I have been followed I am followed by another.

She is a dirigeable.

Four dirigeables

The first.   Have a lesson.

The second.   And a mission.

The third.   And a prison.

The fourth.   And a meal soon.

Twenty eight, I ate what my master. Twenty eight I hate what to be led but to be wed. Twenty eight I wait, to be led. To be wed, I was wed, I am wed. I said I am led.   Twenty eight, I wait to be led.   By she who is all to me.

Can Christians touch much.

First soldier.   I am not a christian.

Second soldier.   I have no wife.

Third soldier.   I am not a christian and I have no wife.

Do be hot to-day.

First Mountain. I am told that words are used in the sense in which they are felt. I am persuaded of nothing else.

Can you effect trees. Yes by gasoline and what is the result. The leaves fall. A great many people are married.

How can flowers sweat.

The dear little thing it just gets hot.

First pound.   I have fallen.

Second pound.   I have not fallen.

Third pound.   I am falling.

And fourth pound. Pound sterling.

A great many riches are riches.

In quiet squares in quiet squares and circles.

How well they love squares and circles.

How can you love squares and circles.

Can you be a witness I am a witness.

Scene II

In a room where is a stove and in summer it is not necessary to keep it lighted as with a glass roof a room with the sun shining upon it is very warm.

Any man who is in the country is a sailor.

First sailor.   How often do you wear my coat.

Not very often.

How often do I take off my hat.

It blows off.

The first sailor is remarkable for the strength of his hands. He hands heavy weights to the men. He is a splendid example of the strength a man has in his hands.

The second sailor is remarkable for the violence with which he remains at home in the mountains. He loves the mountains and he never leaves them.

We are not miserable.

I do hate sentences. I sentence him to have a little rebellion. Why should the public rebel. Why should a stove be known. A stove is known by its name.

Scene III

A mother and a child. How can you tell that a mother has a child.

Let us be in earnest.

A mother has a child. How can you be certain that a mother has her child. The first chauffer. How do you do I forgive you everything and there is nothing to forgive.

Do not repeat yourself.
The first singer. I take lessons.
And what do you do in between.
I mean to be strong and well but really I am not very well.
A Swiss Italian. I am leaving for France. And there.
And there I will be apprenticed to my uncle who is a house painter and is color blind.
What a tragedy.
Not at all he always has some one to assist him.
Georgiana and Louise.
I remember Louise and Georgiana.

Scene IV

It is strange that all the Americans want Carpentier to win and all the Frenchmen want Dempsey to win. Carpentier can win on a foul. That means that Dempsey fouls. Dempsey can win. How.
First Banker. Whose cousins are you.
Second Banker. I am my cousin's cousin.
Third Banker. And who is your cousin.
Fourth Banker. And who is your cousin.
Second Banker. My cousin is Henry James.

Diamonds are not scarce, pearls will not be scarce, no one is interested in coal and gold is virgin. All people rush together.
Be easy.
Be easy be easy.
Mr. Thorndyke was impressive. He said I know who will win. And we all said. Who will win. And he said the winner. And we said the winner will have won but who will win. And he said. The winner.
I can be as stupid as I like because my wife is always right. And my cousin. I have several who are my cousin. Clamor and clamor. No one knew that his name was Macbeth.

Scene III

The Portuguee.
First ribbon maker. I am making ribbons for Mrs. C.
Second ribbon maker. In what color.
Third ribbon maker. Black shot with gold.
Fourth ribbon maker. I have meant to love silk.
All silk and a yard wide. We almost think in meters.

Scene IX

I regret nothing.

Titles make a rejoinder.

First grocer.   I am sincere.

Second grocer. I believe in service.

Third grocer.   I love my mother.

Fourth grocer. I am rich.

The fifth day they all came together and said. How many worlds have men who can fly.

We do not think there is another.

Scene X

Reader I wish you to understand how to speak and return every day. If anybody returns every day we don't want to hear them.

Reader I wish you to understand how to speak and return every day. If every one returns every day we do want to hear them.

Markets are full of greens. Beauty is full of green. There are a great many who do not like green. I remember very well some one being asked if they liked a room full of pictures replied quite simply. But you see I don't like green.

My neck is not thick.

My face is not fat.

My nose is not large.

My mouth is not quiet.

And I have my hair.

My best wishes for your success.

Scene XI

A brilliant Susan.

How can you be elfish.

Enthusiasm and daughters. I am the daughter of enthusiasm.

First record breaker.   How do you date your skies.

Second record breaker. I wish to rest.

Third record breaker. I have a brother.

Fouth record breaker. I am fatigued.

And why do you cherish copper. Or gold. Or silver. Because I love to sell.

Very well.

Scene XII

A horse shoe soothes a Jew.
What can a horse shoe do.
It can ease jealousy.
First sculptor.   How I wish to be read.
Second sculptor.   Reading made easy.
Third sculptor.   Marriage means a daughter.
Fourth sculptor. I love my father.

The market.

A street. Nobody in New York is sweet. A street leads to a girl. How old is Holly.

Scene XIII

I improvise.
The first negro.   It is raining and the sky is blue.
The second negro.   I do not like blue.
The third negro.   And I don't like yellow.
The fourth negro.   I am very fond of colors.
A little nose and a tired eye and a broad yellow face and thin Jewish hair, and lovely hands and a strong physique and sensitive ears and a shortish chin, and a heavy head and a curly neck, and no reason to sin. He does not win a gold watch nor a torch but he is a print and I say that much. He is not a print. He carries what he carries. He loves grammar and sadness. He is a reproach to grammar and sadness. I do not despair. Read me easily.
The first author.   I am.
The second author. I am too.
The third author.   I was very happily finished.
The fourth author was a painter.
Miss Constant Lounsberry present me.
Can you love all of the painting, can you love a little Christ. Can you love the roar of weasels can you love the little wife. I do see what makes me thunder when the words are not repressed. I do love the little Jesus I do really love him best. You mean of all the pictures. Yes I mean of all the pictures.

Scene XIV

Little words of a queen.

The american army.

I will be ordered like the American army and I will like it.

Say yes.

First boy.   I am awake.

Second boy.   I am awake nicely.

Third boy.   I am waking up very nicely.

Thank you very much. I seem to be pleased.

False smile. False smiler.

Scene XV

Why does a tail curl.

First girl.   I see the hair.

Second girl.   I see the greek.

Third girl.   I see fishes.

Scene XVI

How does French make French. How do French make french.

The first imitation imitates very well.

The second imitation is very well imitated. The third imitation is not useless. The fourth imitation urges you to be exact.

Scene XVII

I recognise a bust.

Do you.

I recognise a crust.

Do you.

I recognise that I must.

Do you always.

I recognise animals.

Birds and mouse a mouse. We have so carefully forgotten mice.

Will we ever remember birds.

It is astonishing how suddenly we are pleased.

And so many people may marry for pleasure and for words because really religiously speaking words are nearly always spoken.

Scene XVIII

Everytime I mention a number I am lightened. And a great many numbers

are nodded.
First reunion.   A message to Anne.
Second reunion.   A message to Emma.
Third reunion.   A message to Mary.
Fourth reunion.   A message to please.
   Please enlighten me about how dark the room is at midnight. In these days it is not very dark. In these nights it is not very dark.

Scene XIX

How can you.
How can you.
Let me lead you gently.
Where to.
Anywhere I want to.
The battle reader.
How many pictures are sold.
Do you know what a discussion is.
Do you know whom a discussion is with.
I am very happy here.
I am so much happier than to-day.
Than yesterday.
Than every day.

Scene XX

Don't you like to make it.
Do you not like to make it.
A continued story is one that continues when it is begun.
This is very nearly done.

Scene XXI

A door and a man.
He says a woman inspires him more.

Scene XXII

I love my love with a z because she is exact.
I love him with a z because he is candid.
How very funny you are.

The first pearl.   I am from the country of rivers and factories.
The second pearl.   Are the factories near the rivers.
The third pearl.   Almost always.
The fourth pearl.   They are not in big cities but in large villages.
    That must be very pleasant.
    I have almost meant to be kind.
    I like that kind.
    Now I can tell you about another man.
    She does not say I have left my purse she always says I have left my gold
purse. And she often had.

Scene XXIII

    Catherine of Russia.
    Hildegarde of Prussia.
    Gertrude of Roanne.
    And Michael of Bavaria.
    And Alice of England.
    And Henry of Armenia.
    And Rupert of Bologna.
    And Richard of Savoy.
    Which is your toy.
    I do not care for places.
    The first building put in America was larger than a house.

Scene XXIV

    My memory does not tell me how and what to remember and so what do
I do. I remember everything. How kind you are.
    I do very nearly love you. So do the friends of France.

END

CIVILIZATION.

A Play

In Three Acts

Characters in Act I

George Couleur and his mother Marietta.
Therese Manner and her nephew John and her niece Pauline and her sister Ivy.
Therese Manner and her mother and her father.
Therese Manner and her brother John and her brother Frank.
Jenny Henry and her husband William Henry.
Then the landscape. And the animals.
An old woman from the mountains who should sell raspberries but sells mushrooms and her brother. The nephews are not seen.

Act I

They speak of it. As is natural. Not that they are very interested. As is natural. But they do not say. Exactly. What. Makes it. And therefor. They are. Not interested in it.

No one speaks of George Couleur and his mother any more. Than they speak of his mother and George Couleur, except those who have been interested, or else those who have something to do with it. One may say. That some one with whom. Some of them. Are very pleasantly. One may say. They are friendly. Say she is very well. At least. Not very far. From very well.

These may not connect these with others.

After all the only thing he says is. That he would be glad to see him. Even then. Though. Actually. It is undoubted. That getting richer. And therefor working harder. Does not happen to interfere. With. Coming. When. They do not come. And so. They are finally. Not ready. Not to come. After all. They have been. Not without. A wish.

Act I

George Couleur and his mother.
Marietta Couleur and her son.

Act I

Therese Manner may be. Without hope.

She may. Or she may not be. Without hope. She has no obligation. And no obligations. To be of aid. To her nephew John and her niece Pauline because they have a father and a mother, a mother and a father, industrious, painstaking. And probably. Not richer than they have been. But as rich. As they will have been. And everybody is prospering.

Therese Manner. Is thinking of everything. And no one. Has been beguiled. By anything. But every one. She has a brother John, he is a man tall and thin and he likes hunting and is successfully. Incidentally, the best shot. Never shot. This was surprising. We asked him why. He said he did not. He never had.

Therese Manner is not avoided. By women. Or by men. She is devoted. To her mother and her brother John and her nephew John and her niece Pauline and her brother Frank and her sister Ivy. She is not older than all of them. One may say she is not extravagant.

Jenny Henry and her husband William Henry. She has lost her husband William Henry and has been seduced by a man working. This made no difference as she was serenely prosperous and could like sheep. And always be pleasantly prepared. In no way was there any interference. And now Act I.

George Couleur. One and one.

Act I

Therese will be. Credited with devotion. To her family. By those. Who follow her. She will. Not be denied. Hope and resistance.

Act I

Therese will amount. To a belief. In their respect. She will not know. That they say so. Either to go there or here.

Act I

George Couleur. May never have met her. Nor will he yet and again.

Act I

George Couleur will not trouble to wonder but he has a mother. No mother has a mother nor has any mother more than their mother. George Couleur had a father and they resemble their mother and one another. She may not be selfish if they say it. She may be prosperous. And a good manager. She may be lonesome with the company and accompanied later. Indeed. They may say that it is selfish. No one need know who knows. It is all who have hopes. Of wholesome. And a wedding. And they will be willing. To be helping. If a milliner or either a dressmaker or either a helper or either forbidding. Who means whom. They must be at once.

George Couleur is no misanthrope and he manages well, that is industriously and twice they have seasons of seeding clover, that is it is better.

Act I

It is in land. May they. May they indeed. For. If they should be only with. The riches. Of it. Always. Not having been. Very lately. Acquired.
How can riches have been very lately acquired.
Nor may they have been acquired if he listens.
Which may they do. In not turning.
All of which. They feel.
A marriage can come to mean anything.
And so. They will influence them to their hurt.
In which they deprive them of obligation.
Nor need they mind. What they deprive.
Of what they are deprived.

Act I

In meditation. Florence Descotes. Is not resting. Nor indeed. Is she working. Nor preparing. And so they. Witness it.

Act I

A brother can replace a mother. Or not.
If the mother is faithful to. The brother.

They may be more particularly. With. One.
After all. Who may account. For their. Denial.
And they were eager. And they were.
She may be seen to have coats.

Act I

Florence Descotes. Has not been one.

Act I

It is very well known that they are not happy.
It is very well known that. They are not happy.
Each one is content in unison.

Act I

A father and a mother. May make either parent.
A mother and her father.
A sister and her mother and a brother.
Nor may they.

Act I

George Couleur has his mother. She is living. They will have an attraction.
But they may be. Said as yet.

Act I

She may be without doubt allowed.

Act I

Marrying. Or. Religion.

Act I

Would they could they. Or cause. Or rest because.

Act I

They were marrying and he came with her.

Act I

Florence Descotes is fairly busy. With her farming.

Act I

Could all who call call them to come.

Act I

Be men. Or be. Men. Be men or be men. And so George Couleur knew when to go. He had a very good reputation. And he. Had a very good reputation. George Couleur and his mother were prospering. They were rich. And they were buying.

George Couleur was rich. His mother was rich. They were rich. And they were buying. Land and a house. A house and land. And they already had some. And they were buying. Land. And a house. And they already had one. George Couleur and his mother was prospering and he was marrying. And this. Was lengthening. And so they meant to be women. That is. Women meant to be women.

Act I

Therese would not marry any one and no one had wanted to marry any one. She had not known George Couleur. And never knew him. She had met his mother. But that was natural. As she went to market. And saw her. And why. Should she see her. She never answered any question. That is to say. She never asked any question. She always answered every one. And this makes no connection. Naturally not. Any connection.

Act I

George Couleur and his mother were prospering.

Act I

Have no have no help to know. That they have no one to know, that they have no one.

Therese is one and one.

Act I

She may be wedded. With one. And no one. With. No one.

She may be added. With one. With. Any one. She may be added. In adding any more than any one. And so they have a pleasure in their ending adding one.

Act I

Therese having one. Begun.
She may be added. As. Any one.
And so they may be of use. And she may be of use and they. May be of use. In one. As. In one.

Act I

Therese may be the necessary one.

Act I

No err Couleur, she never knew one.
There was no reason not to know some one.
She did not she did not know any one. She had met one. One of one of the two of them. And there is no connection. They live there and they live there.

Act I

George Couleur is married to his wife he has a mother, she is a mother and he is married to his wife and his mother they will be ready with. Any one. And they live as they may say one and one. And not narrowly. And any one. Working in the fields works hard with grain and corn and nuts and wine and oxen and help and any one.

Act I

It was a chance that she looked well.
It was a chance that she looked well spoken rapidly.

Act I

It was a chance that she looked well. She did not mind the cold although she appeared to suffer from it. This was not because she said she minded it. She said she did not mind it.

Act I

She said. She was ready to stay in order not to go away but she wanted to go away rather as she wanted to go away and she wanted to be there. Where. She was. Where she was When she. Was. She wanted to go away where. She was. She wanted. Where she was to stay. And so. They say. Timidity won the day. Timidity. Won the day.

Act I

George Couleur and his mother and his wife he had no sister never knew her. There are a great many who do not know every one. One and one. Everywhere they eat they eat with some one. Some eat with some and some eat with some one one and one.

Act I

Therese was easily pleased by forgetting no one. Easily pleased. By not. Forgetting any one. Therese was easily pleased by not forgetting not any one of any of them.

Act I

No one does know any one of them because although they do not come together there are not very many. There. At any one time. At any one time. There are. All of them who are there there but not to know them. This is easy to understand. By them. Of them. And not. Of everybody. Who does not know any of all or one of them.

Act I

Therese may make a mountain out of a molehill.

Act I

Molehill. May be. A whole. May be.

Act I

May be. A pleasure. Or may be. A pleasure. But. She met her. And aided her. That is they asked her.

Act I

George Couleur was never to be an orphan. He had had a father and he had a mother. And they had one another. And he worked very often. And whenever. He gathered the harvest later and earlier. It is very well to work well. George Couleur and his mother worked well. And his wife worked as well.

Act I

No one. Places. Faces. As having been met.

Act I

Very well met.

Act

Therese will not leave often. May be she will not.

Act I

Who may they be. They may be.

Act I

May be they will be. Ready. To end. Act one.

Act II

All out but you.
Therese has taken pains.

Act II

Therese. Is not ruled by you. She is influenced by you. She will be ready to be through. And come to be. Ready for whoever should be better than ever.

Therese. May be inclined to be thoughtful and older any one could meet and collect them in their clover. That is the seed need be filled. With what. They need when they sweep. A road. And so. Which may be. That they will. A third. They have a third more or two thirds less than are needed.

Therese. She may be able to come too.

Act II

No or no more. Because they will not question. Nor need they. As they. Do not. Ever think. Of George Couleur. Who had a mother. Who heard her.

Act II

May she be three. Or readily free. Or made a mother. One two three. Who needs wishes.

Act II

George Couleur has a hope of a mother who is a mother to her father which may call mother mother may they help with them as farther. They may exist. May they. With warning. Or may they. Be equal. In with. Farming. Farming is a station with out shaping their destinies. She may be thought. That. She may be. In. Amount. And would a brother and a mother desert her.

Act II

It may be heard to be hard. To leave them. For two.

Act II

Therese never comes as a witness.

Act II

Because she never had been in that place.

Act II

And that was natural. As it was not in that way that she went when she went to her home.

When she went. To any place. Where. She went. No one allows them. To have been.

Act II

Thinking. Of winking.

Act II

Many could be one or two.

Act II

George Couleur had a mother and she could press a pigeon to be or rather. They could be there with her. She had a husband and a father. She was a mother and a sister and a daughter. Her son had a mother. They may be outlined.

More which. Is it. As made. With which. They call. That it is. Well. To be. Very often present. As well. When they will. Arrange. For it. As well. Which they may. When they. Are ready. As well. As when they are thought. They were married.

Act II

She might like. Seeing at a distance. And like. She might like. Which she will see. At a distance and like. She might not like and seeing at a distance she might not like. To see at a distance.
Therese. May be attached to the children of men and women and women and men. And she does say so in not seeing them.

Therese may be an advantage for them to have them come with them to have them coming. May she be. Men and women. And it is early. To have them follow them. She does stay at home not precisely. As she does not move about with them. They never leave them. She does not leave them.

Act II

She will stay to be useful too. They do not need to need two.

Act II

Therese. Could she smile. Awhile. If she was met by two. Or yet. Not new. Therese. Could she think as well. As if there were more than a few. But not two. She is not very happy as well. Therese will be well met by three and two. And not by seeing through four or two. As much. Therese will be joined by them. This makes it useful. She may not be imagining. Therese will not be hurt. By questioning nor wait as she is waiting. She will come again. They may be ready yet. And she is waiting. It might that they might not might be there but might be here. She might be here.

Act II

Could anybody know through George Couleur leaving anybody who is

with which without a complaint as they mean will they touch which they yield
for themselves in and on around and they might include. George Couleur and
his mother or. Might they have another than the mother than their mother.
Than any than a mother. George Couleur.

Act II

It is easy to think that Therese. May be in place. Of her half sister. Ivy.
Who after all. May be not at all. The child of her mother or of her older brother
or of her older sister or not at all. Just the youngest of all. And therefor tall.
Therese. I am going away.
Question. To stay.
Therese. No not to stay away.
Therese. I am not only going away.
Therese. I am not going to stay away.
Therese. I am not going away.
Therese. I am not going away.
Therese. I am going away not to-day.
Therese. But she went.
Therese. Went away the day that is two days for four days anyway. And
there is a survival.

Act II

Of many which. They may be rich. To think of which. They will be selfish.
They may be where. They will not care. They may be there. They may be
selfish. She may be there. She may be where. She may have come. She may
be won. She may not think. She may not blink. The facts.
Therese. Is not away.

Act II

George Couleur, fastens a rabbit, that is he does not shoot, nor does he
wish nor does his brother-in-law, nor does his brother-in-law shoot although
both of them are capable.

Act II

One two one two. They leave two.

Act II

Not as much as they were.
With care.

Act II

New who. Who can be through. Who means to.
Be better there than two. And though two.
May make it easy for two. Two may not.
Make it easy for two. Or more. Or through.

Act II

Therese. May not be. Attracted either.
By a mountain. Nor. By a big city.

Act II

Therese. May wish. That walking. At a distance.
Therese. That walking a considerable distance.
Therese. That walking a very considerable distance.
Therese. May or may not be walking.
Therese. A very considerable distance.
Therese. In either case.
Therese. It makes no difference in either case.
Therese. Nor will they be a pleasure.
Therese. Nor will they be without pleasure.
Therese. Whether. They will. Or whether.
Therese. They will be. With pleasure.
Therese. Will in any case. Be a pleasure.
Therese. Will return. As a pleasure.
Therese. In any case.

Act II

George Couleur. Has whether. It may be. In.
May have been. Not in. A suit. Of clothing.
Because it could. Not have been.
He could not have been. It could not have been.
It could not have been. Him.

Act II

Not finely because of one or two.
George Couleur, could be. As if. He.
She his mother could be. As if indeed.
They could be as if they were more.
Than if indeed. They were. Remembered.
Than if. One or two. They were.
Could everybody. Be a mother and son.
One two.

Act II

Otherwise are you through. Practically.

Act II

Therese.   When they will dwindle and have one.
Therese.   When they may. Or better one.
Therese.   Let us see certainly. They ask to see.
Therese.   And whether they may. They ask. To say.
Therese.   That she will move around. In moving away.

Act II

A button. Or a fire. Or a sheep. Or a sound.
Therese.   She will be present. When they are around.
Therese.   And strangely. The hearing is acute.
Therese.   Because they will not be selfish.
Therese.   And so they hope so.

Act II

Therese makes three more useful.

Act II

It is not there. But here.
They will be here. And there. And may they sell.
Or give with them. None can give them.
Or plainly.

Act II

Three words are selfish. Fish. The same. And meant.
Therese. She may have a sister.
Therese. And indeed many.
Therese. And they may count.
Therese. As one more.

Act II

Therese. May she be meant. For you.

Act II

Therese. But that has been her wish.
Therese. Ever since she was a little girl.

Act II

May George Couleur never be deceived. In having been as well known. As his mother with him. Not without a father with him, nor indeed marrying with him and no father with him. A mother and a mother without with him.

Act II

They need two to be two.

Act II

Therese. Will be they may be indeed they will be.
It is well to be able to be of avail.
Therese. She may be naturally without fail.
Therese. There without fail.
Therese. Not very likely.
Therese. That she may be.
Therese. Be able to disregard a sister.
Therese. Or likely to place at a disadvantage.
Therese. Who missed her.

Act II

Therese. What is the difference.

Therese. Nor might they go.
Therese. For which they will change.

Act II

Or through. Do not disturb. Nor hesitate to detain. Those who might.

Act II

Therese. For them it is a choice as well as a chance.

Act II

Therese. She may be equal to gratitude or gratefully.

Act II

George Couleur may be with her. That is may be with her. He was made to a purpose and believe. Or need it. She may or need it or deceive.

George Couleur regret very much to having forced it to give him a meal.

George Couleur. Or should. May they be when they come or carry out their intention for which they disturb no one. George Couleur is a tiller, of the soil and owner of very many who have not added to being leant or given. No one lends anything. And they are careful to be left to mine. May they carry as they call. Or either be thorough carefully.

Act II

Therese. Has not arrived in her place.
Therese. Nor will she know him.
Therese. Nor indeed might any one.
Therese. For this is as safe as natural.

Act II

Therese. May be easily an older woman older.

Act II

No one need think of anything.

Act II

Therese.   Yvonne is agreeable and condescending but it is very nice that it is you.

Therese.   Because in any case it is very nice that it is you.

Therese.   Because Yvonne who is very pleasant one by one it is very nice that it is you.

Therese.   Because of them that is they are as old as they were to become when they were to go with them.

Therese.   They may be lent to be made then to come for them.

Therese.   It is why and they will wish.

Therese.   For which they mean as well as meant them.

Therese.   Any little while they will go as they did when they will go and part.

Therese.   May not be pleasant as a witness but she is pleasant as a witness.

Therese.   For them or more than for them.

Therese.   She will be more as a witness that they went there with and without and for them.

Therese.   Should she be better able to be asking more for them than she would if she were by them with them. And so they married. Certainly not they. Or more with them. It is very strange how many in the country are not willing to be married although it is necessary and yet is it necessary not if they have house with a window and they may have them.

Therese.   She may be mentioned with them or she may be not mentioned she may not be with them.

Therese.   Which she mentioned with them.

Act II

Therese.   May be and may be mentioned with them.

Therese.   Is here with them.

Therese.   Is here is here with them.

Therese.   Could it be easily found that she was happy without and with them as she was happy without them as she was happy with them.

Act II

George Couleur may dream of the mother of a sister or either of the sister of the mother or either of a father of a mother as a mother and a sister and a mother. George Couleur may dream of one another.

Act II

Civilization follows every season.

Act II

George Couleur said that he still expects guests. Nor need he. Trouble to be questioned. Nor left alone. He will be able to be advised. And they will. Never apply what had been devised. For their entertainment or their pleasure. George Couleur would willingly wait. He speaks as if he were silent or out loud.

Act II

Therese. Has really heard. That they were more than a third. Not there. Or nearly there. Or not behind.
Therese. It is strange to see her anxious.
Therese. No one need know any one.
Therese. She might be left to have been or to leave it to be left.
Therese. May listen if they mean after or before then.
She has heard what they are saying.

Act II

There is no door they have no door therefor they have no floor. Therefor they are near the door therefor they do have to clean the floor and open the door. This may be for them.

Act II

They will please whoever they will have seen known them.

Act II

Civilization all through.
George Couleur known to have had a mother too and still they are to blame. Who is to blame because. After a pause. They will satisfy any one.

Act II

Will they come George Couleur and not his mother. Naturally not he will come George Couleur will come and not his mother or naturally not. Neither will come as a sister ought or a mother ought or a mother or a brother. Ought.

Act II

It may be true that if it is stronger there is no comfort and if it is not stronger there is no use.

Therese.   Dwell evenly upon it. Be proud of a sister and be a comfort to a mother.

Therese.   They be capable of obtaining more than they gave them.

Therese.   For which they will wish not to thank them but to see them.

Therese.   Because they will include that they went there with them.

Therese.   Many do not mention who went there for them.

Therese.   But they will remember whether they went there and not without them.

Therese.   For them in asking them anything.

Therese.   And they will answer as they like them.

Therese.   But all of it for all of it for them.

Therese.   They should have been allowed to see them with them.

Therese.   They may be all of it for more of more without them.

Therese.   May be they may have been with them before they may be out side near them.

Therese.   It is plainly just what they would like as they do like them to have it as it is given to them to keep for them.

Therese.   It is very well for all of them.

Therese.   Just as she will.

Therese.   They may in the way.

Therese.   Come if they can.

Therese.   Which is why they are able to come.

Therese.   In no trouble.

Therese.   Without any difficulty.

Therese.   And when they go away again.

Therese.   They will have it there for them.

Therese.   It is very easy to be there with them.

Therese.   If they are not there again.

Therese.   When they have not gone away with them.

Therese.   Just yet.

Therese.   All may be.

Therese.   Just here when they left.

Therese.   May she be missed or left.

Therese.   By once in a while fairly.

Therese.   When they knew.

Therese.   It makes no difference in coming.

Therese.   They come just the same to go away.

Therese. About this time.
Therese. Will willows fall.
Therese. By them they will be here by then.
Therese. They and by them they will be finished by then.
Therese. Accurately or registered.
Therese. Just when will they like.
Therese. Even if they are not alone.

Act III

George Couleur saw a door and they stood and they were oxen. More than if they were alone.

Act III

George Couleur there is a difference between scissors and a thimble between oxen and wool and between various ways of welcoming.
George Couleur. They change.

Act III

George Couleur. May be for. For which it is better. That it is for. For them. Would he be. That they had may may she be spoiled or not be better for. For them.
George Couleur may not be asking any or for them. In eclipse or brown or a starry night or and. It may be called collection or collecting. For with them.

Act III

There may or they may be no mission nor or mention or motion nor no mention of nor or. For them.

Act III

George Couleur. Which a wish or oxen.

Act III

Each which may or did not mind or in a mid or manage he with she. Three. May they motion or mention with them. George Couleur could or was with or with oxen.

George Couleur is young with or without or waiting with a wedding or adding oxen to adding mention or adding mention with without wedding or nor with oxen.

Act III

It is often with or without a or without or waiting. If. Visiting.

Act III

They may call girls girlish. With or with or without mention or nor no adding waiting. Could they carry a that they may.

Act III

George Couleur.   May or may be or or has not to do with or or oxen.

Act III

George Couleur. She meant to be very careful with reading the paper. Which it did matter. This was no need of knowing her or Therese. He was older that is younger and so he would not know the family beside did they live there.

Act III

Therese. She is properly proud of her sister.

Act III

George Couleur, I love my love with a d because she is a darling I love her with a y because she is beautiful.

Act III

George Couleur may be with a large or larger not hesitation or eagerness but made nor indeed may eagerness.

Fill feel or ought a color be white or felt a fail. George Couleur is not as avoided as within hail.

He meant to be. And no attendant to her attend for her could be fail. George Couleur has a mother his wife has a mother George Couleur has a mother a mother has a wife that is George Couleur has a wife and mother he has a mother George Couleur and a father he is not faded. A father is faded not a mother. George Couleur and a mother the mother which is his mother. To the mother.

Act III

Therese. Has nothing to do with leaving or demeaning. It is called early or brother. One sister and a brother or a sister and a brother and a brother and there may be three.

Act III

Civilization suggests enters.

Act III

A moon. They need to have good weather.

Act III

George Couleur. May share. And he may wear. Or nearly. A suit of clothes. And they. May be. With which they will relish. That he is more than leave it. As a pleasure. It is a wife who has joined with a mother and they need not be neat because or gather that they will add neither. A father.

The grandfather having been dead.

Act III

Should no one. Shown.

Act III

Therese. Shone. Or wood. Or would she. Be fond of leaving. Open. But not after night fall. The entrance as a door.

Act III

Therese. There is no care to have them share anything with her as her sister will be longer in not adding more or longer. Can you see that they are not the members of the family.

Act III

She may be easily heard to be. One of four or of three.

Act III

Therese. May more quietly and noisily. This may be not only is not the habit of the country.

Act III

Therese.   Ours and hours in their country.

Act III

Therese.   If they will remember one another.
            If they father and her brother.
            Come back as they shall.
            With less or more than ever.
            But best because there is no doubt.
            She will need when. They had.
            Better come to eight.

Act III

It is strange not to be timid but not to go alone. Because.   He is timid.
And he does not go nor go not go without them.

Act III

Therese.   May be well and not willing.
            She may be well and willing.
            She may be well and she may be willing.
            They will go with some some go.
            They go and it is as well.
            That they are well.
            They are well and they are willing.
            Some go and some are willing.
            Some go and some are well.

Act III

It is very easily forgotten. Who was going.
As easily forgotten. Who was well.
As easily forgotten Jenny William.
And as easily forgotten. Jenny. William.

Act III

It is as easily forgotten. Jenny William.

It is as easily forgotten. Any money.
It is as easily forgotten. Mushrooms.
It is as easily forgotten and Jenny William.

Act III

George Couleur. She may be often told less. Anybody may be an orphan. That is with women. With a mother and a wife and any other. Anybody may be an aid to any. Be women. Two may. Be. Women. Anybody may aid any orphan to be of women. He had a mother and a wife living.
George Couleur. If they did. Stay and nobody went away. Which one went with them. He went with oxen and they went with and with him. He stayed with oxen and did not they did not they went with them. It is easy to resemble men and women and oxen with them.

Act III

Therese. Two many twos whose. Which went with them. She had a mother and a father and two brothers with them. Very often as much.
Therese. All who are timid with them.
May be they will for them.
As many as stay with them.
They will be ready with them.
They add it with them for them.
It ought to be eight or them.
And so with any for them.

Act III

It takes several weeks for it to pass away.

Act III

Therese. She shall be certainly sharing her quarter. And they will like blankets.

Act III

I have decided that only the timid.
Are eating. Only the timid are eating.

Act III

Therese.   Either whether. They will. Gather.
Therese.   Will not tell whether he is very well.
Therese.   Because he will have heard it heard that he is very well.
Therese.   Should they be careful or with them cautioning or with them caution.
Therese.   If they are leaving or not leaving as well.
Therese.   Will. Tell.

Act III

Therese.   May need no as a distinction and she will come as well. She will not need no not need no as a distinction she will come as well.
Therese.   And now do I need my life.

Act III

Therese.   Any day or any day I may stay with them all of every day.
           And so gradually.

Act III

George Couleur needs more to be obeyed or as they are more. To be obeyed.
George Couleur.   Leaves no one to add more to each one. To leave more with each one. To come one.
George Couleur.   Feels often healthier.
George Couleur.   May join exactly always in their way as never, or indeed. George Couleur may think and have as need. May be they do require a wife and mother.
George Couleur or one another.

Act III

George Couleur.   Will work with his oxen as hard will work with his oxen as hard. Will work with his oxen as hard.
George Couleur.   May they be there for her with her.
                  And still waiting for a visit to her.
                  To them to her.
George Couleur.   May be they do.

Act III

George Couleur.   For when her. For the love of for when her.

Act III

Therese.   Has been thought very even may even have come.

Act III

No one knowing any one or Jenny and William. They may be many of them and they will who will be going by then or marry William. Not as Jenny.

Act III

Therese.   May have added coming to women.
Her sister with ambition.
She herself with any feeling.
Or nearly when they were needing.
It is easy to remember them with angry feeling.

Act III

She chews gently at her food.

Act III

Therese.   If asked would it be a gain.
It would be very plain.
That they meant to remain.
And it would not be a pleasure to remain.
But to remain. All the same.

Act III

Therese.   It will or they must with their care be very busy.
Therese.   She may be often left to be aware.
Therese.   She may be often there.
Therese.   Or with them they may be not often.
Therese.   They may not be as often there.
Therese.   But which with them. They will not be.
Therese.   They will not be often there.
Therese.   Just at one time.
Therese.   They may not be as often not there.
Therese.   They may be not as often and not there.

Therese.   They may be there.

Therese.   Would they have heard.

Therese.   That they would go again.

Therese.   Only one.

Therese.   They would be there.

Therese.   Just when they were as well there.

Therese.   As often there.

Therese.   They were there.

Therese.   Which was not but it was by the time there.

Act III

Therese.   In consequence.

Therese.   They were there.

Therese.   As they were not there.

Therese.   In answer to not there.

Therese.   But which in answer.

Therese.   With it is it is.

Act III

George Couleur.   Mountains and might then.

George Couleur.   If a mountain is covered with snow I have not seen it.

George Couleur.   Nor with them in wedding.

George Couleur.   In summer.

George Couleur.   May in the middle.

George Couleur.   Of winter.

George Couleur.   Nor what is winter or weather.

George Couleur.   How many acres can be as a mother. Nor any father.

George Couleur.   They never think together.

George Couleur.   Or any other.

George Couleur.   Please think of it with it.

George Couleur.   A great many read a mother for a father.

George Couleur.   With one a mother.

George Couleur.   Or as or father.

George Couleur.   With as or mother.

George Couleur is married and resumes well, being well he resumes being well.

George Couleur is married and he resumes being made very well by winter and by summer.

George Couleur has no use for a difference in oxen he knows very well well.

George Couleur for they may take pains.

Act III

At last they change, they may be made to change red to blue all out but you, and so they think well, of resting. They may be feeble with pleasure and excellent at most.

Act III

Anxiously for their investigation in order to please and be pleased with more there. With which. They may plan. With which. They may plan with. More there. Or for it. And so anybody which may as pleases.

Act III

If George Couleur married to her may be with her married to her or rather her married to her or rather a mother who rather no brother or rather a brother with whoever or other which they may have as a care.

Act III

Come welcome or most which when they can rest with all as they may in guidance.

And now contentedly eat slowly as often as more.

Act III

They may be meant not be meant to be restless.

Act III

George Couleur. Please be without pleasure for three.

Act III

Therese. Having gone and stayed may remain and in neatly and frame.

Act III

Therese. Would never know that there had been. George Couleur.
Nor would Therese leave when they went investigating.

Act III

Therese.   They may be religious or met at once.
Therese.   For will they be met or may they be met or may they be met at once.
Therese.   They may not ease be met at once.

Act III

George Couleur.   It is as easy to be cold with when they will be a plain chain of well or rather not as much as left. To have a fire. They will speak loudly. And not mutter.
George Couleur.   Be met very often as a name.
George Couleur.   It is hopeless to be cold and warm.

Act III

George Couleur.   Is rather.
George Couleur.   That they disturb is rather.
George Couleur.   He had no brother not even a brother Henry nor a sister not even a brother Henry a sister Clara or a father not even a brother a sister Clara or a father William Couleur.
George Couleur.   He had a mother and a father.
George Couleur.   He had a wife her name is Florence and she may be rested or eating not with or without not with or without them.

Act III

George Couleur.   More startling.
George Couleur.   Or interesting.
George Couleur.   Or breathing.
George Couleur.   Or explaining.
George Couleur.   Or planning.
George Couleur.   Or laying.
George Couleur.   May they be three in occasion.

Act III

Therese.   May or may not have heard.
Therese.   Any Therese may or may have heard.
Therese.   She may be with them.
Therese.   As alone.

Therese. Or a little.
Therese. Just when.
Therese. Timid in the scope.
Therese. Would they wait.

Act III

Therese may inhabit any two or village.
Therese.   May inhabit two. A village.
Therese.   In not moving from one she.
Therese.   In inhabit one.
Therese.   Therese can inhabit two a village.
Therese.   In visiting a third.
Therese.   Not two and a third.
Therese.   A third village.
Therese.   Two a village.
Therese.   Can inhabit two. Village.

Act III

George Couleur has been. A street car conductor he has not been. Because he is rich he has been. And had a wife and he has been. Not left to grow more than they have been. His brother that is wedding a wedding.

No more will George Couleur try to cry.

It is easy not to have a fire in autumn.

Act III

Therese.   She will be older in case.

Act III

She will not in place.
She will be older in case.
She will not be older.

Act III

When you will be with me still.
In which way they will.
Which they may.

Will or stay.
Which they will be which or will.
Will they.
Will they stay.
Or will they must.
Stay.
Which way.
A. Thousand.

FINIS

THEY MUST. BE WEDDED.
TO THEIR WIFE.

A Play

Any name. Of which. One. Has known. At least two.

> Josephine
> Ernest
> Therese
> Julia
> and
> Guy and Paul and John.

Of all these. Two or more. Except Guy.
And this. By. One brother.
Two separate brothers. Of two. Separate brothers.
They must hurry and get. Their wagons. With their harvest in. Before
the rain. Can. Pour.

> Also.

It would be well. If. No. Hail fell.
To hurt. The other things. That have been planted.

Act I

Three brothers. Of which. One. Saved. The two. One. By one. From
drowning.

Act I

Reminding. Of. The names. Which. Have been chosen.
Josephine Ernest Therese Julia Guy Paul and John.

Act I

Josephine. Has been known by that name.
Ernest. Has meant more. Than. That claim.
Therese. Will be faintly neat. And they close.
Julia. Name which welcomes a valley.
Guy. It is a funeral. To be. Well.
Paul. She says. It has. Charm.
John. Will they cover. Endeavor.

All in a barn.

Act I

Scene I

Mary. Why will. They hope. That she. Is the mother of Etienne.
Josephine. Because. I am married.
Ernest. Why will they hurry.
Therese. They smile quietly in a gain.
Julia. May she. Have heard. Birds.
Guy. He saved my life.
Paul. And mine.
John. I claim. No. Shame.

Scene II

They see a river. Which. Runs through a marsh. One might think. That the mother was unhappy. But not at all. She has hopes. For her future.

They have. Not forgotten. The sister. And daughter. Neither. Will they. Like it.

Marcelle. Who has known. When. He. Can smile.
　　　　All who remain. Come in.
　　He is. Sure. To dance. Well. If not. Now.
　　And so. The month. Of July. Opens. And closes.

Scene III

This scene is in a place where. They are.
Violet. Oh will you. Ask. Him. To marry me.
Marcel. He laughed.
Josephine. After many opposite to. It.

Ernest.   Politeness.
Therese.   I am older. Than a boat.
             And there. Can be no folly. In owning. It.
             There can. Be no. Hesitation. In. Working.
             Like. And. Unlike. May. They. Come in.
They all wish. That they. Had been there. When. They would. Have
been. Surely. Not. So frightened.
       After this. They may be proud. Of themselves.

Scene IV

She may be wearing a gown newly washed and pressed. Not in any other
language this would be written differently.
Josephine. Oh Josephine.
Ernest. May be a victim. Of himself. He may be delightful. Or not. As it
happens.
Therese. Will always know. That she. Is not a disappointment. Nor whether.
There. Will be. Her. Share.
Julia. Julia could be called Julia Arthur only this. Would make. A dog.
Uneasy.
Guy. Would it. Be possible. To believe it. Of three.
Paul. She says. He is charming.
John. He rescued. Them. One by one. From. Drowning.

Scene IV

All of them having come to the door.
This is now. Scene IV.
They all. Talk. As if. It were alarming.
Also. As if. They expected. Him. Not to be. Charming.
They also. Make preparations. For an. Exception. They will. Gladly.
Wait. For his. Impatience. And. For his reception. They will also confuse.
A bird calling. With a dog. Squeaking.
       And so. They resume. Their. Usual. Expression.

Scene V

Will she be alive. And will. They thrive.
       They may best. Be. Best. And. Most.
Josephine is not. Astonishing.
Ernest. Is obedient. And. Developing.

Therese. Is quiet. And not. Depressing.
Julia. Is harmonious. And. Impatient. And willing.
Guy Paul and John.
May. Or may not. Come.
They will. Hope. That it is. Their wish.
Which they welcome.

Scene I

Pretty soon. They will think. Of some one.

Scene I

It is going on nicely.
The place in which they stay is this one which surrounds. In the midst of suspicion that they will leave without them they may be an audience. As a reception of a difficulty they may manage to stammer. They will. Incline. To oblige. Only one. When they stare.
This is how millions mean.
This is a little a scene.
Just when will they go by adapting.
Nor may they be merrily there. To share.
Justly. In why.
It is a round movement this. Because. Declared.
For it. It is. A wonder. Because. They. Were. Spared.
Might it be agreeable if it were a mistake.
Josephine. May not attend. A. Wedding.
Ernest. Has been widened. By attention. To misers. In their misery.
Therese. Is always sure. To have. The key. In her bag.
Julia. Julia is known as forlorn.
John. An elder brother who regrets the illness of his father because it deprives them of traveling as a vacation.
Guy. Who has not been drowned Although he was very nearly not saved.
Paul. Whom she says always has. Charm.
They will come together to vote as to whether they will be often. Without weddings. All who look. Are wealthy. As found.
Josephine hesitates. More than they do. She chooses her air.
Julia. Has been not only better but really well.
Therese. Is patient and calm.
Ernest. Purposeful.
John. Devoted.
Guy. Unknown.

and Paul. Pleasant vivacious and quarrelsome.
Bitterness is entertained by them all.

Scene I

Josephine.	Will leave.
	Patience will yield.
	She will employ.
	They will enjoy.
Josephine.	Josephine is called. And she has. Displaced. Xenobie. Also. She has well said. That. She will not stay. That is. She. May be. There. All. Are. Pleased.
Josephine.	All. Are. Pleased.
	And kisses. Two. On either cheek.
	May be accepted. Or. Refused.
	By. Two. Josephine.
Julia.	Julia loves to be. Above. With her. Yes. With a pleasure. They will. Be their care. Or. Julia. Other. Than. With them. Or. Another. Julia. Has made it clear. With them. Here. Julia.
Therese.	Will blindly keep. Not only. But. Also. With welcome. As from. The time. With one. Welcome. Indeed made. In the. Interval. With them. Therese. Can. In face. Of. Therese.
Ernest.	Should it. Present. Presently. There. May. Should they. Form coldly. With. And. An amount. A. Clergy. All who should. Place grace. Or. Disgrace. They may be forty to four fairly. It is well always to mistake a name.
John.	Did all. See John.
	All who. And. Whom. Would come and soon see Josephine. See John.
Guy.	They may recognise places.
Paul.	All who did know Julia said Julia would try.

Scene II

They add gayety and gayly.

Scene III

Josephine.	Meant Joseph was once free.
	Did he think for them.

Scene IV

Therese.   May she be thought well of, by all who are made clearly in their
              prayers as brother and their brother. She may shut. It. Without
              them. By the time. That they. Are cautious. In this case. No.
              One. Is mentioned.

Julia.   Julia who has won Guy to be welcome to them. Welcome to them.
              Julia who has been unwilling to be unwelcome to them. Julia
              who has been unwilling to be with them unwelcome for them.
              Julia who has been with them welcome for them. With them.
              By them.

Julia and Guy. One. Two. Three.

Ernest.   And a pause. A pleasure. And a pause.

John.   A pleasure without a pause without them.

              Scene in which they second them.

Scene I

It is our right. To be. Our delight.

Scene I

     Just why they would.

Josephine.   Differs from Fanny and Catherine.

Ernest.   Therese differs from Josephine and Mercedes.

Therese.   Ernest. Fastening. Audibly. Ernest. Fastening. They in conclu-
              sion. Audibly. Josephine.

Julia.   May they. Who by. And by. Who. By and by.

Julia.   May they. Who. By and by.

John.   Webster. Was a name. That was spoken.

Guy.   All who call a wall.
              Very well I thank you.

Guy.   All who tell that. It is. Brightly. A concert.

Guy.   Who have been happy.

Paul.   Forget-me-not.

Scene II

Act I

Forget me not.

Josephine.   They have hurt them. By. Leaving.

	Are they afraid of leaving.
Josephine.	Have they minded sleeping.
	And been bothered. By sleeping.
Josephine.	Have they heard of meant. With them. Mentioning and trembling. Both lost.
Therese.	It is always at last.
	Ernest. Should have been. First.
	They will. Have been. Made. By them.
	For him.
Ernest.	Do they mind him.
Julia.	As all. He was disturbed.
John.	It makes no difference. It is not that.
	It makes a difference.
	Because. Of which.
Guy.	Orphans. Profit. By mischance.
Paul.	I call. For all.
They all	May be they do.
come together.	Will they.
They have	For them. To think.
known each	Whichever
other.	It is very clearly.
	Autocratic.
	And angrily.
	As well. As they say.

Act II

They may very well be equal.

Scene I

Josephine.　I like it as it has been begun.

Scene II

Josephine.　A very beautiful day succeeds in summer.

Scene III

Josephine.　May we be well. Forgotten.

Scene IV

Josephine. I should be thankful. That. He. Has made it possible.
Therese.   I. May be silent. And. Simple.
Julia.   Come smile. And be. A. Half. Of. Will.
Ernest.   How are Howards. Known. Alone.
John.   Disturb. Them. As. Known.
Guy.   Do not distress. Or cause distress.
Guy.   Or cause distress. Do not distress.
Paul.   A brother. Paul has. No brother.
            The time comes for one of them.

Act II

Josephine. Who has held Josephine.
Julia.   Who has beheld Julia.
Therese.   Who has been Therese.
Paul.   Who has loved Paul.
John.   Who has learned of John.
Ernest.   Who has followed Marcel.
Guy.   Who can think well of Guy.
All together.   And all the same they will be disappointed.
Josephine. May has met. With wet. Weather.
Josephine. And they will think well. Of me.
Josephine. For them to close. At once. Is a. Mistake.
Josephine. I have thought of three.
Julia.   Be relieved of perplexity. And for which fortune and fortunately
            in thoughts of plunder. For the same. In there. In. Perplexity.
            With. Guidance. It is a hope. That they have made. With them.
            Their mistake. In guidance.
Julia.   It is easy to see a shadow. And with. And will he. Withdraw.
Julia.   They may be often. Exactly. They. Answer.
Julia.   It is our aloud. All of which. They. State.
Julia.   It is not. By that time. That. They are. In error.
Julia.   By that time. Which. They have called. As hospitable. As their.
            Or. Are there. All in told. And having. Told.
Julia.   Should it be hurt.
Julia.   Coming.
Therese.   Esther. Should it. A volume of. White. And relieving. All. As
            it. Was it. A color.
Therese.   Should she allow.

Therese.	Them to go.
Therese.	Where they would if they went.
Therese.	It is. Obliging.
John.	Do they.
John.	Believe in a mining for them.
John.	They have broken nothing.
John.	I say. Nothing.
John.	They have.
John.	Nothing here with them.
Guy.	Believe it all.
Paul.	One of them call.
Ernest.	May attach mention.
Ernest.	They sometimes say. Honorable mention.

Scene II

Josephine may establish who may.

Josephine.	They will announce declare.
Josephine.	A will wonder where.
Josephine.	More say more. See.
Josephine.	With this. And. With. Me.
Josephine.	As. Best. Us. ·

Scene II

Josephine and Therese.	She led. More. Than. Their.
	May be helped. To. Send her.
Josephine and Therese.	Will she be. With them.
	Will she. Be. Dismayed. Excuse.
	Will she be disenchanting.
	Just made. In sofar. Justly made.
Josephine and Therese.	Insofar justly made to prepare.
	For them with them alone.
Josephine and Therese.	It is. A pleasure. To see. Delicacy.
	Which makes it. She is. Sweetness itself.
	As she. Appears.

It is pleasant that balsamine has a fragrance.

Josephine and	May she be tall. And true.

Julia.	May she also. Be new.
	May she. Also. Be. One of few.
	May she come. To see. Them.
Josephine and Julia.	Very nicely.
Julia and Therese.	They have not met. To meet.
	Will they. Be surely. As.
	Will they be. Better. With.
	Them. As made it. Be all.
	Fortunately for them.
	It is pleasant to have a white table.
	Only naturally.
Therese and Josephine.	May be. In why. Of. They. Mention their wonder. Of. About. Well.
	Funnily too hot.
Therese and Julia.	Should have been. As they were. Inviting.
Julia and Ernest.	More. Will be precious. As. Well.
Julia and Ernest.	For them. To have. In time.
Julia and Ernest.	Always helped.
Julia and Ernest.	A little. Once. At a time.
Julia and Ernest and Therese.	Once. At a time. A little. As helped.
	Much of the time. They do.
	Refuse. Crowns.
Josephine and Therese.	By their help. Are they anxious. For it.

Josephine
  and   In no hurry.
Therese.

Scene II

Josephine.   It is very inappropriate. To have it. Made. With them. By them.
Therese.   Or as they feel well.
Therese.   Which it is. No. No. Which. With. An applied. In their. Credit.
Josephine
  to   No wonder. That. They greet. With pleasure. Their. Boat.
Therese.
Therese
  and   Have many heard. Of dances. Dancers. Make dances. And.
Francis.   Dances. For themselves.
Therese
  to   Josephine speaks first. It. Is widely. Unknown. That they are.
Josephine.   Troubled.
Josephine
  to   It is mine.
Ernest.
Therese
  to   It is mine.
Ernest.
Therese
  to   With whom.
John.
Therese
  to   Claude is a name and also Ernest.
Guy.
Therese
  to   Should they manage. To urge. Them.
Ernest.
Josephine
  to   Or with their yellow. Wishes. Or. Cravats.
Ernest.
Josephine
  to
Guy   It is of very extraordinary importance. That. They. Give this.
  and
Therese.

Therese and Josephine to Ernest and Guy.	Should they be often induced. Induced. Introduced. Should they. Be often. Induced. To change more. Than formerly.
Therese and Josephine and Julia to Edward.	It is in vain. That they count. The amount. For which. They manage. To leave. And open. More often. Themselves. To their lambs.
All of them together.	Little dogs resemble little girls.
Julia to Ernest and Guy.	They may have chances. They. May. Have chances. They. May. Have. Chances.
Julia to John and Guy.	They may have had chances.
Julia to Guy.	Or with it. They may have been there.
Julia to John.	With them.

Scene II

Julia to Guy and John.	It is a. Wheelbarrow. That makes. One anxious.

Julia to Guy and John.	They may know. That. One is one.
Julia to Guy and John.	In made. To punish them. With one.
Guy to Julia and John.	It is. An anxious thing. To say. The month. Of May.
Guy to Julia.	With which. They will. Please. Me.
Guy to Therese.	After all. It was not what. I had expected. It. Was you.
Guy to Therese.	It was you. And. They. Will have pleasure. In that case.
Therese to Julia.	Will all. Who will. Make it. A pleasure too.
Therese to Guy.	They will be anxious. That they have. Seen me.
Therese to Julia and Guy.	All of a wall. Is wet. When they. See me.
Therese to Julia and	Or has been. And now. Is dry. This has been. Because. Of the action. Of the sun. On water. And pleasure. And quiet.

John and Guy.	And a noise. Which. When. It came alone. After.
Therese to John and Guy and Julia and Ernest.	Was not what they. Would have. As an interference. And my niece and nephew. Knew. That. Aloud.
Ernest and Josephine.	All who may know. A march. Will know. That willows blow. When they mean.
Ernest and Josephine.	It is all. Made at all. By them. As. They mean.
Josephine and Ernest and Guy.	It is mine. When. Is it. Mine.
Josephine and Julia and Ernest and Guy.	When is. It mine.
Josephine and Julia and Ernest and Guy.	When is it. Mine.
Josephine and Julia and	

Ernest
and
John
and
Guy.
Josephine
and
Ernest   When is it mine.
and
John.
Josephine.   Or which. Is mine.
Josephine.   Is it mine.
Josephine
and   They may be. Thought. As well.
John.
Josephine.   Naturally.

Scene III

Julia
and   It is three.
Guy.
Julia.   We three. It is. Three.
Julia
and   No one. Has known. They know. That hail. Can hurt. What.
Therese.   It falls. Upon.
Josephine.   I have been. With. I mean.
Julia.   And with. Josephine.
Therese.   It is. Of no importance. To be timid.
Josephine.   With them. They are. Induced.
Josephine.   To introduce. Mind. Them.

Scene IV

Guy.   It is an advantage. To hope. That it. Is true.
John.   Who can. Be seen. By two.
Guy.   Be welcoming. Them. As they come through.

Scene V

Therese.   Has curtains. And has. Refused. Curtains.

Has wells. And. Has. Refused wells.
Has aprons. And. Has not. Refused aprons.
Has wealth. And has not either. Refused. Or not refused. Wealth.

Scene VI

Therese. Shall be. Met.
Julia. In. On their. Account.
Josephine. May calculate. Four. To a measure.

Act III

It may be beautiful to resemble them most.
Therese. Is occupied in writing.
Josephine. Is occupied at once.
Julia. Is not warned to be cautious.
John. Is sensitive to impressions.
Guy. Is managed by singing.
Ernest. Is variable because of their at all.
All who mention what is left to leave them and so they sit quietly while the curtain goes up.

Scene I

Josephine. Many many have been here.
Julia. To see me.
Therese. When this you see believe in me.
John. With pleasure.
Paul. Has charm.
Ernest. Is not betrayed.
Guy. More than enough.
Josephine. Replaces one.
Julia. Replaces one.
Therese. Replaces one.
One and one and one.

Scene II

Cora. Which one of it. Should.
Dora. Or could.
Josephine. Or. Would.

Scene III

Josephine	Play well. For Dora.
Therese	May they. Call Cora.
and	She may come. For her.
Cora.	
John.	Favor Freddy.
Ernest	And believe well. Of. A melody.
Guy	And think. And. Swim.
and	And meditate. And. Destroy.
Paul.	And think. Well again. Of. Their. Joy.
Josephine	
and	It is of no use thinking of this.
John.	As they amount. To the same.
Therese	
and	She may be. Angrily.
Guy.	With them. They. May be.
Julia	
and	Should it be. Well. For them. To like it.
Paul.	Would it be. Well. In them. To. Like it.
Cora	
and	It is inestimable.
Ernest.	They remind them. Of their amusements.
Josephine	
and	Confine riches.
A Place.	Confine. Riches.
Josephine	
and	Confine places. In. That way.
Cora.	Confine. The place. In that. Way.
Josephine	
and	Compare love. To them.
Guy.	Compare love. With them.
Josephine	
and	They will compare. Their.
Ernest.	They will. Compare. Their.
Josephine	
and	They will. Compare. It. With their. Advantage.
Paul.	
Paul	
and	They will even. Compare.
Josephine.	They. Will even compare.

Paul
  and   Compare add. And they. Compare.
Josephine   Comparison.
  and   They will compare. Adding. With. Seen.
Adding.   Them.
Josephine
  and   It is astonishing. That asking.
Nichole.   Is it. A name. For a. Woman.

Scene IV

Josephine. Julia may be. With. And succeeding.
Julia.   Cora is not. Patient.
Josephine. They may align. Making.
Julia.   Just made. Harbingers.
Julia.   Of a. Reason.
Josephine
  in   They may dance together.
pleasure.

Scene V

Josephine. She might be late.
Josephine. Or rather more. At. Their behest.
Josephine. In a chance. Of an allowance.
Josephine. Just when. They went. And well. Alone.
Julia
  and
Cora   They will. Will. He.
  meeting   May she.
Guy.   They will.

Scene VI

Practicing.

John.   Could know all.
Guy
  and   They will call.
Paul.
Ernest
  and   One.
John.

John.	They may. And could. Count.
John and Ernest.	It was. It was. Too.
John.	Two more.
Walter and Paul.	The youngest. For. Water.
Paul.	May they. A wall.
Walter and	
Walter and	Will they. Or. Will they.
Paul.	Be tall.
	Because they. Are. Tall.
Paul and	She may be.
Guy	They may. Be. As. They. May. Be.
Paul.	With it. She might. Be united.

Scene VII

Josephine.	Can be. Respectfully. Left free.
Julia.	She may be. Respectfully. Free.
Guy.	She. May be. Respectfully. Left free.
Paul.	She may be. Respectfully left free.
Josephine.	May be. Respectfully left free.
Josephine.	May be. With three Josephine Julia and Guy.
Josephine.	May be. With them. With the. Three Josephine Therese John and Guy.
Josephine.	She may be. One of. Three. Josephine Julia John and Guy.
Julia and	They may be. Very sleepy.
Guy.	And again. They may not be.

Scene VIII

Therese.	But and budget.
Josephine and Therese.	But and budget.

Therese
   and   Be careful of three.
Guy.
Julia
   and   May they repair places.
John.
Cora
   and   It is very easy to be fearful.
Guy.   And they will provide themselves with it.
Therese
   and   They will either ease with ease.
Paul.   Or not with ease.
Julia
   and   Not without an easy access.
Ernest.   Not with and with it.
Cora
   and   They use names.
Hilda.
Julia
   and   It should be wide.
Therese.   With them.
Therese
   and   Wild with them.
Julia.

Scene IX

Julia.   I. Julia.

Scene X

Therese
   and   Twenty or three.
Guy.

Scene XI

Josephine
   and   It may be a dish. Or which.
John.   It may. Be a wish. Or. Which.
Therese
   and   It might nearly have been a stain.
John.

Scene XII

Julia and Josephine.	By choosing. A mine. They will. Find time.
Josephine and John.	But will it. Have been. A net. No. At once.
John and Guy.	It is not certain or sure. Of having an older brother. Or daughter. It should be tried.

Act IV

Scene I

Therese.	Who will. Who will. It will. They may. If they will.
Therese.	A circumstance that was not intermitting in embrace. Their. Clarity.
Therese.	She should be sent. That is. It is. She that is. They are sent.
Therese.	No. When. They are. Welcome.
Josephine.	It is a bandage. She will. Be very. Anxious. To know. That she. Is. All well.
Josephine.	She may be often. All made ready. And then. It rains.
Josephine.	She can be all. Ready. And when. She has gone. She has hesitated. But really. She had better. Go.
Josephine.	She may be. Unaccountable. If there has been. No difference. For that. Which. It is not at all. Extraordinary. To have happen.
Josephine.	She may be. Without doubt. Better prepared. Than ever. They were. But it will be. All of it. At. One time. And assiduously. In their. Rebound. She may not be worthy. Of all. They wish.
Josephine.	It is of course. Of no account. Not for them.
Julia.	All changes. Are made. By liking. It. Best. By liking. It best. By liking it best. All changes. Are felt. By liking it best. All changes are felt by liking it best.
Julia.	She may. Easily. Be anxious to please.
Julia.	They will turn around. If they think. They hear a sound.
Julia.	It is. A disadvantage.
Cora.	Do be pleasantly with me. To see. Do be pleasantly to see. With me.
Cora.	They in that in it that they.

Cora.	It is an extra or an. Extra order.
Cora.	It if she may. Have it. To-day.
Cora.	Should they. Have it. To-day.
Therese	
Julia	They will. And may. Have heard. Them say. They will. Have
Josephine	been. When. They. Went away.
and	
Cora.	
John.	It is. No doubt. Alright.
John.	No doubt about what they were doing.
John.	In. At once.
John.	By themselves.
Paul.	It may be at all.
Paul.	All change. To have them call.
Paul.	Our having it. They having it.
Paul.	Which they.
Paul.	Once for all.
Paul.	It is. Of no importance.
Guy.	Shiny as they will.
Guy.	Exchange it.
Ernest	
and	Fairly one two three.
Guy.	

Scene II

Therese.	She may be clouded. Or cowed.
Julia.	And they will trace. And. They will shape. Their destiny.
Guy	
and	It is well. To carefully tell. In the meantime. That. They may
Walter.	be often closed to have it. Closed to them.
John.	May they be precious to us.
Josephine.	As they. Are telling.
	All who told. Are with our consent.
	Left carefully. To be. Attentive.
Paul	
and	It may be. That they. Are willing. To be an authority. About
Ernest.	vainglory.
Guy.	She may be. Attached jealously.
Josephine.	For they may like. It all. To be suddenly. Left only. To
	them. As they may like. When they have it all about. Them.

Therese.	Children are told to be. About to be. Happy. They are equally. Careful.
Julia.	Made to call them in a minute.
Ernest and Paul.	Neither of them are drowned have been drowned.
John.	With them.

Scene III

William can call call Cora.

Scene IV

With welcome. As they deplore. Their arrival.

Scene V

Should be anxiously careful.

Act II

Therese.	Be well. And frightened.
Therese.	Let no one deceive. By. Smiling.
Therese.	Make my claim. Mine.
Therese.	Which they will. Incline. To mean it.
Julia.	With whether. It is. All. A purpose.
Josephine.	By which. They will. Be. Without.
Julia.	Just as much. As a desire.
Therese.	By waiting. Or. For. As well.
Julia.	They may. Be patient.
Josephine.	And. A value.
John.	By. Or. Rather. Or. A calling.
Guy.	They will add. We. In plenty of time.
Ernest.	With all of it. And. Wait.
Guy.	Just by. It. As. They. May. Accuse.
Paul.	A blessing. To be. Promise.
John.	About.
Therese.	With. Mellow.
Josephine.	About. As they. Change.
Julia.	Very likely. They will. Very likely. Take place.
Josephine.	It will very likely take place.

Scene II

By the time that they are welcome they wish.

Josephine.	They wish for it.
Paul.	They. Will. Be pleased. To have it.
Guy.	To wish for it.
Julia.	With them. They must. Be. At once.
Josephine.	Not only chosen.
Therese.	Very well. I thank you.

Scene III

Therese.	Very much. They will.
Julia.	Very much.
Josephine.	Will the will. Violets. Very much.
Julia and Josephine.	Which they please. Play. As. They find it. A very pleasant dish. With.
John.	And without sea shells.
Guy.	But would they affect us.
Paul.	Adversely.
Ernest.	If they do they lead to having seen. A very enormous. Spider in the morning.
John.	Never mention a name.
Guy.	It is in vain. That they. Or we. Mention a name.
Paul.	For their pleasure.
Guy.	As early as they measure.
Paul.	And once again. They sing.
Paul.	As they mean. Sunshine.
Josephine.	She may be taught. That if. She can tell it. As twenty. Or ought. She to be obliged.
Julia.	To be fairly anxious about it.
Josephine.	Or fairly well. Anxious about it.
Therese.	May she come in.
Julia and Josephine.	She may come in.

Scene IV

Julia.	It is rightly. That is it. Or. That it is. Or that. Is it.

Josephine.	By which. They wish.
Julia.	And full of. Might they. Be. Without. A calling of. More than they. Further.
Josephine.	Should have thought likely.
Therese.	It is. A credit. And a pleasure.
Paul.	To wait for. Her.
Guy.	With pleasure.
Ernest.	Beside this. Will they be willing to have it as well a give it beside this.
Paul.	Manifestly. As to origin.
Marguerite.	Has been introduced vainly.
John.	And never again.
Paul.	Will they.
Paul.	Have any.
Paul.	Of one.
Paul.	Of them.
Paul.	Not ever again. Will. They have. Any. Of one. Of them.
Ernest.	It is. In time.
Julia.	When they thank.
Josephine.	As much as they like.
Therese.	When they thank Josephine as much as they like.
Therese.	When they. Thank me.

Scene Three.

Therese.	Will.
Therese.	See John.
Therese.	Will see John.
Therese.	Soon.
Therese.	She will see John soon.
Therese.	Believe all who call.
Therese.	That they come.
Therese.	When they.
Therese.	Call.
Therese.	They will come.
Therese.	When they call.
Therese.	They will come.
Therese.	When they.
Therese.	Call.
Therese.	They will see John.
Therese.	When they.

Therese.   Call.
John.   May be. Without. A pleasure.
John.   They may be. Without. A pleasure.
Guy.   Unless. Hunting. That is. Shooting.
Walter.   Is a pleasure.
Paul.   They may easily. Learn.
Paul.   That there. Is no. Hope.
Paul.   Of their coming.
Paul.   In the morning.
Paul.   As well.
Paul.   As they.
Paul.   Will come.
Paul.   But not be able.
Ernest.   To come.
Paul.   Because Tuesday Thursday and Saturday.
Paul.   Afternoons.
John.   Are partly.
John.   When they.
Paul.   Are not. At liberty.
John.   And often.
Paul.   With them.
Julia.   They may be pleased.
Julia.   To be. Allowed.
Julia.   To play. Theirs.
Julia.   As with them.
Therese.   An account.
Therese.   For which they please.
Therese.   An account for which they please.
Julia.   Be added. To. Effrontery.
Josephine.   Or with them.
Josephine.   As. A plain.
Julia.   But begging.
Therese.   Or may be.
Therese.   On account of their bother.
John.   But with it.
John.   Or. Better.
John.   Than with it.
Therese.   It is. Their. Pleasure.
Therese.   As plainly.
Therese.   As their pleasure.
Therese.   May be. Useful. For them.

Julia
  and   Forty make. Forty four. A conundrum.
Josephine.
Julia.   It is a pleasure to witness.
Josephine. That they are balanced.
Therese.   And preserved.
Julia.   As more than. They mind.
Josephine. As it will. Allow.
Josephine. Them to be. At ease.
John.   But do they need. To surprise them.
John.   Or even itself.
Guy.   They may be happily.
Guy.   At their ease.

Scene two.

Guy.   They recollect. That they were. Apprised.
Guy.   Of which. They were determined.
John.   In place of their inattention.
John
  and   May be. An authority.
Paul.
Therese.   Has never known. John. To know. Paul.
Therese.   How many Johns are there.
Therese.   But which. Acceptably.
Julia.   But all of it. Amounting.
Josephine. To their hope.
Julia.   In which they share.

Scene One.

John.   Makes no mention. Of annoying.
Therese.   Of annoyance.
Julia.   Of being. Annoyed.
Josephine. Of preparation.
Paul.   Of trouble.
Guy.   Of withstanding.
Ernest.   Or affecting them. In opposite ways.
Julia.   They will not annoy them.
Josephine. They will wonder. Why they have not left.
Therese.   The answer is simple.

John.   May have been it may have been.
John.   Important.
Ernest.   And they may have been. Advised.
Guy.   Because it is.
Walter.   Their hope as well as their wish.
Therese.   Reminded by understanding.
Julia.   As well. As apart.
Josephine. Which is why. They are favored.

Act III

Therese.   Crowned in glory.
Therese.   Crowning glory.
Therese.   Trained Therese.
Therese.   With them with seen.
Therese.   With lace.
Therese.   Crowned with lace.
Therese.   With grace.
Therese.   Gracefully remembered.
Therese.   Silently respected.
Therese.   Separately placed.
Therese.   Saving it. In place.
Therese.   Of lace.
Therese.   They will surround. It.
Therese.   By leaving. It.
Therese.   Saving it.
Therese.   With. Their. Saving it.
Therese.   And they will. Be. Accepted.
Therese.   As having done it.
Therese.   Quietly. And they mean.
Therese.   My name.
Julia.   They make pleasure.
Josephine. For them.
Julia.   For them.
Julia.   With them.
Julia.   They make.
Julia.   And give.
Julia.   Pleasure.
Julia.   To them.
Josephine. For them.
Josephine. Before.

Josephine.	Or because.
Josephine.	Of them.
John.	When.
John.	With them.
John.	They may.
John.	Give pleasure.
John.	To all.
John.	Or any.
John.	Of them.
Paul.	Because.
Paul.	With all.
Paul.	They will give.
Paul.	Pleasure.
Paul.	To some.
Paul.	Of all of them.
Guy.	They may make.
Guy.	It.
Guy.	A pleasurable occasion.
Guy.	For them.
Ernest.	And they may.
Ernest.	Abide.
Ernest.	By their.
Ernest.	Leaving it all.
Ernest.	There with them.
Ernest.	For them.
Ernest.	Or.
Ernest.	Without.
Ernest.	Them.

Scene II

Therese and Julia.	She may. Add what. They have. Here. And they will. Be disappointed.
Therese.	May they. Have been.
Therese.	Nor. May. They have been there with. And.
Therese.	Without. They know. Best.
Therese.	What. Day. They choose.
Julia to Therese.	Please see. To it. And please. Be very much. Please. Pleased.

Julia
   to   Plainly as well. As. If. They. Have to have it. Back.
Josephine.
Julia
   to   They may be. With them. Or. They may be. Since they have
Therese   come. They may be. There.
  and
Josephine.
Julia
   to   It is. Not useless. To have them. Come to. Be there. With
Josephine. them. As. They well know.
Josephine
   to   May you like feathers. No one mentions anything.
John.
All   A turkey can be killed.
together. By a dog.

Scene III

Julia.   She asked. For. Their wish.
Julia
  and   But it was a pleasure to give them whatever. They wished.
Josephine.
Julia
  and   It could be. With. A pleasure. That. It. Could be. Easy. To
Josephine. give. Them. Whatever. They wish.
Julia
  and   They wish. That. They.
John.   Will not. Bother. Not to. Deprive them. Of it.
John   But it might be. A denial. To not. Give them pleasure. For.
  and   them. To give them. Not. A desirable. Pleasure. As they.
Josephine. Come too.
Guy   Should be hurt. If they came. Through. The way. That. By the
  and   way. That. Will they. May. Have. It. As a pleasure.
Paul.
Guy   Have never seen. That they like. May they. Beg. Them. To be
  and   disinterested.
Therese.
Guy.   Should naturally mean.
John.   That they will. Love. To come along.

| John and Julia. | They have not met. Yet. Nor will they. |

John
and
Julia.   They have not met. Yet.
           Nor will they.

Julia
and
John.   It is politeness. Or their perusal. And a pleasure. To have been.
           Away. As. Long.

John
and
William.   Long. May they. Be about it.
           So long. May be natural.

John
and
Ernest.   To remember. That they. Bought.
           A boat.

John
and
Ernest.   With tears. And prayers. They knew that. The birds. Who have
           been known as not being shown. As a brown. Swan.
Julia.   May be they do but. Without it.

Julia
and
John.   She meant that Mary a river, Mary, a day and Mary, is a care.

Julia
and
John.   They remember. That. There are four. When two. Are two more.

Josephine. Having never seen them again.
Josephine. Not. To have. Gone away.
John.   But very freshly.
Therese.   They do. Or do not. Marry.
Therese.   In order to please them.

Act IV

Guy.   Should clearly make a mistake.
           Antagonise clearly. Or they will.
Guy.   Please whether. They will. Antagonise. Clearly.
Guy.   They may join. Thoughts. By union.
Guy.   Clearly.
John   They may. Place. Pressure. And.
and   Perhaps. Explain. That. They must.
Julia   Please. Them.
and   Place. Them.
Guy.
John.   And for this. And.

John.	Asking.
John.	Or else.
John.	They may. Make pleasure.
Paul.	A pastime.
All	They may.
four	Place more.
join in	There where they have.
saying.	More than they. Yet had.
John.	In no way. Do they resemble.
John.	Them.

Scene I

John.	Forty. Is an address.
John.	For them to think well. Of winning.
Guy.	Should be succeeding.
Paul.	By which. They climb.
Paul.	As well. On.
Paul.	As when they are sent out.
John.	In and about.
Guy.	To succeed. To rocking.
John.	In a pleasure. They have weeded.
John.	Weeds thickly. As a memory.
John.	In feeling.
John.	Exhausted.
John	But she may be. Easily.
and	Troubled. Not by. Their success.
Guy.	Just as they would fruitfully.
	Know exactly how. They should count.
Guy.	And blunder.
Guy.	Or fortunately.
Guy.	Or blunder.
John	They may be more.
and	They may not be.
Paul.	More hurried.
Therese.	Should be reminded.
Therese.	That fellow-ship.
Therese.	Means accomplishment.
Julia.	But she may be less there.
Josephine.	As if unknown.
Julia.	By their sheer hope.

Julia.	Of letting. It be as likely.
John.	But which may be thought.
Guy.	Just when. They shall. . Devise.
Paul.	That they will authorise.
Ernest.	Them to go.

Scene II

Julia.	I told you so.
Therese.	With their address.
Therese.	But which they will.
Therese.	But she. May be. Very well fitted.
Therese.	To be clothed. For the winter.
Therese.	To be. Admittedly. Not. In pretension.
Therese.	Nor as well.
Therese.	She will.
Julia.	Adhere. To her family.
Therese.	She will.
Josephine.	Be even pleased.
Therese.	To have them come.
Josephine.	To have been. Left. To them.
Therese.	As they will manage.
Julia.	But which they.
Josephine.	Will suggest.
Julia.	It is an appointment and a disappointment.
Julia.	They will deny. That they will.
Julia.	Be with them.
Therese.	Nor very selfish.
Josephine.	As well as will.
Julia.	But they may plan.
Josephine.	And will. And can.
Therese.	In which way.
Julia.	They say.
John.	That they listen with interest.
John.	To what is said.
John.	Is being said.
Guy.	But may.
John.	Having lost. Nothing.
John.	As well. As. Being.
John.	For them. It is. A pleasure.
Guy.	Should. When. They would.

John.	In. Finally. Leaving it.
Guy.	As well. As delight.
Paul.	They will rest. There.
John.	As much. As in. In their interest.
Guy.	But which. They will. Provide.
Guy.	As an instance.
Guy.	Of their. With willing.
Guy.	Should have. As. Well. As. Have been.
Guy.	As much. Thought well.
Guy.	Of. In an instance.

Scene II

Therese.	May talk. Of it.
Therese.	And take. More. Of it.
Therese.	As they will. Please. Be with it.
Therese.	Here. With it.
Julia.	For them. To have no one.
Josephine.	Or just more. Than ever.
Josephine.	More than. Alike.
John.	Should.
Guy.	Which they mean.
Paul.	Maintain.
Ernest.	One. At one time.

FINIS

A BOUQUET. THEIR WILLS.

The Art of Making a Bouquet

The way to make a bouquet or to receive flowers the way to make drawings acceptable or a needle make points of different additional distances which result in a man and a basket at an advantage in consequence of which drawings of calla lilies and green trees and plums all in white and a plan of realising the fancifulness of adaptability when having made azaleas prominent they were more delightful than ever before both as to cherubims and isthmus and alas plenty of time planted in dispersal of the unification of their maligning it by penetrating without a doubt that it was an elaboration of their without having divided what was not only not sent but meanwhile in their enlargement a quarter of it this is what she had when they were entitled to have domes domes and better than ever it is not which when in and letting it have fairly thought making it be with joining it prevailing that it is a chance of a balance by reason of their contradiction inespecial reconciling it more with having introduced not because of prevailing theirs in genuine consideration of it pointedly more than it is made hearts be black upon a brick in color that without doubt and lines made it in straining it from without that most of it coming letting it be seen not with but in the reason for this in said to be made into another purse and language because maidenly can be on account of when willing should it be theirs as an indication of delight that they were fountain of iniquity to change this with aside next to be near that without some to have triumphant netting it more precariously need it for this when is it in appointing that two things made making it from there to have a cactus blend behind in a night with when it is made of which that two make four mainly behind the never have it make it see which can when whether in and altogether they will be beside beside in kings kings have been known as horses and more which can there in place the change of have it for the most of it left to them that is whether it is on account of fed to them in rectifying it by the employment of when a dromedary could be lasting made it have it nor is it considerably named more than come to the persuasion of not more which is confessed at most than there sweetness in allowance because within remained may be as soon as when became left to the undivided elaboration of vindication to be unabridged continuation of whether it is precarious as they single charms as larger than as lambs make it to do unduly in the welcome that is not justified by justifiable inauguration of their will it be not for this and for that alone in the collection of their most and whether if when it is what is what they had which is that the beside and the closest in the main which whenever as they like it is when they do wish to wish what they what they wish that they wish which is what they wish what is the wish which is what which they wish to be a date is when retrospectively in an avoidance of their meteor meteorologically in forbearance that is in no exacting identification of the readily to be not because of the five fifty that it is without it choosing to be so. And so and so. What is it. It is what they wish which is which is which is it.

Their Wills, a bouquet.

In Six Acts

Pauline and Charles Daniel and Dolene Chorus of Baltimoreans.
Food fusses me as blowing wind fusses you.
Chorus of Baltimoreans.
Have not had a habit of wills. Let us make wills. He and she hurried.
Not Saturday but Thursday.
If Charles had no children and only a half brother and half sister and Pauline had two children one of them a daughter and the other one a daughter and they had not a child of one another and Charles left his money to Pauline and Pauline left her money to him and they were both killed together who would inherit everything the half brother and half sister and this was what was as unexpected as it was startling and she Pauline had done that thinking. This makes no account of anything of accomplishing and examination this is finally predicting that if two are killed it is assumed that the husband will outlive everything and so nothing goes to the daughters and this is surprising. Let it be changed so that thing will not be happening and it was done but it took a long time.
Chorus of Baltimoreans had heard nothing.
Pauline. Authorise made easy with a care for them. It is a very welcome for the thing which can that it is plain in conspicuous management of demean

in estuary as can fairly make sensibly fortunes consist in conclusion for the main management. It is all call that a home is what is can contemplate not be for which in coupled to be made might with fortune in conclusion.

Charles may be a banker he has heard vainly of a candidly compelled in collection of reconsider in partly that a chicken country has one kind of architecture and wine country has one kind of architecture and fall of the year that which when makes it a claim.

Chorus of Baltimoreans are distinguished by their management.

In Baltimore there is traffic management in spite of of every country prefer the United States of America of every state prefer the state of Maryland of every city prefer the city of Baltimore of every house prefer his house of every wife prefer his wife and their use.

Chorus of Baltimoreans do not see either the brilliance or the necessity.

Bouquet of rose very tiny daisies made to fit in a receptacle.

Who has pressure to bear.

Dolene and Henry, Amy and Simon Hilda and RoseEllen Nimrod and Caesar. They call classes.

It is a bit whether they go or stay.

Dolene and Charles.

Doline detained and undecided.

Charles made courteous by hovering and detaining Helen and RoseEllen.

Caesar respected by a sophistication in memory of reputed roses. John and Albert married to Amy and Hilda.

Who has been thoughtful.

Very well I thank you. Coupled to clauses.

In every hand on any hand in every hand hand in hand.

It is very certain that if they had been killed together they would have if they had made their wills in favor of each other that the half sister and half brother of the husband would have altogether succeeded to all that either of them had had and that the children of the mother would have had no inheritance and rather it would have been an extraordinary pleasure in a way for the half sister and the half brother because there had been some question that had nothing to do with either either or the father who was not their father and the mother who was their mother.

Chorus of Baltimoreans have not been rather have not been induced matter that it does not follow mortgage in a picnic for the summer with fur gloves which have been won one before the other in a way made much after either altogether.

It is not well to think about what they want when they want it.

Charles and Helen are happily married in spite of the fact that Helen has headaches. Helen and RoseEllen Nimrod and Ceasar Charles and Hilda Doline

and Simon Ida and Llewelen Eglantine and Kleber withstand and made much
of as they were. As they were in circumstance.

The lawyer of Helen is Herbert Walter.

They had different lawyers but neither of the lawyers had realised the
matter and when their attention was called to it they were able to remedy it
after a sufficiently long time.

Chorus of Baltimoreans have indefinable resignation and insistance and they
may be never the less succeptible to the symbol of recovery.

How many Baltimoreans have flushes and may be they do and may be
they may be may be forsooth.

Charles and Helen may have a little son named Julian.

They will be careful to have it and hurried with every afternoon a nap.
May or may be not.

May be they will if they are to go about it.

A scene in which they are to learn the art of arranging a bouquet.

Find flowers which grow and mix them with grasses known as the bread
of birds.

Charles and Helen make banking a profession not because of succeeding
but because of Llewelen.

Stones and streams make a change in house and home.

Chorus of Baltimoreans have meant very much to them.

Susan, Who is known as the mother of Elizabeth one at a time.

They have no hope.

Hope and no hope.

They have no hand in hope.

They have not held out any hope.

Who has heard of hours and they meant.

It happens that men's hats are made.

ACT TWO

Simon is a brother of a banker. He is very well off.

Simons a bouquet will be an interlude.

After the third act.

Charles and Helen who are the father and the mother of Julian and Helen
is the mother of Kate and RoseEllen.

Claribel and Etta are relations. There is intermarriage. There are plenty of pleasant circumstances. There have been names such as Hortense Louis Caesar Clarence Jonas Henry and Bernard. Any rule is made for Baltimoreans.

A blonde boy can be appointed and maltreated by West Point Cadets. There is no need of probably searching for abbreviation.
Chorus of Baltimoreans in allowance.

Nobody likes a bargain.

If one were in a desert and wanted a glass of water and there was no possibility of having it what would they do.

Baltimore integrally.

Do please do do please do please do do please.

Baltimore Chorus of Baltimore Baltimoreans.

If Charles and Helen were married and Helen had had two daughters and their son Julian was not yet born and they had made wills in favor of each other and Charles had a half brother and a half sister and if Charles and Helen should be killed while they were together nothing would be left to any daughter even if they the daughters were the half sisters of the boy Julian who had not yet been born. Nobody had thought that it would happen as it would happen if they were killed together because altogether the presumption is that the man will live longer. How do they like their two per cent they would not even have this sent. Come Thursday not Saturday because of thinking. Thinking one one one one one makes two and San Francisco is made miles of soften.

She sleeps by day day by day she says day by day she says day by day she says day by day to-day now to-day day to day. Which one is it the one that is doing that is to doing to sleep to-day sleep in the day. Bertha Helen Simon Julian RoseEllen Caesar Nimrod Bernard Hilda and Constance and Llewelen.

A list can be filling. They all say.
Chorus of Baltimoreans which is it in forsooth interlude.

They did not matter to a mother who has arranged it differently. Could stocks see.
Chorus of Baltimoreans. Never sing flowers as they are not fond of flowers, they prefer oysters with widening areas. They leave out which is way amount.

A will which is in a reason that it was not brought about may be that two brothers and their half brother and half sister if they have a mother two and mother they will unless it is promised refuse to do so even so.

Might it be for rain.

They like food on the table and screens in the window even when it is necessary.

Think about which came first.

Their wills in forget-me-nots.

Forget-me-nots a bouquet.

Not Charles and not Helen not Julian and not RoseEllen.

When this we see two see one see he sees further than that.

A very little clouded withdrawn.

Charles and Helen who has misnamed Helen. Helen is a nightingale with petals of which with plenty of copper balls of noises in a gather with when speckled of finery. She dresses simply.

Charles and Helen Belle and Belles which could have been pressed with a leaf like a wild pansy is an herb.

A scene in which willows turned into poplars and olives into willows.

Without their having made a will they would not have left their money to each other. Having made a will each of them with their own lawyer they left it to one another and if they should be killed together the assumption would be that the man had lived longer and so if their son had not yet been born their property would not be left to her two daughters but to his half brother and half sister. Thinking of this and laughing is not only what might have happened but would have happened if they had been killed together presuming that the husband lived the longer and their son then had not been born and her two daughters would have been left with nothing and his half brother and his half sister would have had everything.

Simon and William were not half brothers Simon was a brother think of Simons a bouquet think of Simons a bouquet think of everything to say think of a boat rocking made of earthenware and signed and numbered. This is an exact pressure of their widening in the hope of a president.

A scene in which they have dinner quietly.

Chorus of Baltimoreans have no detail which is missing it is not missing because Charles street avenue extended is not any longer.

Means made to go.

If in an auction there are places where they do not hear one another bronzes are pictures and pictures are boats and boats are nets and nets are doves and doves are do and dove tailed.

Chorus of Baltimoreans consist of men and women.

The sergeant said fire fire while you can.

They were not perturbed.

A collection of excellencies.

There are many excellencies in definite delight in handling formally which is without a pleasant time with which to plan to prey upon the saturday in practically for this with the sown of which it is the happy way of dangling in between the four leaf clover a heart and is it well to see it to to see it.

They made miles.

One two and three.

The last time is the worst. Chorus of Baltimoreans consist in men and women.

Have had across.

Consecrated to leaves of wheat.

Made miles in very much that they knew.

Do you know why he thought.

Because he flushed.

Do you know why he smiled.

Because he flushed.

Do you know why he went.

Because he was bent upon it.

ACT III

After Act three there will be an interlude Simons a bouquet.

Helen and Simon.

Would Helen be considered wrong if she was a leader.

Would Helen be considered wrongly not to have been a leader.

Their wills a bouquet.

Would Helen have been considered to have been wrong in not being a leader.

Charles is a banker and he is not cautious he says that one state follows another and he leaves out which one.

They are thoughtful.

If they had made a will in which they left everything to one another and their son had not been born and they had been killed together it would be assumed that the man lived longer so all would have been inherited by his half brother and his half sister and not by her daughter and her own daughter not even what she had inherited she her mother from the father who had been her husband and was the father while she was the mother of the daughter. Thursday not Saturday. Thursday instead of Saturday. She said come out Thursday instead of Saturday, she had been thinking she said come out Thursday come out Thursday which is a little before Saturday. She had been thinking and had thought out this matter.

There is no difference between one daughter and another except that one of them is older.

Chorus of Baltimoreans are all very quiet in the home although they are gay and talk in laughing and laugh in talking. Chorus of Baltimoreans can be slowly tangible.

There is no need for half indeed when they make honey suckles consist in various colors. There is a great deal of happiness in might is right.

Having forgotten every name how can they count when they see the fame that they have earned.

Charles and Helen now.

Simon and Julian and Horace and Hattie and Hilda and Caesar and Nathan and Claribel and Hortense Hortense is her name and Carrie and Eveline. Jonas makes many. It is delightful. They are after all at peace.

Plainly sanctioning.

A scene wherein they have decided to be very certain that they have decided correctly.

They are leaving everything to them.

This is in that amount.

They are not without doubt. Without doubt. A readily felt very well.

A baker should always have a school teacher as his wife.

This is not included in Baltimore.

Does my baby love blue or who. Does that look like a hundred and ten. Stitches when counted silk and wool on tortoiseshell nearer a hundred and ten than a hundred and fifty. A hundred and fifty means four persons.

My baby loves blue and so do you.

Connection between beneath and above. Regularly envisage.

If a million is two hundred and three how many Michaels make a Simon and how many RoseEllens make a melon. Three ages in three.

It is a meadow which makes cake.

It is no matter whether grain has been given or taken. Give and take.

RoseEllen and Julian are travelling they have nothing to do before leaving. They are not going to die. They are fairly certain and there is not hesitation.

Julian. How many days are there in April. How many days are there in May.

RoseEllen. How many days are there in April May and either June or July.

If you are comfortable you had better stay where you are.

Chorus of Baltimoreans. An appreciable difference between hotter in the sun and cooler in the shade and the heat off of a sunny field the more or less hot shade under the trees tree shade is never permanent the only shade that is permanent is a wall of a house or a wall which is a wall, prominent like the, y in Byrne.

End of Act Three

AN INTERLUDE

Simons a Bouquet

Necessary.
Necessary said light, necessary.
Necessary.

Needles in pins.
Pains not knits. Knits necessary.
Necessary. Needles and inns.
In ins, necessary. Needles and necessary.

Celluloid.
Suppose b, c, meant you and he would that shut up. In the best way I will say that there is a short gate. Another wine. Yes. Ick Icktoburns.
A lease.
Clean susans with pallor and a rude cross rude across a smother with a little lang and old chest up. The belief is pain. Yes I died.
Too ducks what. A little suse susianah. It is hutch. All pine.
A sheating.
Poor light, make a mixed stall, show the illuminating lantern and whether not, it was a question. When I came again I come to fastener. This is a good please. Show what shut. Entirely when. It is come in. All the same let.
A cool bay.
What please. If it is near why let the center sound her. This is a little new sense. A bean is arched a little left. All the same Sunday.
A cool bag.
A cool bag has a goal hole.
A bud book lay.
A bud by lay saw if soon to shed a looking sight a tremendous soon. This got out. A left was rest ladled. This made a key soon.
Not necessary.

Simons
A Bouquet

Go in deer. Dear what. A saleing soon. This was a boat.
In. Knows. Necessary.
Noes necessary.
No s necessary.

Knows. Necessary.
No necessary.
No. Necessary.

In climbs and gopher sheds and little keys, large boats wore shells.
Bull put perspire.
No c in me. A last tinned.
Put loud.
Nest oh where cut it spell. Lean more show white. A violin in in.
A walk.
Lay lea a little green. Let it be horses. Horses and a practice, a called practice. Practice not. A least excrescence into the foreseen hillside with two waters not show height. No such peas neglect.
Not walk.
Not walk pot. A pot is a loud sized pea with a nail thimble and a join knot.
Break fast.
Breaking fast so that glasses, glasses, are nets and a thin tongue is glowed glowed with sand and hammer and a noise nail.
A bouquet.
All the bank old dinners are shouted and little cools little cools fishes and big negroes big negroes cigars.
Paid red.
Paid red is a sash not a sash on but a little atlantic. Atlantic what atlantic sit the and lever when, when it is a mother. A mother and a sister. All tracks and leaf leaf of why more should extend so sew more.
Any shade.
Sharp not necessary for a stool. A maid a made where. All this to be boat and a cat less not it necessary not it occasion.
Window, brother, leave call. This is the rate of the road. It makes heavy. It makes what, not carrying this is pass.
Each bone.
Each bone care and a change heat, a change and heat, heat is heat.
A care less.
Suppose it came that by a reason which is beside the shock it happens that sisters are wives, very neatly then mothers are calling. This is disgrace at least in a fashion which makes it necessary that there is a disagreement. Take herd, take it so that there is a kind candle and little blight moon and it is nearly so, it comes to be winter, not winter it has rust and little seizes of the same sam sand stone and hole pieces. This is a bother. Then came to see saturday. All the rest is in the hose. Real bean is oblique.

Neglect of gorge.

A real smell, a real smell is tight, it is stout too and nearly painted.

A real smell is a sticked not so after chandelier. It is a page of birds and little little were trimmed corsets. Nearly all.

This is the mean, meaning in and a question a question of ladling of ladling is ill.

No old clothes make a sash, wet.

Simon.

A bouquet.

(Necessary)

Necessary be when, a violin.

Simons.

Be necessary.

A, follow that with sprain. A leave a rain.

Suppose a cute a cute flute. Be quaver, that is getter.

Simons, not boo.

Simons not bouquet.

Simons a boot quay.

Please claque claque pen, pen with hogs, sticks and stacks.

Simons not bouquet.

Simons tickle.

Simons be such lay.

Simons seat sir.

Simons say nickle.

Simons say.

Simons in why mow. Simons set set let, set, let.

Simons not re leaving.

Simons sit in go shade by a sit so.

Simon.

Simon.

Simon is Simon is Simon is is.

Simons

(A bouquet)

Pleasanting the language of the hat makes tobacco makes it a green shutter. Lively and leaves and let us sundries, sundries is what is.

Suppose a wooden a wooden nickle, suppose it so carried that fruit and vegetables are jewelry. Is this a heard case and it is necessary to keep a pencil in books. Is it neglected.

So that fourteen ninety two makes percent. So that there is a violin.

Perspire. What is perspire. Perspire is not not moon on a light and needs a hundred needs a 100 mills needs a little sandy lea and row needs a sandy needs a lea and row needs a sandy land row.

All gall is dealed with in and much. It is to gay.

Simons, a sin to say.

Simons, grief. Simons dishes. Simons a real little oil and lard stir. A real little steal.

Suppose Simons a bucket to pay. Suppose Simons a real advertiser. See it in furls and in a house paint and a proof a proof of roof. It is a such such touch, touch tough thick pealed oysters and a blessing a blessing is money, money, mealed money, a silent pea season.

Sup in a cap and show it show it farther. A little turn a stage plenty plenty full of going back to breack fast break fast dinner. This is the time. No use, no use in spots.

Simons, a bouquet.

Re lease a little large prod, prod of what, pave in, between, select bin.

A cool large, a loan, a seed bread, a bolt a bolt a bolt of black brown all brown, all pulled brown all cut.

Leak bet with sheds, sheds roof let net. Limb own seen no limb no own no seen no, limb own seen know, limb know seen know, own no seen limb own seen.

Nick naked and a bloat a bloat hammer a shuckle a shuckle thing a limb own a limb seen own. Go last. Wetness. Go last witness, wit, wit chest wit wit.

A bouquet of Simons.

Leak leak mut, leak a stool a graduated glass, a poison a pill a little grange, a moat, a pile a change, a salt fat, a grain fight, a change bust, a laugh whet, a chill chapper, a chill chapper, a kind horse back, a loaf best, a vexed sugar, a share, a share pony, a pile a put sand, a counsel.

Bouquet of Simons.

Necessarily, not, necessarily not, not not.

A bouquet.

Simons.

Simes whens, siming, siming no song, sung, sung sung sung.

Sing sing sing, singing. Sing sing sing, sing sing sing, sing a sing sing, sing sing sing, sing sing, sing.

A bold bat, bat in batting.

Little wolves hen, hen and hen, lead wolves when, hin and hin, hin up, hinder hinder a peach a peach.

Little wolves.

A roll a roll of pasting with heaven snatches and sups sups and apples.

It makes a baker's pie.

Lead colored light the bouquet has no buttons, not buttons and not limb buttons, a chance leg, a followed piece with little pots, pots of pull, pull, tell.

Please set, set up cold, cold choice beef steak, beef steak not blind, blind not to be all, not a paid egg, six eggs ten.

Not a but.

Part of three, blue black. Part of one, Simon, simoon, must mutter, blue black.

Blue Black.

Blue Black.

Part of one, must mutter.

Part of one.

Must mutter, sitter, sitter in on weighed water, water is weighed black. Sitter in weighed water. Watter is weighed, sitter in.

Weighed Water.

Weighed water not weighing water, not weighing paint and coal and excellent cream, not weighing a turkey, weighing ducks, weighed breath and bale water, weighed in weight.

Part in one. Part in one excellent exceedingly managed by a returned train that has an omnibus that is to say wheels. Wheels are betired. This is a spin a spin in, a spin in in.

Here is a shed to beef.

In beef. Here is a shed in beef.

Supper in a call. Call in and pass a button a little button with a size of a cap and nearly, nearly. To be all.

Leaf in a hand.

A leaf in a hand and much vegetables much vegetable capable.

Much vegetable capable.

Leave a gold pipe leave a gold pipe in a glass fitting strange older be wired arranger with a neglected pocket case such which is a comb.

Not a nursery, not a nursery and a place and a piece of water and careless, able to guess pleasant cutters, cutters with. Not a coloring beetle not nearly so exhausted.

This is a little higher than that higher than sugar or birds or molasses or real gates or the selected radishes which have tons, tons share. A whole eighty and it sent is an inclined day, a day behind more than fertile in inches. More bellowing.

Boots are not polite blessings. They easily pack in.

Please get let sentences so sunk. A collected extra pin is not what makes sham and pain, it is lordly, lard what it is, come in, come in, come in. Come in. Come in.

Nor a bouquet.

Nor a bouquet, not to lay not to lay. Nor in a bouquet.

A blank gall.

Least Mays seventy nine.

A piece of May warm cream warm cream shutter smash late bycicle jest custard and a sweater, really oats and lark trees and twins in quails, twins and barns and all mice and a kind of stick lantern, really all a joint a joint of eggs more eggs in a wagon in a wagon in.

This is both.

Both what both soup soup late.

Suppose a done can boat and place a right station in a meadow, does grass wind in to fat, does it. Come in.

Leaves of chest, best water rusher, animal eleven dotters and leg late not served in state, more shoes is. Rest or quiet or pale gold or real little water green or a chatter later or a grand and exchanged word room and nearly please and nearly please nervous. What are eye glasses in winter, there are in thin, golden go, go at shoe full and nice screens on tables and mended water. All of it drink, drink a pleased tough reasonable and altogether a travel and more suits. Pale gall with a yellow ribbon and clothes, james clothes. Be go stupid wake land in a house where if a door is a relief a whole door is better than next. Come to distate that coincidence new bell in. On ease sit with bales.

Six and simons and a birth plate and a loaf of leather.

One and Simons and a back sheet and a last cape and a dog gold cellar.

Three and Simons and a real egged black gold and more stress more stress why linked beads guess.

Go shame a glad and garfield season and beds and bakers and let a horse know, let in by spots spots glued and mounted and nervous and really what, why meals are poked and a gallon a gallon is forever forever what, pickles, salt water stranger, beer. No glass is wooden and more deeper collided and a violin a violin is in in a smell.

What is a son, a son is a careful concealed revolving autograph with little saddles and mounted may blossoms and real pay poodles and more selections.

No such walk.

What is a day stake. A day stake is a direct dark dimple and a real question is there talk, is there white siphons, are there pieces of beet sugar placed cups, curls.

What is a careful extinction. A careful extinction is no supper and twelve eggs and really that really that something.

A bouquet of Simons.

In Simons, A bouquet of Simons, Simons. In Simons.

A bouquet in Simons.

Simons. A bouquet, A bouquet. Simons, A bouquet. Simons.

Color in lobsters, release vegetables, please ripe pears, keep a flannel, flannel, keep a kind dog, keep a place for a cigar a cigar green, a green stand, a stand crackers, crackers and crackers.

A bouquet of Simons, all and bellow, all and below, all and, all and and and, all and and and, all and and and.

All call it with a spoon a, all call it with a with a spoon, with a, with a stepper, in a stepper and a rain a rain clearly a clearly startle, a noise soon, a girl beef, a slept height, a real round and a piggle a piggle in between dinner. No bow, no bow caution, not a grease bottle and ache house, not a little light arctic, not a please old carry all in buds and oysters, not in it.

No coat is a pew.

Failing pearl ground and little lilacs and never mentioned in the hand when left in that she by the right long, in the sea shine and search preceeded and little oregon left by separation and more buttons any more indicated more is a baked key a key with an eye glass and fine any fine lap, lap full of of eaten lasts and really old fired reread moistness with a second in plain and much in the collect.

Collect what, it is not edible, not be for and more grown more grown by between and left in the piece of valise which is a case, all in a trunk which is where there is that date that date to be ate sweet. Sweet. Sweet.

Many tickle some one thin, many tickle many tickle with a fellow fat, fat with a pecked old bank stake which means a house. Many tickle some one in. Many tickle some in. Some in bouquet, bouquet of Simons, some in Simons, some in Simons.

Necessary.

Necessary pick out chairs.

Necessary called photographs.

Necessary give gas lamps electric gas lamps.

Necessary go chambers, left in chins and gowns.

Necessary bind cups with lots of dotted dark little poodles and not any dogs.

Necessary read ss.

Necessary put in legs.

Necessary leave on it.

Necessary.

Simons a bouquet. A bouquet of Simons.

Necessary.

Not necessary to be an owl with eggs and sashes. Not necessary. Not necessary to be old and candy. Not necessary to be like like. Not necessary to

show oh be wasted. Not necessary to please simple chimneys. Not necessary
to have useful bold and between cases. Not necessary to rechange more glasses
than to be a ribbon and an inclined hand. Not necessary to be an only wide
sheet. Not necessary to be in a seat. Not necessary to relieve old watches and
new boats and wide sleeves and old oysters and real butter and extra pears and
left over apricots and more white bites and nearly outer with draws. Not
necessary to double roosters. Not necessary to see in grate. Not necessary
to make nils nils and sheds sheds and brown brown. Not necessary to under
reliver moisture. Not necessary to breathe baths and real paste steps and
more shapes. Not necessary to reconsider purchases. Not necessary to miss
stems. Not necessary to have it to be set. Not necessary. Simons a bouquet.

If they will all they have to one another and they are killed together the
man is supposed to live longer and his relatives will have everything that they
had before they had it together if her children have had another father who
has not been killed but who has died altogether. Altogether is better than
country bread. Bread which not been eaten but which has dried and when it
is refreshed is sweeter and eaten.

One two three. Swim.

Do they doubt that they are hurt if they are not cakeless. Can those who
said they would sell suffer.

Arthur and almonds.

Give and take.

Scene II

Red white and blue all about you.
Remy.

Scene III

Establishment.

If they were pleased that they were white would they like it.

Julian and RoseEllen and fifty million speaking of oxen as pears.

Not in maiden aid in Reagan.

RoseEllen Reagan Joseph Philip and as a wedding. It is very difficult
to be unalloyed.

RoseEllen Helen Margaret Lewis and Francine.

If they had made their wills in each others favor and nobody had been
there and they would have been accidentally killed it would be presumed that
the man had lasted longer.

Who makes chocolate cake out of cocoa once in a while but when they
were resigned to having it it had not been made.

Gaston is a name that goes with Berard.

Gaston Berard.

Live and learn.

Chorus of Baltimoreans are exchanged for chorus of Washington and Kansas cities.

Not a cherry a cherry not a cherry not a cherry not a cherry a strawberry.

Chorus of Washington city district of Columbia exchanged for chorus of Baltimoreans state of Maryland.

Chorus of Kansas city changed for chorus of Independence chorus of Independence Iowa changed for chorus of Grant Virginia. And so all day.

If they had made a will come earlier Thursday not Saturday they have been thinking.

Scene III

Did you my precious pet say not yet.

Interlude

Simons a bouquet.

ACT IV

Anybody with a wife has to have and in a couple of lending lamps lamp a jacket with a cause because do be noon at a day. A day calls caterpillars.

Julian RoseEllen Dorothy Robert Remy Winthrop a little reason for a name and two syllables.

If a man and his wife and she and he had made a will each one in favor of the other and they had thought about it they would have known that if she had children and he had none and he was fond of them and then they have had that if they could she did think that if they were to be alike and came to an accident accidentally and she would be known that is the concurrence that it is presumed that he lives longer not by the time that and she were killed. So that they would be pronounced identical in after all. Perhaps they would not be be left yet.

RoseEllen and Julian. Mother is a mother of one or two and father father is a father of one or two one or two.

The little pasture which has not given place given place.

They made a made a made a wailing down.

Remy. Fastens flowers in broken badly in account for the waiting that it had blown away.

Just as at a finally they must do.

Dorothy. Dorothy had three brothers Etienne John and Ernest. She was known as Annabel and he was known as Hannibal. They had not been doubled in collusion.

Anybody can print a will.

Scene II

Bother ably dislike amiable with a key stone held handle may be. May be they do but do doubt it.

Elsa more head with italic.

RoseEllen had a pretty very much held by and wall.

He made her think oxen were tall and all if they come down hill will.

They made a lake betake better take a lake.

With wishes and crosses and shawls and alls alls bells balls cover how do you do deniably.

Singing RoseEllen as Ellen.

Playful with a take be mine monkey shine lay low have a shadow of realise wise.

Ernest Wise Henry Wise and Edgar Wise. They were all three three of five brothers.

It is by luck and not by management that Julian was a man.

Their wills made in favor and for shade not for shadow because it is likely supposing that there was an accident and they were found and he was alive and she was not the presumption would correctly be that he had lived longer and so to believe so to do so and it was so.

Everything which is not lost is brought in and very often even if it is lost it is brought in. Bring in.

What do they do when nothing happens.

Scene III

When this you see remember me to them.

There is no use in saying so in saying so in saying so there is no use in saying so if he does not move in then. There is no use in saying so in saying so in saying so there is no use in saying so in looking as well then.

There is no use in saying so in saying so in saying so. There is no use in saying so in hearing it in them.

Wills are a curious subject. When they are made she can say come to-day

Wills are a curious subject he can say when he has heard her say come to-day he can say I am coming in a day.

Wills are a curious subject they can say that after all she was right.

Wills are a curious subject they can say that it is told at once.

Wills are a curious subject it may be that her lawyer for her and his lawyer for him were mistaken.

Wills are a curious subject they can be very careful after she was thinking.

Wills are a curious subject it is very easy to move from one side of a sunny tree to another side of a sunny tree and still be in the sun even if it is a hot day and they which is may be they are separately avoiding being in the sun.

Chorus of Baltimoreans are very reserved they tell nothing about pictures photographs fortunes rays of lanterns and dress. They are terrified if any one is beckoning they also feed upon their very delicious food.

Chorus of amiability.

Very many changed Howards for Birds and Freds for Henriettas and Julians for Claribels and RoseEllens for abruptly and belike for forsooth and predict predicate Julia for Joellen and Booth for beside. This is made Rose.

Chorus of Baltimoreans are intermediary and intimidated.

A voice natural to Godiva.

Heard in the distance when made in succession.

RoseEllen and Julian have arranged with their lawyers that their wills are as they should be.

They think of everything.

No interest in do very well very well I thank you.

Scene IV

Chorus of Baltimoreans have a mixture of their seeing religion.

Chorus of Baltimoreans. Have a conscience about sun on Sunday.

Baby might baby might baby baby baby baby baby baby baby might baby might baby baby baby might.

Very near to tears.

Scene V

Judith and Judy and wildly and sell.

Better very well.

If they were cautioned that they had to wait and they had waited waited with them.

Julian Mary Bernard and soothing.

Would they call the process of elimination that they had inherited. Socially yes.

Chorus of Baltimoreans are mentioned before.

They make satelites in market tamely and sundries.

One one in a single with a stretched as they may be out with them in ferocious conceptions of amalgamated does it suffice with pleasure.

RoseEllen. A with as with confess consent comforted let a melon be an accountable by with a time to be for it.

Supposing they were finally never killed together and they both lived longer how times are they to keep with it.
Chorus of Wellingtonians. Here have a chance to present a lake and let it make a fasten with a catapult and see. Seeds are flown flying and harshly a lake is a jet of water.

There are fifteen women. Fifteen weakening weakening Mabel. Mabel marble distract heather.

Julian is bold whether there is or is not not accountable.

Helen is meadowed with out or with hospitality.

Arthur is felt tightly in redress.

John is nearly succeeding and would look.

Camille cool if a man has a name a man named Camille a man named Camille yet.

RoseEllen is astonished.

Ellen comes to be amount to it.

Gessler made allow.

Fasten a double with welcome and Friday they will come welcome.

Scene VI

If they had made their wills they had and they had left it to each other which they did they might have been killed together and if they had the children of which he was not the father would not have inherited anything from their mother nor from their father their mother having inherited from their father and the law presuming that if they are killed together the man lives longer.
Chorus of Baltimoreans.

Nothing is found out ably.

They believe that seeing is believing.

They believe that if they wait they are waiting.

They believe that may be they do.

They believe that outwardly with care they will come Thursday and not wait until Saturday.

Make a dent.

Scene VII

It is doubtful whether they are one and one.
It is doubtful whether they are one and one.
It is doubtful whether they are one and one. It is doubtful whether they are one and one.
It is doubtful whether they are one and one.
Railroad time railroad time.
A railroad in a tunnel.
A railroad within and in a tunnel. A railroad within and in a tunnel. A railroad within in within in a railroad with in in within. A railroad within a within a tunnel without a tunnel a railroad without a tunnel.

Scene VIII

Called credit.

Scene IX

Creditable.

Scene X

He prefers her in Baltimore. She prefers her in Baltimore.

Scene XI

Very likely they are to move about.
Very likely they are to move about.
A scene in Baltimore with Baltimore a scene with Baltimore a scene in Baltimore a scene a scene of a scene with and of seen Baltimore.
Fast and wound fast and wound they must do their share.
Say much in stretches.
Scene Baltimore.
Baltimore May marry.

Scene XII

Not lost it.
RoseEllen with well in a point in appoint a councilor or a counselor or a tutor or a better feeling authority in propositions in relation to saving and by all with merriment plenty of course advantages with Friday a man and Ferdinand colors hopes and hopeful and at last and remained if they were willing to be welcome inadmissable without oriole a complaint.

Scene XIII

An advantage.

Harry who is ill.

Ella who is after every little while very comfortable.

Nelly who owns remaining very far reaching.

Frank who has a return every day in the fastening of a ribbon in an attachment for the reunion of palaces and appointments within call.

After that many manage to have the time to be always ready.

Scene XIV

If in between they care to be Europeans if in between they care to be Europeans in Atlanta there will be after all Geneva in Africa. And about what about what are they referring to.

RoseEllen is always happy to hear and Europeans know that they are after all not having a beginning a middle an ending on a black butterfly without fluttering a black and a butterfly without floating a butterfly black with a grey white border which is not fluttering but flying, a butterfly can fly very high over the water and over the trees and not so well with a very little breeze any solution can be indeed indeed carry all, they may have a train going in and out.

ACT LAST

Because without with carry a train in and out of a tunnel well tunnel well.

ACT FIVE

Farther.

Father than an act.

Farther in farther.

Than another act.

Makes a medicine seemingly audacious and perused.

Peruvia and precluded.

Rather precautionary in supper and surprise supple in competition in rectilinear in counterpane and at a most than wither a cloud unsupportably dismay with sweeter for the nine in eradication they make mine whine in appliances for the most cause as pronounceably irreplaceable for the financeer.

Helen did they call aloud and say what makes it partake of left to right in vertical with and without their plan if they have not heard of it.

Very nearly Julian.

Come Jonas come and plan half come and to be troubled with a cannot land in interrogation with might it be found irreplaceable in their on their account.

Avery never does believe in twins.

Scene II

If they were accidentally killed together it would be allowed that it could be believed that if it were possible he would have been living longer and now it would not make any difference and she would could be killed first.

RoseEllen is never hurried.

Neither is Julian.

Chorus of Baltimoreans is never not prevailed for the moment in commission which did if it happens make plenty of in detail with particular in appointment that they were fancied as by nearly really display gracious if so Mary.

Mary.   Mary is so gracious.

Desdina.   Will they have to have a talk with them.

Raymond.   Let out without a brother who is tall when they are very much better than if they could be called about in Rome. Rome is a distance. So is Switzerland and Italy and so is Scotland and England.

RoseEllen Ellen Ferdinand and Maybelle. How are happier happinesses in happen to be fair.

They are fair in leaving it without doubt not as they used to.

Chorus of willows and also of little pears.

How are Howard and his cousin with a cousin as a man. With his cousin and have it just couple it out of return in regard to advancing lain for a restful in interdependence they reclothed.

A little Julian.

A larger Louis.

Allowed Amy.

All but very well.

Very well I thank you.

How are Howards left to pale. She is very excitable.

If it does not make any difference will he will she marry them will they will they provide cloth for part of the time.

There is no to do.

Chorus of Baltimoreans not any more in a twitter that time has passed.

One thousand or two framed friendly or few with ready recall of appearing with a winter and window in repairs.

And so out loud.

Their many.

If it is veritable that if they die by an accident they will be killed sooner as much with out Howard and loaves of wishes. Loaves of wishes make water melon. In a hurry. A chorus of Baltimoreans may do may be they may do.

OLD AND OLD

OLD AND OLD

I. CONDITIONS.

House plants.

Cousin to cousin the same is a brother.

Collected tumblers.

Pretty well so called, pretty careful and going all the detention.

Hopping.

Pretty well Charlie, pretty sour poison in pears, pretty well henny soon most soon bent.

Collect.

In do pot soon, in loud coal bust, in do pot soon, in chalk what.

In do pot soon in hold hot. In do pot soon, in due point, in die point. In due point and most visible.

In vain, in vain, in a vein, in a vein. In do point that. Bay weight and balk and be wet. Be wake and white and be wet. Be count and lunge and see wall, be how, be how but can than.

Be how not inches, be have no cone grass, be who come in tear, be who coat.

Collect.

Couple calling, call cuts, call peaches and way laden and brim, brims and climate, a whole paper, little holes, and little hole, little holes.

Crowd a collection with large layers, ages, ages and ages, ten, control, kill hen, hurry in, hurry. Hold up. Saw a case cool most, come with him. Come with him. Come and trim, come in, come. Come, come, come.

Call all coupling just that please and a way to irrigate is a fountain, a folding dish and a head meadow, a folding glass and a heated moan, a brittle orange and a soon, all so soon, acres sideling. Acres sudden and a pole mischurch, miss olives, miss old age collars and cuffs and rhubarb, rub roads, roll extras, rule a case of set smashes and no pillows, no pleasure pillows. No waking cases, no closed colors, no colored suddens, no votes, no viols, no mixed peas, no regular soap stones, no regular stools, no regular ones, no such bad eggs, no cold chicken no shadow, no winter seen, no bowls, no carrots, no joints, no slender peals, no cape cuts, no batter and always more, always a season.

The grass, the grass is a tall sudden calendar with oats with means, only with cages, only with colors and mounds and little blooms and countless happy eggs to stay away and eat, eat that. The high arrangement which makes colds is that. A grand stand a real old grand stand and means and trees and coats and bars and cherries and wheels and boxes and cooking and limes and bowels and butter and points and points.

Cold wets and cold woods and cold cow harness and cold in the stretch and more pleasing reason with the cheque in the book and a dress and a dress and a medium choice and a blooming chest and a passing supper and a little cheese and a white a white and a wet white tool and a pole and a straw and a little chicking bean and a little toe white and a little cow soon. A little kew a little piece of an hopeless pre barometer and jelly cups, a way both heat, a way they heat cold. A single thing is dandy, a soiled monkey eating ahead. A spoon, a coat, a collided blotter and a case.

2.   TREATMENT.

A whole eggs in stout muds. A vest sand, a lime eater, a cold saw, a kind of stammer, a little shade, a new opera glass, a colored mule, a best winter, a spoon, a wetness, a jelly, a window and a fruit season and a ripe pear and a point in pudding in a pudding being a pudding and sometime anytime, in being a pudding and necessary and reasonable and mostly judicious and particularly flattering and seasoned, really seasoned and almost always too bad.

Cunning next.

Cunning is to be too easy to be funny. Cunning enough and a whole extra change is not necessary and all the time and particular.

A best stand is minus and it is, it just is more and any way is there a road, is there a whole way to have a belly and a bycicle and measles and oats and oranges and little whistles and balloons and old things and necessary and a pleasant day to stay and bycicles and old stretches and cold stuck and bodies and little cheeses and meat balls and sandwiches and closets and collected oils and balls and sweet breads and toads and colored choice sticks and little steady mirrors and little puddings and almost any pies and between handies and mittens and clouds and old things and butter and a soiled omelette and pieces of oat meal and a stage. Can there be any difference in any way. Can there be necessary.

A bouncing release from a whole water country and more than that makes a bed-room. It does that. It shines by day-light. It makes all the pins steal. It does show. It has moons, it has more, it had mind and molasses and everything in a thing. It is so hold.

A little be seen by a dent.

Any dent is a past time and a coach a coach why when there is wood and old iron and little things and readily quite readily.

3. COLLECTING POLES.

Old mans and a cost in corsets and a grand guard and a good gold flour, a good flour, a cold flower, a bad flavor, a certain decent and a request a request for a distant smell, a request for a smell, a request, a distant smell, a smell distant, a request, a smell, a smell distant, a smell, a distant smell.

That is the end of a solid tree in a fog, that is the end in noon, that is the end of a chance to sit in change, that is the end spinach and an egg much more egg, much more green.

Collected poles.

A little bit of spoiled choice, the little bit of wood and gold, the little bit of old baked gold, a little bit of water which is cake.

Then comes the decision. Supposing the utter meaning is that a loose dog is a fellow and a piece of certain exchange is places where there is a return, suppose all that necessarily, is it not soon beside that each is were in a tall and natural cane, is it not more so. A distribution.

We and cake, wake cake, wake, walk, cake, cool, sun, pale, rich, hold with a piece of half and half, whole, hold in with a canter and a choice and a little piece of clean and not too old soda.

We in between, cold spores, cool and we, so allowed wonder struck and so glass, so glass in previous notices. We change what. In when.

We in between, a button, a log, a handle, a burnt heading, a changed charlie an altogether neglected tub street.

Weak in the glass worn in the nose, perceived in the gold, chosen in the waste, and tuneless, quite coldless.

Collecting poles.

Come, come, no no no, no no no no, come, no no no, come. Come no no no come. Come, no no no, come, no no no no. Come.

Come no no no no, come. A loaf a whole little lamp shade that has a bottle, a kind of a bottle in it and is used, is used in a way, is used in a way splendidly.

Collecting poles.

A way to suggest restraint and alarm and reserve and a mistake and a single kind of neglect and a softened order to remove pieces and a messed sadness and an exchange is in the beginning and in the end definitely, is definitely useful.

Invite.

Bounce, to bounce, a head, to lead, to squeeze, to wander about, to neglect, to assuage, to please, to refuse a cold, to engage furnaces, to collect a roll of paper and to remove a best part of a snatch, all this and the whole real place, the whole real place.

A kind of business, a ready handle and a sold penny and a leading string and a powder any old returned cover, all the courtesy and a half of napkin, all this so suddenly. What is bleeding.

Cool gate, a sand lot and a sudden key and a house bent and a pleaser.

Cold thimble and agitation, a best fit and a boast and a harsh man.

Question. A lively turkey and a feather. Real hosts, ready hose. A basted clothes manger.

Age in girls age in cakes, age in opera glasses, aged plastered stools.

A coincidence that is a deal a great deal of patience and hold enough and wind out often in above. All the cow herds are stuffed. They are wide. In the cane there is a cover, a long thin cover of excellence and how is it.

Invite in a way.

Help a hook and a clothes button. Help it in a spell. Help a hangar. Help way in the nucleus of a particular delight and a change, changed hurry, or sudden white ship a little linen cheese.

Invite in a way.

Clean, clean in a horizon of rich red milk and made high made a way and a lifted helper, all that, a cousin is a bit, it is so reckless, it is so collected in a puddle, it is so seasonable with survey chants.

Beam, loaf, electricity in left cleans, extraordinary water spoons and sullen clocks secretly, sullen clocks not so seen as they are why so. So much animal roast leaves in mutton.

Colored janes and a high lip ruddy, a gook in soft bees and little holders.

Give in birdie, go on to artichokes suddenly in mean and in collections, go on to this sense, go on mind in so.

Go on particularly, night in.

Go on particularly nickels strange. Go in pour the chain for it full of china. Full of china choice up. Full of china crossed in. Full of china. Full of chin that has china. Chin and china. China.

5. A TOLD HIGH FLOWS, COLLOSAL, SMELL, BELL.

A tucking only a silver hose, a white lip a single tin, a solid reasoning arch representative, a single arch representative.

A single arch representative, this is so. A told countenance, this is the personnel exactly and considerately.

Curve the second to place collecting and mere ways all right. Which in bear cases and neglected suit tracks and white sails and kind of vagrant wellies and collecting verses and beads and called plates and places with soon more and white, might there, and with, all the cow bright laugh in sounds and laughter.

Heap and combine killed captures and the blame bone and the illustrious station the steady water flame breaking the called way in a change, in a silly veil storm and clutches and a time when a time table utterly and noise and nearly all the estranged speats and later spreads and last vexed coats all coats.

A ladder viciously and a keen collected wood pen and a coaxed cat in a rack and a combination, a climbed call at.

Hard all, hem stitch centrally cooled with cables in a place and strong, strong elevated horrid stones and nearly why and more the which is able to and no.

Cousins in and coal beds on and coal beds there and why the half stead which relates that which when than more go to horrid exchange.

A told in that all which has mine and beads the same which shall be shut and more to wait and all the candy, all the habited exchanged wonder resources in the best condition vacationally reduced and rectified more in that change.

Lend a stand and little eases and the whole resolved exchange of wild-nesses and a lease and peas and a chat related and the nut and but to make the water steal.

Cone in cousins is bleeding with the exchange of letting out palings and whole seeds and all the little ways. Tenderly. To be let.

Cold acres, cold couches in three cities, colored cups one readily and much must be resumed and let out with magazines and care taken with takers remedy and a whole speech readily very readily external and more extra than by the side of a shirts. By the side of half and more in the miserable seat of a whole interchange between education and visit between education and visit. More in than before the last prints and idless becomings and more aged mending and little pieces. All extra.

Put in the most and delighted and believe the hay mound and little classes, believe big classes clouding and cowardly weather spittoons and grass mere, merely the same, merely believe that change, merely show towels, merely be in that gaining collapse and article.

Be wet in a chest of sucks where there is a grasp and a close a half close cup of excellent refusings a cup so more readily and behind that. Behind that.

A gentleman that vindicates addresses and pearls and loose cards and shoes and puffs and little seas and a great deal of necessary able colored watches and behind any little thing is so likely very much that benumbing and reclosed, all this means a bed room and a single center and more beneath, and not climbing with paste and crevasses and any little thing. This is no neglect of spades and all the ways and like that and orderly and a best way to sputter when there is a distraction which a doubt can make beam, can make beam.

A little in that white wonder place which shows the slight indication of more necessarily reduced and disturbed and loosening all the regular manipulation of lessening the challenges which make plenty a disgrace with a booth. The real thing is beside that when the return is pleased with cloth and more nearly on the sweet hold of the change which makes these.

That then more cultivated in a slight union of a viciousness which is the very best representative of an incline and a message and really utility is the indication of much that is neglected by harmony and mingling and a little chapter and no counter leaving.

The best union to fit is in the shut and not in that neglected by cold scratches and a little there. Not at all then.

Peeling changes makes ready and left brooms are called that reliably and with that fair division that makes it cold and potatoey in the meadow light and in the ground and all of it, all of it.

A case to know.

Singly is enough, any way it is splendidly and be that in a way and a hold a wide hold and old told, old told in a loaf of told batter and green pleases and all that. No dirt, no copper no doubt, no doubt no dirt, no doubt, no doubt that, no doubt that that copper, no doubt that, no copper, no copper, no doubt that no doubt no copper. No copper, no copper, no doubt. No doubt. No doubt no copper, no doubt.

6. WIDOWS.

A cold state, a kind of stable life, a kind of boiler and a gold skate, a choice hearty delicate underneath water builder and muttons muttons of useful ardent oat cakes apron. A cold state and meat pants and little losses and beneath water apples and doors and jerked barbers and little hens and leaders. All that and a best halt and little goes and wheat staffs and miss curls and hard chests and all best and little mutters. Little mutters to salt wet words, little mutters in the dew. Little is the case. Little is the case.

Go belt, go in there copiously and within and strong sudden salt works, strong sudden salt works, have cold wet nurses and cold wet noises and cold wet nuts and cold wet nurses. Cold wet nurses and cold wet noises, cold wet noses, cold wet nurses.

Cup spaces.

Cup spaces are readily seen to be local and back and never stolen and always always coincident, coincident with long angels and much much passes, much so. A little gain is a squeal it is a squeal so addedly it is a squeal, it is a squeal. It is more than the first apron it is the second. It is.

Collusion.

Collidable and covered and with stead and sturdy and neglected occasion, with neglected occasions there comes meaning and every measure with stalk.

Kinds in tables.

A learned collection of more places once, a learned recollection comes from springs and lanterns and little sides, a learned recollection of more places once, a learned recollection of more places once comes in to the kinds of a first exchange and then collectedness and then a table a piece of expression steadily and really what is the exchange between glueing, what is the select action of real neat and sold pieces of cork. What is the best standing and more shoulders in nearly application to a rain that is stubborn and relaxed and so torn so torn with with water places and real corns with very blue soldiers and little really tall colors with blue. All the same growing is with steady and ridiculous furs, monthly the cup kind and the grass, really the grass and the considered window and any way what is crossness for, crossness is for a reason and a little change to make a bell and ringing, ringing is all the same as knocking and any way a little difference is not necessary is not more necessary than freezing not really more necessary than a settled shawl. A real way to make fingers is rather by that and that. The real white way is with a color and powders are green and roses are vacant and beets real beets have balls. Suppose there are quick ways suppose they are and a memory is told by asking in change what was the case in dream what was the case in a tall decanter what was the last case that had puddings. The answer is already.

A little afternoon makes the sun and then if there is a circumstance and the real shout is called right in with a splendid and regular delay then surely there is in between more comforts more real comforts readily. A question is a dozen. A question is the case of the revolving butter and last train and secretly really secretly, all that, and no consideration for spells and little tiny white eggs and the same in blue and in a center color. The rest is in exchange collected by long and satisfactory installation and dusting.

All pages and white thistles and little torn berries and little mass means, and the time of the stretch and a plan to carry poles and little searches and a couple of condies with a sudden best stick, and last met with a sign of a place to show touches and a little climb and a sweet hold of a more excellent and reseen oleander, a most excellent hurling, a most sand paper and a glass which shows a change in cultivating rare trees and little things which are mutton and a pet all the same close bent share of cut a way clothes brush.

The season is best with wheels.

7. GRASS TREES.

Always satisfying the labor of exacting the recognition of lost references to the long case which has structure elevation and disgrace and surely there is a bald sacrament that means an extrapiece of lamp with a glass shade certainly clean. The best excuse is this. Let the right corner see more great pauses then there are practical places to search out cups and saucers. Let there remain little things nice things and exact works and little quite the best time exactly and more in the wick and sold more there and there there is doleful examples of ever ready hydrangeas. In the ease which makes all the disturbance and a center concentrated all this makes a reason why any distance is a street and a street is mathematical and wise really wise and this makes a hole makes a hole so that coming in is in.

Great bay waters and left in there makes a swim a tank and makes bugs real bugs that is bugs that have a lesson and an organ and an approach and a light change and a miserable a quite miserable interchange most readily.

Making a change quite readily is peaceable. Any cold is a species of least resemblance and love. Love is a cool cat which has them. A grain a grain is established and hesitation is so learned that almost any is put in the house patiently with no hesitation, none, no one.

Cold up with the expression of the reason when a glance and a little paste all the newly joined is in the particular clear use of more than organs.

Cold up with a climb and an ox and a sensitive birthday of pieces of cheese and a lost a long lost specimen of rose. A rose is streak a streak mentionedly and like a current which shows the circumstance of light and a cap. A cap is surrounded by blind clause which shows rain and the same.

Rest with it and make a tall mind show it. Rest with it and make no man tall more likely. The best is in the soot, a large dress shows that, a large dress is made with him.

Ground left.

Cunning seas so sweet in being little nice and covered with one. All the tough apple makes a piece of raisin all of it and eye glasses are exchanged by nearly everything naturally and in legs, again a week, any tuck makes a different thing tremble and show electricity with a vim with a lovely dog and feet, heels are careful with bursts and kindly in with black.

A mouse cow and a strange half cram filled with a surging that is particular with sound. A relief a whole church a whole lean bag necessarily.

Waist in a little piece of hurt with a head and covered covered with an ear and a long a long oar or a long a long cat called a collision. A real meet, a real met land which is copied by a latterly arranged cut up resemblance to not more than a relief from more mixing than the chance. A time climate and religion and sweet use and a pill in and a whole sound which is called met and which seems chair and which is conwheeled.

Left in when and leave leave a corn starch with a heather that is red and a pin and a likely cooled in frozen.

Cut in. Hinges.

Close to all the wide reason that there is cold and a happy warm table and a little biting egger and a puzzle mentally, in spite of despite of, relight from, all this wade later and later in lie which is the.

The rest is popular. The rest is a pole teller. The rest is pope and wheeler and a page flated, in the pay of august and more waiter and mind in page whiter, and in whiter, in whiter page straight in later page in later. Page. Later.

8. CUT INDIANS.

Come in little cubicle stern old wet places. Come in by the long excuse of more in place of bandages which send a little leaf to cut a whole condition with a pan, all the can all that can see the pen of pigs wide.

All this man is a make of chins which is to be tall and most many women, in the directory that shows why the state which is absolutely with plaster absolutely with plastering received with boast. All this in bedding.

Cut circles in Indians.

A cubicle with a reserved center and little spades and a large shade and a colored hour glass and little pieces, grand.

Colored up with bet let, leen glass cage. Colored up with let keen girk clink gage, colored up with keen get call up be seen in when call up when in bend that more wheezily. Colored up in when call that up if cost, call it up in when call that wake west, call it up in when that when it is in call and call it up in when it is when it is in when, when it is in when it is in when when it is in, when it is in when, when, it is in, in. When it is in when.

When it is in when call it up in when.

When it is in when call it up in when it is in when. It is in by the perulean repetition of amalgamated recreation of more integral and less solidifying rudeness. It is paul.

Baby mine, baby mine, have a cow come out of have a cow come out of baby mine baby mine have a cow come out with time, baby mine baby mine have a cow come neatly have a cow come sweetly baby mine baby mine have a cow come out in mine. Baby mine baby mine have a cow come out of have a cow come out of baby mine baby mine have a cow come out of have a cow come out of, have a cow come have a cow come have a cow come come come come.

THEY WEIGHED WEIGHED-LAYED

A Drama of Aphorisms

Maurice I

Way-laid makes speeches.

Maurice II

If a tree at all it is an adventure to come back in the night with a white dog.

Maurice III

If at a distance they come near.

Who has been heard to care for this.

That they will leave to them they are not there whether it is not left either.

For them. They will be that they announce neither either other farther whether rather neglect.

Maurice IV

Odder than the door.

The dog is at the door.

But not at a door.

A melon can ripen.

There are three things that have a fragrance melon chocolate and chestnut but not as eaten.

Maurice V

Birds have dahlias.

Drink dahlias.

Maurice VI

If all of it goes away.

We are here.

In refusing mingling separation.

Maurice VII

A blue sky who may say reply.

Maurice VIII

Far from follow it.

Eugene I

Follow with it.

Eugene II and Maurice I

A dagger is dead when a door which is a dog is living yet.

Eugene III Maurice II

It does not make any difference who is regal if they are all for it which naturally it is not.

Eugene IV and Maurice III

Why will they sigh When they sleep.

Marcel I Maurice IV

Why will they sigh and not die.

Marcel II Maurice V

When they sigh they think of defeat.

They have followed previous prayers.

They will compete.

They will see no one near she can hear that he is meant for four they will have it as a change for their then without men. He is dead but not or men.

Remain here.

Maurice VI Bernard I

Do leave marble alone.

Marble is a rare stone.

Maurice VII Bernard II

Eugene is not eleven.

Eleven how eleven.

Maurice seven.

Maurice VIII Bernard III

With them with this with purses.

With enchanting victory.

Marguerite I Maurice VII

Buy Marcel a joy.

He is a sorrow not to annoy.

But to exchange pears.

Marguerite II Maurice VI

They will have rest for dogs.

Marguerite III Maurice V

When they rest they sigh.

This is a sign of their rest.

Marguerite IV Maurice IV

When the sun shines the clouds form they may be scattered by the wind that depends upon others.

Marguerite V Maurice III

He was not grateful to me.

Maurice II Leon I

They have supper for some.

Maurice I Leon II

It is useful to be made for two.

Leon III Eugene I

There are often two who are there with one. They make as if they saw that bulbs can dry if there is sun.

Leon IV Eugene II

He needs what he can leave for instance they might like it better.

Leon V Eugene III

They have thought that all of it was lost.

Leon VI Eugene IV

They were better informed.

Leon VI Eugene IV

They will be fought for.

Leon VII Maurice I

But it is a remedy.

Maurice II Marcel I

Coming and come.

They can have been working in the sun.

They will be the same when they have some.

Which they will have given by some one.

Which they have as they will have been met by some one.

In the care care and case is learning, they like fastening.

They will be presently with everything.

They will make that with an escape of changing.

Why will they like being here.

Maurice III Marcel II

Thoughts are a happiness to them.

Maurice IV Bernard I

Pardon for one.

Maurice V Bernard II

Welcome for one.

One of them.

Maurice VI Bernard III

They have nothing to puzzle any one.

                    Maurice VII Marguerite I
Violets and a name for them.
                    Maurice VIII Marguerite II
The best thing they can do is this.
                    Marguerite III Leon I
Why is it more.
                    Marguerite IV Leon II
Than it was.
                    Marguerite V Leon III
They have no hope of seeing it continue.
                    Leon IV Maurice I
Reach and riches.
                    Leon V Maurice II
They leave liking them.
                    Leon VI Maurice III
Two sounds for one.
                    Leon VII Maurice IV
Live like one.
                    Maurice V Marcel I
Better be here to do it.
                    Maurice V Marcel II
He is a poet too.

Scene II

Little dogs should not eat flies.
They come in between.
They think about how mountains come.
Men of severing them.
This is a tragedy.
To make them see through.
Mouths and mouths.
A dog vomits once.
A man is very careful of his health.
A son is irritated by admiration.
They come together.
And they sing.
All the names are included in the song.
In this scene they make an unexpected acquaintance.
                    Maurice VI Bernard I
There is an appointment.

Birds will need balls.

Maurice VII Bernard II

In this scene they will have it left for them.

Maurice VIII Bernard III

Birds and balls and trout and seagulls and their nests follow me.

The unexpected acquaintance is Eugene.

Eugene I and Marcel I

They will patiently wait while they have hopes of leaving.

They leave and one does not become a soldier either because it is better to leave his mother.

One has a father.

A father who is often made more nearly his father.

They both hope to hear that either one is to be a soldier which they are because a soldier does go and come with more than a regiment. They leave trees to be tall.

It is finally their aim.

Eugene II and Marcel II

It is a pity that they must stop here stop here.

Eugene III Bernard I

Too many days make of it too much which they will do as widowed. Dissemble. They will add it as gain. They need to emphasise first letters. Gain and realise.   And be employed.

Eugene IV Bernard II

There is no insistence.

Bernard III Marguerite I

Many have been happily married.

Marguerite II and Leon I

They will think kindly of their circumstances.

Marguerite III and Leon II

A birthday unites birds.

Bertie Applegarth

He is or was a help to them in arithmetic.

Marguerite IV and Leon III

It was in there that they saw a help to them.

Marguerite V and Leon IV

They have their scissors unreliably left.

Leon V Maurice I

Be kind to and for them.

Leon VI Maurice II

In opportunity to be useful to those who have need of having it without them.

Leon VII Maurice III

There is no difference between them.

Maurice IV and Marcel I

There is no difference between when and sudden. They change.

Maurice V and Marcel II

Change all of it for you.

ACT II

Maurice VI Eugene I Marcel I

Our which are ours.

Do be obscured by ours.

They must be waiting to be well.

Maurice VII Eugene II Marcel II

It is a hope in thousands.

Counting.

As acceptable.

Will Marcel be as well.

Maurice VIII Eugene III Bernard I

In reason including one.

Eugene IV Bernard II Marguerite I

With thorough distaste.

For lettering.

Which they bring with holding.

Withholding quiescence.

In bridges.

And lays.

They made it without hers.

She meant to be in a reversion.

Of an added gather.

They gather them.

With them.

To be around.

In their avoidance.

Ration with reluctantly.

And envisage.

They adjoin dress.

And train to treasure.

Tresasure in a margin of their being here with and without attempt to
attempt to clear them.

Bernard III Marguerite II Leon I

By politeness they sing to me.

Marguerite III Leon II Maurice I

Just why they have to ask that they will by the time they are themselves almost at once.

Marguerite IV Leon III Maurice II

Should choices be left to other ones which they mean.

Marguerite V Leon IV Maurice III

It is obliging for that made to be orderly for an arrangement of their I mean.

Leon V Maurice IV Eugene I

In apt to be asked for them.

Leon VI Maurice V Eugene II

But why do they make it regrettable.

Leon VII Maurice VI Eugene III

In brought with reference to their bestowal without their use with length.

Maurice VII Eugene IV

They introduce them or themselves.

Maurice VIII

Wait.

Scene II

Bernard I Marguerite I Marcel I

It is best to plant them one by one.

Two at a time is temporary, three are carefully thoughtful.

Bernard II Marguerite II Marcel II

They lost them by loving.

Marcel I

Better then always leaving because of accepting.

Bernard III Marguerite III Marcel II

They made hands press down roses.

Marcel I

Without ostentation.

Bernard I

With final regret.

Marcel II Bernard II Marguerite IV

But whether with revision.

Marcel.

There is no hope in heaven.

Marcel II Bernard III Marguerite V
It was better to be thought careless.
Marcel I
Just divided justly divided judging divided and dividing and defence of division.
Bernard I and Marguerite I
A pleasure in deceit.
Marguerite II
Praise of precision.
Bernard II
Made with them as it were with their capability.
Marcel II Bernard III Marguerite III
Hours precious hours which they have used with pleasure. Pleasure is so agreable so selected and so fairly denied.
Marguerite IV
She should be joined by leaving one.
Leon I
One of them.
Leon II Marcel I Marguerite V
It is fairly provocative of sunshine.
Marcel II
Three hoping they are altogether.
Leon III Maurice I Eugene I
Birds are hoping that they have to stay.
Leon IV Maurice II Eugene II
They will be sadder with their death.
Leon V Maurice III Eugene III
Come cautiously.
Leon VI Maurice IV Eugene IV
Does he mean Edward Glasgow.
Does he indeed.
Leon VII Maurice V Marcel I
They will be left to pray.
Maurice VI Bernard I Marcel II
A habit of sitting is not changed.
Marcel I
Let me not choose roses.
Maurice VII Bernard II Marcel II
They will they have an opportunity to be older in having a mother a grand-mother and no habit of having hope. Hope they will.

Marcel I

It is an education to have pleasant thoughts.

Maurice VIII Marcel II Bernard III

Just in a way of having had this as a reason. They will mind if they hear a request. They will be well received. It is always alright.

Scene III

The parlor widened they did buy the road.

Scene IV

She was not the same as she had been.

ACT III

Leon I Marguerite I

With no objecting to avoidance.

And with no pleasure in success.

With and without hope in their reason.

With them with which they gratify.

They will change their thought and their alliance.

They will urge them to do very well for them.

They will habituate them in leaving.

They will count in years.

Marguerite II Leon II

They will try to have it do.

They will please themselves with you.

They will join themselves with their and them nicely.

They will seem to be almost made happily by the time they have been hearing them or they come.

They come with noisy welcome.

We are so glad to see them.

Marguerite III and Leon III

He was disappointed as well as she.

Marguerite IV Leon IV

It is inexplicable.

They do and are careful and at hand.

Marguerite V Leon V

Should they move slowly.

And ask it to be a little more.
And have the habit of reminding them.
That it just as well they came.
They are as careful as that of it.

Leon VI Maurice I
She should make some use of it.
Leon VII Maurice II
It was as much as they knew what had happened.
Leon VII
With which.
They neglect.
To make.
It be.
Their hope.
Of joining.
In a little while.
Now.
It is often that they ask is it so a week ago.
In spite of all it is sad.
So he says.
She might.
Think well.
Of them.
As much.
As more.
Than they.
Did think.
Of it.
First.
It is hard to be sad in english.
Maurice II and Eugene I
They know that they do.
Whatever they do.
Maurice III Eugene II
With them.
Maurice IV Eugene III
As lightly.
Maurice V Eugene IV
As they knew.
Maurice VII Marcel I
With distribution.

Maurice VII Marcel II

As a climax.

Maurice VIII Bernard I

They like it.

Maurice VIII

As much as ever.

Bernard II Marguerite I Leon I

And Louis who is gone.

Bernard III Marguerite II Leon II

They will welcome yeilding of one.

Bernard II

Louis and they will add each one one.

Bernard I

Which one.

Marguerite III Leon III

Forty are thirty for one.

Marguerite IV Leon IV

Fifty more and they are always four and more.

Marguerite V Leon V

They pass more than they have seen before.

Marguerite IV

Which they like.

Marguerite III

To like.

Marguerite II

To be like.

Marguerite I

After and like.

Leon VI

They might measure six.

Leon VII

All good children go to heaven.

ACT IV

Maurice I

He stops and asks if asking is the same as leaving. He knows leaving is an occasion.

Maurice II Eugene I

They will ask if they ask it if they have it when they mention coming.

Maurice III Eugene II

Both are brave they light it as well as if they knew that they will go if they do before they come with sugar which they have eaten with bread and does it disturb them as much as then.

Maurice IV Eugene III

They ask it as well as better and as much as differently.

Maurice V Eugene IV

Do please open the door so that they can go out better than before.

Eugene III

They make an allowance for happiness.

Eugene II

They follow themselves with wishes.

Eugene I

They welcome them home.

Maurice VI Marcel I

They will be with them presently too.

Maurice VII Marcel II

Think well and think that they thought that it had been bought for them.

Marcel I

Leave it as a present.

Maurice VIII Bernard I

They change so that seven is one.

Maurice VII

They will prepare this for them.

Maurice VI

They have prepared something so that they will leave it alone when they do.

Maurice V

It is a plan they have.
They have a plan.

Maurice IV

Which they enjoy when they can.

Maurice III

It is a likelihood of their being very much alike.

Maurice II

It is not any use to beg them to go there.

Maurice

To go away is made necessary for them here.

Bernard II Marguerite I

You know that we think of you.

Bernard III Marguerite II

We hope you do.

Bernard II

Be very certain that we do.

Bernard I

And that we never neglect it whatever we may do.

Marguerite II Leon I

It is useless to know that Louis is not Leon.

Marguerite III Leon II

Which they hope with them who do. They will settle nothing for you. They will give it to them for you. They will hope that this will do.

Scene II

Marguerite IV Leon III

She was just as sweet.

Marguerite V Leon IV

As they were together.

Marguerite IV

Was it indeed by having or without that they counted that they would do without.

Marguerite III

She made it be that it was tenderly that he went to see whether he could be better than he had been.

Marguerite II

She said she was necessary to him.

Marguerite I

She might be withheld as she would have been.

Leon V Maurice I

He heard him say that he went away.

Leon VI Maurice II

And did it matter.

Leon VII Maurice III

To him.

Scene III

Maurice III

Maurice call him.

Maurice IV

Eugene call him.

Maurice V Eugene I

They made a meadow inundated by the sun.
The meadow was sinking.
It was under water like anything.

Maurice VI Eugene II

It was in the hope of swimming that were engaging between leaving and welcoming milking.

Maurice VII Eugene III

It was agreeable to be neglectful.

Maurice VIII Eugene IV

They will sing about wedding women.

Maurice VII

She made a hope that they would be there.

Maurice VI

It was valuable to have it heard from here to there.

Maurice V

They made women wait.

Maurice IV

They sang too late.

Maurice III

They sang that they are singing.

Maurice II

Which they were as women.

Maurice I

Which they were with humming.

Eugene III

And they think.

Eugene II

That it is best.

Eugene I

To leave it now.

Marcel I Bernard I

As they do.

Marcel II Bernard II

It is not easy to be cruel in thinking that it is different that they left with out an allowance of more than that which is everything. Let it be ready for them.

Marcel I

There is a hope that it is cooler than that there has been one.

Bernard III Marguerite I

They like it when they think that they have been advising.

Bernard II

Which they do.

Bernard I

One for one.

Marguerite II Leon I

What is a tragedy when he is lonesome.

Marguerite III Leon II

She dropped the shears.

Marguerite IV Leon III

For him.

Marguerite V Leon IV

With help.

Marguerite IV

Withheld help.

Marguerite III

In acquaintance.

Marguerite II

As much as which they will when he is held.

Marguerite I

Withheld.

Leon V Maurice I

They will account for his having run.

Leon VI Maurice II

Which they have in the need of one.
And they without.

Leon VII Maurice III

It is as alike as they like.

Maurice IV

There is no need of being one.

Maurice V

Which they examine.

Maurice VI

By hope.

Maurice VII

And wishes.

Maurice VIII

Too late.

ACT V

Eugene I Marcel I

Prepare to ask why will they come with me.

Eugene II Marcel II

He went yesterday if not to-day.

Marcel II

With circumstances of delay.

Eugene III Bernard I

Will no one give any one more than just one.

Eugene IV Bernard II

Yes when they ask three to be four.

Eugene III

When this you see remember me.

Eugene II

They refuse cakes because they have not eaten.

Eugene I

I was touched by their sorrow.

Bernard II Marguerite I Leon I

As many as they have been without they will refrain from exacting it for them.

Bernard III Marguerite II Leon II

She was in no hurry.

Bernard II

They make excuses for having relish for wishes.

Bernard I

By the time they question.

Marguerite II Leon II

They might be faithful to themselves here.

Marguerite III Leon III

They all died but not all in poverty.

Marguerite IV Leon IV

They were relegated to this that they could be separated.

Marguerite V Leon V

In which they please.

Marguerite IV

May I be chosen.

Marguerite III

To have it please.

Marguerite II

That they like to give.

Marguerite I

It to them.

Leon VI Maurice I

They are happy in the thought.

Leon VII Maurice II

That they will not go away.

Leon VI

They please me.

Leon V

In themselves.

Leon IV

They displease me.

Leon III

In themselves.

Leon II

They remain with them.

Leon I

By themselves.

Maurice II Eugene I

In happily having had it prepared they make it be a chance to be with them as their kind.

Maurice III Eugene II

They are kind.

Maurice IV Eugene III

Which they own.

Maurice V Eugene IV

In a minute with their care. They will be careful to prepare their hoping to be left to-day which may be by the time that it is arranged. They will not do it if they know better, they will be persuaded that it is useful and in hoping for a refusal they are generous and flurried they will be anxious for a dismissal. They will be without doubt eager for an appointment which will consolidate their reunion.

Maurice IV Eugene III

How do they like their liberty.

Scene II

Maurice V Eugene IV

They hope for this as they did.

Maurice VI Marcel I

Maurice and Marcel very well that only they are left Maurice and Marcel, all the others very well that they are left Maurice is left and Marcel, Marcel is left and Maurice.

Maurice III Marcel II

They think they like to disturb hopes.
They will be imaginative in requisition.
They will recite their pleasure.
They will arrange substance.
They will incite them to go.
None are left.
They are without this arrangement.
They save it.
They like it in the place of their arrangement.

Maurice VIII

Too late.

Marcel II

They are through.

Eugene IV

It is remarkable.

Bernard III

They imagine that state.

Marguerite V

They wish for me.

Leon VII

Hope of heaven.
Now they all sit and without that there is tragedy.
Remember the occasion of their denial.

Maurice VIII Eugene IV
Marcel II Bernard III Marguerite V Leon VII

They think with me.

Scene III

The mushrooms were delicious at lunch.

FINIS.

LYNN AND THE COLLEGE DE FRANCE

The scene is layed in the small village of Perpignan or Billignin.
The characters are Lynn

The College de France

Madame Rose

Marcelle Mariot

and

Henry Clay.
What they ask they ask together.
This is the condition. Of the Play.
What. They do not. Question. Interests them. They will. Be pleased.
To be conversational.
Lynn commences and Henry Clay finishes.
There is no order. In nationality.
Thank everybody. For their expression.
What will. They like. And admire. Most.
Very pleasantly.
A privilege.
They often commence speaking.
Henry Clay leaves the College de France to decide.
Everything is calm.
They sing well.
And tunnels. Are encouraged.
Place it conveniently. If. They please.

All who have hoped. To. As to. Perhaps. Pass. Have. Asked to. Perhaps. As. In this. To be. A pleasure.
Lynn. Had. Come. In.

It would. Have been.

A pleasure.

Now think well how an event. Comes to pass. And who. Has. Not been. Aware. Of asking.

She will come in.

With. An. In. Them.

They may have been suspicious. Of linking.

It was. Ours. Toward.

In there. Prevailed. Invariably.

The first act, commences in Bilignin.

Was Lynn. A. Available as Lena. Who. Was. Gone.

With them. In pearls. And. A. Little silk blue. Not little. At all. At a loss.

The College de France. Is caught. At. A. Cross. It.

Forty men. Feel fought.

The great hope in respect to Lena is that they may not hurry manage. Pearly.

Pearly is a color and characters are a quantity. And so. The college of France. Opens. Gloriously.

In this. Which. In their way.

All who. Have held. Poles.

With crying.

All. Who. Have. Held.

Poles with crying.

And all. Who. Have. Held.

Men. Meant. With. Trying.

Leave. Act one. To one.

Act two. Which. They do.

Act three. Sea-shore. And. Liberty.

Act four. Name. And. A. Door.

Act five. They. Will. Thrive.

Act six. They. May. Mix.

Success with glory.

Four and forty. Two and twenty.

Three and thirty. Six and seventy.

The college of France. Lynn and Henry Clay. And. In memory.

Always knowing which a name. Will they keep it all the same. In. Memory.

Beatrice Glory.

Henry Clay.
General Wallace and Arthur Thorn.
Who went to school with Henry Clay.
They will say. They saw Lynn to-day.
What is the difference between village life and city life.
Village life. Which. Will. They. Have. It come.
City life.
Bilignin and Perpignan.
They knew better. Than that a. Hill. Is a. Cone.
Should. All who have.
Thought well. Of them.
Believe in. Tears.
Believe. In knowing. Fears.
Gather. In. Cares.
Named. Gather. In theirs.
Or much. As much. In. Glowing.

Act One.
All. Begun. Act one.

In this act. The characters have not met. They have not known. That they. Should recite. Love of the city.
She has just found out. The name. Of the. Village.
Beatrice Glory and Lynn. They will exist with suffering.
They may be perishable.
They may be carried farther.
They may be. Ours. Instead.
In which case. It will not matter.
Henry Clay and the College de France. Let me not arouse them apart.
Henry Clay and the College of France and walking and an interim.
Will they blame often.
Will they frighten. Them.
With him.
More than they could.
In a little while Lynn means to turn into Helene.
Which is. A. Mystery.
Henry Clay. Happen. To be. Fast.
With them. And. Miserably.
In a little while. Henry Clay Arthur Thorn and General Wallace. Have been. Indeed. Appointed. In. Their way. By them.
Please may they be. There. To carry.

That is. It should. Have. Been. A. Refusing.
They. Are. Cautioning.
Might. They. Be. In a confusion.
Beatrice Glory is mentioning something.
All of which. They. Are hoping.
It may be that the College de France. Is open.
Henry Clay and General Henry and Henry Thorne.
Lynn and Lena and Leonard and John Lane.
Who refers. To blame.
They will. Nominate. Just. The same.
The College de France has been older than. In commencing.
And now. They bow.
And they. Will succeed.
In which. They mention.
                    Their.
                    Choice.
And there is. Very much. Spoken. To. Their advantage.
Henry Clay. Joins. With. And. Remember.
If there had been.
More than anything.
And they would. Commence. Then.
To join. In. Would they.
Then. Have it. In question.
That. They would. Voice. Everything. As. Their suggestion.
All. The College. De France.
Who have. Been heard. From.
Their is a meeting and they all come together. To-day. They remembered
yesterday. And. Yesterday. They were. In advantage. To separate. To allow.
To-day. Which. They say. They will. Be entirely. Evasive.
Henry Clay. Measured. With telling.
They need. Henry. As a name.
They also. Need. Genevieve. As a name.
They also. Need. James. As a name. They also. Need. Henry and William. As
a name. They also need. Hundred. As a name. They also. Need. Nine. And
in. Them. More. Than. Their name.
Will. They add. With them. As. A name.
The College of France.
Lynn. And Henry Clay.
Think well about it now. And. When. They will. Rejoin. As they call. Him.
Which they may do. As. Easily. As known. In connection. With planting.
And. A dome. It is. An authority. To leave. A half. Alone.

She made a movement. Was it. A gesture. Or was it. A turning. In the way.
Of. A pleasure.
Lynn and General Arthur. Everything you do is a pleasure. To me.
Henry Clay. And a visitor.
They may well be adored.
Henry Clay General Arthur and William Thorne and Lynn.
They will mingle Lynn with Helene and Helene with Lena. They will add.
A crown. To Helen. And Cora. Cora is religious.
Henry Clay visiting the College of France is expressing this thing.
The College of France in the interim.
General Thorne and General Wilder are visiting and Lynn is intending to re-
count that they. Are visiting.
Helen Lynn and General Thorne and Henry Clay are everything.
The College of France. Is closing. For the summer. Vacation.
The anniversary of the founding. Of the. College. Of France.
Should one wait. Or should one. Light. The candles. For which. They. Are
looking.
She has decided correctly.

Scene I

Lynn or Lena. Is hidden. By a wing. Of. A building.
And they. Are serviceable.
And they. Are able.
And it is. A deliverance.
And a pleasure. And. An exchange.

Scene I

The foundation of the College of France is what. They are. Celebrating.
One two three. And they. Choose. Liberty.
Which may flourish.

Scene I

Henry Clay. General Thorne and Lynn. Make no declaration of friendship.
They happen to be very well-known.

Scene I

Many come. Together. In. Scene one.

Henry Clay. And General Thorne. And John Lane. And Herbert Grander. They all. Come. Together in Scene one. Lynn comes in Scene one, as Helen, or as Lynn or as Lena. She comes. In. Scene one.
They may now. Wait. For. A four leaf clover.
They may. Now. Wait. For a pen. And water. They. May wait. Now. For. Jasmine. They. May not wait. In. Receiving. They may accept. In. Receiving. They may. Retire. And think. Very well. Of better.

Scene one.

Very many. Come.

Scene I

Better which. They. Like it. If they may. They will. Not follow. Whether. They will.

Act I

It is very well known. That a name. Governs. With one. Who thanked. Them. Henry Clay. Is very well furnished. By the time. That they were anxious.
Now think very carefully. Of how often they are. By themselves. Gracious.
The College de France makes no mention of names.
Henry Clay. Is not a name.
And so. They feel. Well. In. Establishes.
Henry Clay. Is. Nervous.
General William Thorne. Is suspicious.
Lynn is nominated.
William Paul Gold. Is made silent. By. Their count. And so. They will. Imitate. Delicious.

Act I

Scene one

The College de France. One. By one.
The life of Mary River.
The life of Andrew Dove.
The son of Andrew Dove.
The life of Mary River.
The life of Andrew Dove.
The life of Mary River.

Mary River. Made a mother.
She was startled. When. They asked. Are your children coming. They meant. Her nephews and nieces.

Mary River. Was ordinarily. Patient. And she thought well. Of better and hovering. Hope was equal. To defeat. And their allowance. What she chose. She had. A delightful way. With dogs and children. Andrew Dove went to college. As one. Who has an advantage. In winning. He may be thoughtful. And they neglect. Without them. More than. They are. Cordially winning. And so to proceed.
The College of France has begun existing.
Henry Clay. May murmur.
Mary River and Andrew Dove. Know each other. This will not follow. Upon. Another. Following. In order. They will not meet. In. This way.
The life of Mary River.
General Thorne is in defence of the community. And the continuation. Of everything. In. Building.
A building has been named. The College of France.
The life of Mary River.

Act I

To drop a stitch. Which. The foot. Fell off the frame.
Mary River and Andrew Dove. Heard. That they were willing. To love.
Loving makes. Their. Meaning. They will follow. As if. They were seeming. To understand that General Horn. Was meant. To be. Returning.
When was the College of France founded.
Henry Clay. Prepares to be detained. And in order. To establish a definition. Mary River and Andrew Dove. Feel that they may. Declare themselves. To be indifferent. Which may. Make. A hope of an interference.
The life of Mary River.
The College of France was founded and they will bear this in mind. Whether they are equal to exacting hope. And help. And their. Arrival.
                    Henry Clay.
Whan all is. Perfectly. To-day.

Scene I

The life of Mary River and Andrew Dove.
The life of Mary River.
Forty make.   A. Conundrum.

And they will.   Manage. To leave. Them.
She waited for them to come. And they came.
The life of Mary River.
And of Andrew Dove.
And the College of France.
There is no hope.
Of their remaining.
With and without all.
Mary River has a life.
Andrew Dove. Has a wife.
The College of France is known.
The best. Of all.
It is very merciful. To think well. Of their. Election.
What can. Any one. Imagine.
Hope. And regret. And worthiness.

Act I

The College of France is meeting and celebrating. Their existence. Henry Clay. Andrew Dove and General Thorne are invited. Mary River is present. There are a great many meeting in conclave. And they are very careful. Of. Their memory.
The scene finishes. With their reminding. No one. Of. Their hope. And they will. Think well. And wish well. Alternately.

Scene I

Should they or should they not keep still. In this way Mary River and Andrew Dove. Have no advantage.
Mary River and Andrew Dove. The College of France and their intermission and their permission.

Scene I

Mary River and Andrew Dove. The College of France has precincts. So have all colleges. And they will know. All colleges will know. Mary River and Andrew Dove. The college of France.
She might be thought to be won. By having heard from. Them.
There is often. Not a name. That. Came.
This is why. Mary River can try. To buy.
Will Andrew Dove. Come with her.

The college of France has a beginning and an anniversary.
It may be thought best to count.
Henry Clay. Addresses. Everybody. Mary River is in the audience.

Scene I

Pretty soon he will think. Of. An interruption.
And in this way. A college of France. Arises.
They may have been left to them. General Johns Andrew Dove. And more than. Ever. Velvet.
It has ceased to have been preparatory.
Everybody could be happy.
The College of France.

Act 1

Scene I

Andrew Dove General Thorne and Henry Clay meet. They confer together. They find. They have been meeting. They will be willing. To have it. As much. As they can. As they. Are welcome.
The college of France opens. And the opening is one which may be told. Often. In that way they decide. To plan.
Henry Clay. Has been met. Unexpectedly. It had been assumed that. It would not happen.
How can. There be. A difference. Of opinion. Concerning. The length of it all. The college of France is founded.

Act I

Scene I

Montlucon.
Mary River.
I would be blest. If I had thought. That I would gather. Whether. They were taught. If. In the meanwhile. They may like it. Very well.
Would. An american day laborer, hope to live as well. As. The middle classes. Of France.

And who is perfect. The college of France. Is founded. They have. Had. The curiosity.
To please themselves.

Scene I

Mary River. Has hoped. That. An ornament. Is helpful. Also. That. They will love. To be careful. And helpful. And pleasant. And that. There is more. Pleasure. In working. In the fields. In the evening. The college of France is founded.

Andrew Dove. Meets Mary River. And they will inaugurate. Their meaning. Which. Is. That. One brother. Will save. Two of his brothers. From drowning. Very earnestly. By. Not leaving. And. Making every effort. There. Is happiness. Enough. In. Not being troubled.

Scene I

Mary River. Is helpful. When. They carry with them. Their help. And their. Feeling. That. They will be choosing, between selling milk. Or feeling. That. They will please their father. By making of the milk. Cheese. For the evening.

The college of France was founded. At a time. When. They. Were satisfied to need it.

Scene I

Come. With a. Cousin. Come.

Act I

What is the daily habit.
And the past.
What is the present. Sentence.
And. The last.
What is. The daily. Habit.
And the past.
Which they may. Meet. They. May.

Act II

When. They have heard. That.

Wait. That. They may. Incline.
To think. They will be. However.
As they may around.
Who will be stolen. To have. Their care.

Act II Part II

May they. Be graceful. As. A dog.
Or else. Be welcome. As. They are.

Act III

Furthermore. A college. In. Plenty.
They. Will. Scantily.
Read. More. For fervent.
In their touch.
May. Join. Just. In. Penalty.
They will. Be met. By. Shells.

Act IV

They must. Be invited.
And made. To try.
To leave it nightly. That they may cry.
For their wishing.
It is. All told. Separately.
This is what makes the college delightful.

Scene I

Mary Rivers. Or a conundrum.
Accept this. As a little debt.
Contracted. In your favor. Or. Pray.
Against. You. With a thousand.
Excuses. And desire. To remain.
Unknown.

Scene II

Henry Clay and Andrew Dove.
They may counsel them to discover made. Of. Dove.

Henry Clay. And. Andrew Dove.
There is no meadow in turn.
They will accept: To which. They will. Not. Return.
						Henry Clay and General Horne.
Will they be intimate. With. And on. Their account.
May they respect blessings.
It will finally be taught.
May they. Be gently. Further. Than. Their walk.
Very well. Gardening.
Think well of their wish.

Act I

The college of France and the reunion.

Act I Scene I

Does a crow. Resemble. Or. Be joyous.
For they. May. Be felt.
He. Robert. Might. Have been.
Eagles. For fishes.
A. Bell. Is reserved. And. They will try.

Act I Scene I

Mary River. Pleases. In. Harvest. It. Or rather. He arranges. With it.
By. Them. Or whether. There is an interruption.
In hurriedly. Looking. For. Their door. To them.
The college of France. Has learned.
And will. All. Seats of learning.
Which they do. Having. Been fought.

Act I Scene I

Mary Rivers is astonishing.

Scene II

All for you.

Scene III

They agree.

Scene IV

Open the door.

Scene V

And thrive.

Scene VI

Plainly mix.

Scene VII

All is leaven.

Scene VIII

They will abate.

In which. A countryman insisting. Says. Say so. It will. Be. Rhyming better.

Act I

Mary River. Is made. To be a treasure. So is Andrew Dove.

Scene I

The college of France. Has opened. In its past. Which is. Not past. As all. Present is present. And therefor. There is no delay.

Some day.

Scene II

Why is. The college of France impressive. With. No name. Because they will meet a conundrum presently. With. No name. They will be meant to thrive.

It is a comfort to have a wooden table and a velvet chair.

Act II

They will be without doubt unalloyed.

Scene I

It is auspiciously begun.
From sun to sun.

Scene II

Cherished all through.

Scene III

Made generously.

Scene IV

Without care.

Scene V

Made alive.

Scene VI

With pleasure as a prefix.

Scene VII

Made abundantly with seven.

Scene VIII

They made it especially fortunate.

Act II

Mary River, Allen Dove, Andrew Dove and Angel Dove.
They will not diminish their arousing it for being it in and hope.
Mary River has anxiously been here.

Scene I

The college of France opens. And introduces. Whom. They will.
They will also be often made content with a circumstance.
Their name college of France. Pleases.

Scene I

Confidentially thought well fo.

Scene II

Andrew Dove. Is wedded to imminence. And mine.

Henry Clay. In pleasure. And allowance. In coming. And delight. In voyageing. In enumerating. In winding. And in violence. And in volume. They will. For them. In hope. Of. Is it well.

Scene III

General Horne may remember his childhood. At that time he was interested in chemistry. Also in music. Also in William Tell.

Mary River rejoined.

Scene IV

A number before. Is inevitable.

Act II

They entertain. Their hope.

Scene I

Mary River. And clouds.

Which may. Engage. Manages.

With willing.

Scene I

It is well. To know. That.

They will. Find. It. By evening.

Scene II

More than which. Cost.

They will. Which. Lost.

Scene III

By them.

Scene IV

As a. Custom.

Scene V

Made it.   Leave.   Them.

Scene VI

Certainly this evening it will rain.

Act II

Scene I

How many times. Are there. Explanations.
                    Mary River
If she. Will sing. Please. Be. A name.
                    Andrew Dove
Enters. And she and he. Remain apart.
They both say. What they. Think.
That is this.
It is of great interest not only to hear everything but to keep on telling
about it. Also. To be persistent. In the explanation. And. Finally. If not.
Correctly. They will. Be. Not. Without a solution.
                    Mary River
Will be acceptable. As. The conclusion. She will. Have been led. To be
unhappy.
                    Andrew Dove
Hopes that it will. Be a reproof. To husbandmen. In so far. As they must.
Be willing. To keep. On. Laboring.
Once more. Andrew Dove and Mary River are present.

Scene II

Henry Clay. Has been experiencing. In no way. A revolution in thinking. But happily. A beginning. In. Retrospection.

He will add. In more. Than. With them. Their. Thought.

The college of France meeting has. An anniversary.

Scene III

Do be through. Or make. South. Everything.

Act II

It is often cautious to lose men in an institution. And also. Not. A confusion. To be. Prohibiting nothing. Or even. As. As. They may glance. They will plead. Further. As. Would. And. Be a pleasure.

The college of France having. An anniversary. It is interesting.

Mary River

It is astounding. They will. Be often. Here. May they be called. One of them.

They will manage. Further. That. The summer is over.

Andrew Dove

The summer. Is nearly over.

Mary River

They will. Manage that. That. The summer is.   Not nearly. Over.

Andrew Dove

They will manage that. That the summer is not. Nearly over.

Mary River

In waiting. Is not. Open.

To any value. As when.

They meant. This. That.

They have undertaken.

It is very certain. That a garden. Is affiliated. To. The college of France.

Andrew Dove

Mischance.

Scene I

They may be hesitating.

Act III

Henry Clay. May lightly undertake a burden.

Scene I

Nor will I ever. Be angry. Or even. Distant. Again.

Scene II

Andrew Dove.
It is mine. Not to. Blame. Indeed.
To. Be. Frightened.

Scene III

So they will remain hospitable.

Act III

There is a foundation for this fact.
Also for the length. Of. A volume.

Scene I

For. Of four.
Leave. Five. Of four.
To add. To please. Four. Of four.

Scene II

It is difficult. To scent. The air. From the sun. They may. Leave that.
One and one.
They may even wish. One. And one.
May. They. Be. With them.
May they be with them.
They are with them.
As they are with them. With which. They will be. With them.

Scene III

It is. Very valuable. To beg. Of them.
That they will. Abet them. To. Vanish.
May they. Be believed. To be with them.
Which. They will.
They will. Not. Be. Without them.

Scene IV

Just as much. As. Made.
A ferry. Has been replaced. By. A bridge. To be made.
They will resemble. A place. To be made.
By their leaving. It. To them.
He is very beautiful.

Scene V

It is more than their willingness.
More than their willingness.
A pleasure. In more than their willingness.
It is their pleasure. In more than their willingness.
It is a pleasure in more than their willingness.
It is a pleasure in more than their willingness.

Scene VI

May they come. And have. An avoidance. Of their. Pleasure.
They must refuse.

Scene VII

One. Two. Three. Four. Five. Six. Seven.

Part II

Act I

Mary River has bestowed. Their meaning.
To their place.

For them alone.

Scene I

Mary River knows Henry Clay and Andrew Dove.
May they. Be. All. Welcome.
Mary River. May be permitted. To be welcome.
So may Andrew Dove and Henry Clay.
Mary River Andrew Dove and Henry Clay gradually approach in conversation.

Scene I

It is very often that there is a deception.
Not to every one.
There is very often some deception.
To. No one.
There may be a reception.
There has been one.
Will any one be received.
Only those. Who are accustomed.
To welcome.
They may easily. Be taught.
Always to be ready.
In case. Of their. Reappearance.
What is there. When they differ.
They please rather. Than please themselves.

Scene II

They may be alive to satisfaction.
Andrew Dove and Henry Clay speak not of anniversary but of villages.
They will pray be well.
Andrew Dove and Henry Clay are often present.
They will relieve it as an astonishment.

Scene III

Andrew Dove. Has been. And he has come. And they will. Be. With him. One. By one.
Fear is often placed where they wish.

Henry Clay who is not often. Made clearly ready. May care. For this. Which they. Remain. For it.

Henry Clay. One day. In declaring. Reserve. And denial. They may infuse. Joining. To petition.

They will and there will. Be politeness.

Scene IV

There is astonishment at the door.

Scene V

They are readily surmounted. And now. This introduces. An anniversary. And itself.

Act I

A memorial serves as an individual.
They may reconcile. Their homes.
May she or he be very welcome.

Scene I

It is very doubtful if they will recognise well and will.
Andrew Dove
It is merry and just.
To receive a return. For their. Injustice.
They may not feel very well.
Which is why. They will.
Permit it.
And no one calls. One. One.

Henry Clay addressing. Them. It is bedewed in their reserve that they will measure theirs as theirs.

So many have come away.
Andrew Dove
May we hear more of fortune.

Henry Clay continuing. In their delight. Join hope. With night. Might with delight. And fortune to fortune. With. Them.

Andrew Dove. Knew many. Who were members.

It is very pleasant to have an anniversary very often and every. Four hundred years.

Mary River

She may be apathetic.
Or should she praise.
The house. She lived in.
She had lived. In a house.
When she was born.
And so. And so. To say so.
More that. They will include.
Aid and parade.

Andrew Dove

And so there is no mockery.

Henry Clay

Of any one. Or. Of anything.

Scene I

The anniversary of the College of France to which and to whom many
were invited.

Act I

Scene I

Mary River.
Believe in believing they credit thought with thought. Believe that they
will deliver. It. As well. As taught.
And so they reunite.

Andrew Dove

She may be made to rest within their calling. It. Best.
And might. With mountains.
All which. It is. A politeness.
Called readily.
Heraldry.
May be with a dove.
May be with a glove.
May be with them.
May be with this.
May be they will.

Henry Clay

In honor.
And amount.

In their beguiling.
And in trust.
In they will.
In they have.
In their ought.
In joining yes.
Ceremoniously.
More than four one.
For one.
The college of France had been an advance and a preparation.
So they will unite in their may.
The anniversary of the college of France was not in May but in June.
And this is readily controlled. The college of France.

Andrew Dove

Do believe me by themselves.

Mary River

Or which with pleasure.

Henry Clay

In imagination.
The college of France. For their and mine. In it. A mine. Is made. Made
well. For them. Announcement. In by itself. Alone. As she. May be. Thought.
Influenceably. Precious. They may believe in all. Of it. For their known.
Thought. The college of France has been placed there.

Act II

Welcome through.
Than which they were.

Scene I

For their acquaintance.
Andrew Dove. And. Henry Clay.
Andrew Dove. Will love. To say.
That he knows. Henry Clay.
And there is no difference.
In the way. In which. They.
Will remember to say. In which. Way.
They might. Or they could. Know.
That the College of France.
Is. Made. Creditably. Their. Welfare.

Mary River

It is very often thought.
That. They would be. Industrious.
By. Their practice. Of patience.
In waiting. More. Maybe. They.
Will have more. Than they had.
Maybe. They will have. More.
It is. Hopeless. To think well.
Of sameness. More. Than.
They inclined. To hope. To prosper.
They may be. They might.
With them. They might.
They may be prosperous.

Mary River

Was all. Of them. Enjoined.
In May. In being thought. All thought.
They would come here. Because.
Should they be prosperous.
A very beautiful day to-day.
The college of France may wait.
For them. For me.
And little. A little. They. Will. A little.
They will wait a little. For them.
The college of France will wait a little for them.
And this. Makes. Waiting.
What will colleges say.
On. Their birthday.

Scene I

Because of them.

Scene II

Should two. Be. Often.
With them.

Scene III

Accomplishment. An accomplishment.
Of moving. And of. Movement.
Very much. Which. They wondered.
Whether they would be. With them.

Scene IV

Often with a brother-in-law.

Scene I

I had no doubt. I had not known. Nor even heard. Of whom. There is no doubt. That it was not unfamiliar.

Act I

Who knew Lynn.
The college of France.
They will win.
The college of France.
Will win him.

Scene I

They will multiple will they will they will multiply or die. They will. A beaver. Who has made. Home his mother. A gopher who has made. Home his mother. And. Quickly will. They will. Prepare why. In case. Of numbers. That they change. Or change. Or four. Or change. Forty. For it. How many or rather. A. Number.

May they be gracious in excess.
Or address.
Lynn. Has known. Confiscation.

Scene I

Be always. Or why. Has Lynn.
To cry. She cannot sigh.
In excess.
Mary River. In tenderness.
She cannot try. In bought.
In my. Helping. Her.
To try. In. Tenderness.
      Once. Often.
Also Mary River.
A college of France. In order. May they make. It. Merry. On their birth-day.

Andrew Dove

Who remains. Older. Than Andrew Dove.

Henry Clay

Who has had and heard. Help. From them.

Andrew Dove

May they be often complete.

Andrew Dove

Will they help men. To. Be members. Of it.

Henry Clay

They may. Answer. In. A day. For which. They will. Be welcome. To-day.

Henry Clay

Often. As they wish.

Andrew Dove

Henry Clay

There is a hope. That they will wish. Them. Well.
They can be just. As well. As merciful.
They will come. With. Them as they call it theirs.
Who have many do.
One claims. One. Can claim.
One can claim. Them. As the same.
It is very well-fashioned.

Henry Clay

Who likes Andrew Dove.

Andrew Dove

Who likes Henry Clay.

Scene II

A dog can snore.

Scene III

Men more.

Scene IV

Or four.

Scene V

Or a floor or a door.

Act II

What should Lynn do.

And Mary River too.
Or should they just be welcome.

Scene I

The college of France has its anniversary.

Act III

I could be widen as out loud.
Do they forsake.
As she could with.
As suddenly.
Be beset.
Fortunately with.
As they are drawn.

Andrew Dove

How do you care for love.

Henry Clay

With pleasure.
As fully.
As a table.
Is white.

Scene I

Patience is Plain.
Whose patience.
Patience is not. In vain.
Patience. May they. Be merry.

Scene II

She just drew.
Patience. Because.
He may. Be crying.
Nor may they. Be within.

Scene III

They may. Just. Judge.

Scene IV

That they will enchant.
That they will motion.
Enchantment.

Scene V

They will be. Remarkable.

Scene VI

In forty. As many. Minutes.

Scene VII

Should they. Amount. To much.

Scene VIII

In varying. And built.

Scene IX

They must. Incline.

Scene X

To be numerous.

Scene XI

For an excuse. To mean. Much.

Scene XII

For their. Reminding.
That they will. Exchange.

Act IV

Andrew Dove. Startles.
Henry Clay. May be just.

Mary River. Has satisfaction.
Theodore Earle. Should entertain.
Felix Holmes. Is mainly. There. As a reminder.
Vincent Host.   They shall marry.
Arbuthnot Henry.   In a vine. Or perishable.
Erwin Constable.   They may. Mostly. Love this.

Scene I

Andrew Dove is remarkable.   She may be extravagant.   Andrew and Arthur Dove are remarkable.

Henry Clay and their arrangement. Would it be better. To arrange. It. Or should. They mean. And mind. What they do. General Thorne. May be distinguished. Or in. An abhorence. Which they mind. For them. It is very well done. That they finish.

It should be moved. To be. A room.

Scene I

An abandonment. Called. A moon. An anniversary. Called. Coupled. Or could. They estrange. Their. Amount. It is no. Annoyance. To have. All of it guessed.

Who may understand hearing partly.

Act II

Scene I

Did. He. Will. And. Will. He. Tell.
That the name is renowned.
For them. They cherish less.
All. Who may. Be requested.
To come. And. Remain.

Scene I

How old. Is it.
Four. Hundred. Years. Old.
And how many stay with it.
All. Who. Are. Told.
Told. Is an anachronism.
For bold.

Scene I

Who has joined. Them.
All. Who. Have been. Joined. With them.
They cannot be said to be joined with them because once they are joined
with them. They are. Not with them. Insomuch. As they. Are there. They.
Are. They.
And so the College of France. Changes.
It. Opens.
And. It. Closes.
It closes.
And. It opens.
And it. Remains open.
And it. Remains open.

Scene I

The hundredth anniversary.

Scene I

Andrew Dove.

Scene I

The hundredth Anniversary.

Scene I

Andrew Dove.
A miller. Makes. Mills.
A pleasure. Is a pleasure.
Their nouns. Are their nouns.
Forty make a pleasure.
For forty. To make. Pleasure.

Scene I

There are less than forty-one.

Scene I

Andrew Dove.
Who has carried. A river.
Who has. Carried. It. To a river.
They will be silent. While.
They carry it. To a river.
Andrew Dove and Mary River.
They will be happy to know that a river is a ribbon.
They will be happy. To know also.
They will be pleased with themselves. Nevertheless.
They are accustomed.
To find.
That they will please. Every one. When. They. Come. To be. As much.
Coveted.

                    Andrew Dove
Thanks for their time.

Scene II

The hundredth anniversary. When they looked up they missed a dog.
                    Andrew Dove
It is a mistake. To wait.
                    Andrew Dove
And which.
They all. More. Call.
                    Andrew Dove
By and by.
                    Andrew Dove
A word.
At a time.
The college of France. And an audience.
The hundredth anniversary.

Scene I

It is very fortunate. That they. Were made. To be pleasing.
                    Andrew Dove
It is very fortunate. That they were made. To be pleasing.
              Andrew Dove and Mary River

It is. Was very. Fortunate. That they might be. Thought. Opportune. Or. Of which. They were remarkable.

Scene I

Andrew Dove
It is mine. To be seated.
And carefully. It will. Do me good.
                    Andrew Dove and Mary River
They will be careful. To covet. Their hope.
They will. Be allowed. To investigate. Their. Bench.
And so. A judgment. Rules.

Scene I

One hundredth anniversary.
A college. Is. Of France.
And they. Leave. Them. To chance. And they are carefully chosen.

Scene I

    Andrew Dove General Thorne Henry Clay and Mary River
Oh why should it be all that they ask.
Or leave nations to quarrel.
Or shut. The door. A little. At a time. With welcome.
May they be. There. As they. Finish. In opposition.
In this way. Nobody. Was known.
Or having. To have. Troubled. As a. Resource.
Should they change.
Or join.
Or trouble. Them.
Or mean. More. Than they do.
It is. Not that. They expect this.
With them. Or. Their. Doubt.

Scene I

The hundredth anniversary. And one. Which make a two hundredth anniversary one.

Scene I

Andrew Dove
Who can. Suggest. That they might. Be mine.
Or will they. Welcome. All. Who halt.
May they be. Called.
Wire. Or why.

Andrew Dove
There has been. Little harm.

Mary River
In interruption.

Scene I

The third hundredth Anniversary.

Scene I

Andrew Dove.   Felt. Well.
Andrew Dove.   May join.
Andrew Dove.   Sees Seven.
Andrew Dove.   Waits.
And so the one hundredth anniversary. Passes.

Scene I

One. May be. One. Husbandman.
He may be two. In. Between.
He may be three. With a choice.
And they will request. Well.

Scene II

Mary River.   Arriving.
General Thorne.   Patient.
Mary River.   Believing.
General Thorne.   Pleasant.
Andrew Dove.   Made many care.
                   To be there.

Scene III

Mary River.   May mean.
              Not. Mean. Nor.
     There may be. A door.
     To cover. Or. A door.
     To have open. Or. A door.
     The one hundredth anniversary is not. An anniversary. Any more. This
is a question. The two hundredth anniversary is an anniversary before. The
three hundredth anniversary. Which is. The anniversary before. The four
hundredth anniversary.

Scene I

Andrew Dove
     Many think within. A cousin. Nor may they break. A ball. To be. In
recovery. They may search them. With. In. They may. With them. Search
them. With them. Andrew Dove astonishing.

Scene I

The four hundredth anniversary is the anniversary. They are. Celebrating.

Scene I

              Andrew Dove. Sees. Harmoniously
Andrew Dove.   May they.
Andrew Dove.   With. When.
Andrew Dove.   And shelter.
Andrew Dove.   And leave.
Andrew Dove.   With him.
Andrew Dove.   As they mean.
Andrew Dove.   To like.
Andrew Dove.   And dislike.
Andrew Dove.   And lose.
Andrew Dove.   And excuse.
Andrew Dove.   Their mistaking.
Andrew Dove.   No one.
Andrew Dove.   Nor anything.
Andrew Dove.   Quietly.
Andrew Dove.   With. Him.

Andrew Dove.   Made.
Andrew Dove.   For him.
    And so Mary River seems. To have thought very well. Of mankind.
Henry Clay.   In no intermission.
Henry Clay.   Nor in eight.
Henry Clay.   Fourteen. And refreshing.
Henry Clay.   They will well wait.
Henry Clay.   To be. All used.
Henry Clay.   To it.
Henry Clay.   In a way.
Henry Clay.   Just with them.
Henry Clay.   As they say.
General Thorne.   Tobacco. Is formed.
General Thorne.   By growth.
General Thorne.   Grapes. Which.
General Thorne.   Are bruised.
General Thorne.   Can scar.
General Thorne.   Which they are.
General Thorne.   They may.
General Thorne.   Be very well.
General Thorne.   Then.
Mary River.   May subsist.
Mary River.   By itself.
Mary River.   By elf.
Mary River.   Having not.
Mary River.   Destroyed tube-roses.

Scene II

The four hundredth anniversary.

Scene III

She may seem to read.
But really. She often. Falls.
Asleep.
He may seem to enjoy.
But really. Very often.
He falls asleep.

Scene III

This may be two.
The two. Hundredth anniversary.

Scene IV

The three hundredth anniversary and no more.

Act IV

Andrew Dove.   He does love the difference between dove and dove.
Andrew Dove.   Which may they have. As the difference. Which they love.
Andrew Dove.   They have been meant to be. With no mention. Of their principle time. Of needing. One at a time.
Andrew Dove.   They may need.   More time.   To have.   Laid it.   To their charge. Andrew Dove.
Should she or he be boastful.

Scene I

Why should. Mushrooms resemble seaweed.

Scene I

Andrew Dove.   Mentioned. With an absorbtion of with and withdraw.
Henry Clay.   In indifference they may.
Mary River.   Accustoned their having been gainsaid. Or might they. A mountain. In a life time.
The four hundredth anniversary of the college of France.

Scene I

Andrew Dove.   Mechanically one.
Henry Clay.   With their resemblance.
General Thorne. It might be an escape.
Mary River.   With pleasure for none.

Act IV

Scene I

The four hundredth anniversary of the College of France.

Scene II

Just why. They ate.
They will. They. State.
They enjoy. Their state.
In likelihood. Of their. Intact.
Andrew Dove.   Will. A pleasure.
Henry Clay.   May. Is wine.
General Thorne. Lightly. As one wishes.

Scene III

Mary Rivers.   If. They will see.
That there. Is no fear.
Of their avoiding.
Once. A piece. Is taken.
And a grape is pealed.
And a piece. Which they have.
They enjoy.
It is to refuse. This time.
She made. A paper. Be. Disturbing.
The hundredth anniversary of the college of France.
Guide and. Divide.
They please them. And preside.
They may seem. With them.
That. They are to abide.
By the four hundredth anniversary of the College of France.
And then. They should. Bestow.
Ours. Are all mine.

Scene IV

There is a difference between walking to and fro.

Scene I

Should they be won.

Scene I

Ours are how. Well
Fastened with their. Good.
In nigher. Enjoyment.
For them. Fortunately. At a distance.
Should they choose. For. Or them.

Scene II

They will be just. As. A.
Wife will be. Just. As a.
Place. Where they will have.
Rain instead of thunder.
More than they count.
In theirs. In joining.
May they carry. Their four hundredth anniversary. Pleasurably. Which
they do. All. Who call. On account.

Scene I

The college of France, recognises when, then, in, on, of, as, and, the all
at once.
The college of France plays havoc with their chances.
The college of France pleases. In the. Call. Of stations. The college of
France. Disturbs nothing. They will be welcome. Originally.

Scene I

The college of France.
Who has been with whom.
Think well of feeling well.
Play many with a pleasure. As their care. The four hundredth anniver-
sary. Which they share. With many. Whom. They will. Include in coming.
Not as soon. As noon. And so. They share. Their share.

Scene I

Andrew Dove. It may be thought patient of Andrew Dove. Impatient of Andrew Dove.

Scene II

Henry Clay. May they be separately, well aware of this. That they could call. All. Who call. May. All who call.

Scene III

General Thorne.
May. It be thought evenly willing. And should they mend. Their stand. Evenly willing. As they. May mend. Their. And their stand. Even they. Will be felt. To be. Disturbing.
In looking up and down.

Scene IV

Mary River. May. Or.
Mary River. May or.
Mary River. May or may.

Act V

Every day.

Scene I

It is a pleasure to think well of Henry Irving and William Tarrytown also of Henry Winifred and so every one applies.
Love and cries.
And tender ties.
And they may wish.
To relate. With whatever.
And the care. They take.

Scene II

Armandine River feels that no one can defy mountains. No one can defy meadows. No one realise plans and places them where.

They are there.
Mary Rivers and Charles Noble. They will attach. Me. When they will. Fill.
It full.
Mary Rivers and Arthur Dove. They will be pleased with joining as they
love to join it. And never by the arrangement. In their. Accomplishment.
It is not sudden. Nor is there. In meaning.

Scene III

At a banquet, they may share, what they have, and what they bear, and a
hare, may be they may be in no distress, to arrange with them with tenderness,
and chocolate, has a pleasant, flavor, to the pleasure, of their. Intention.
Mary River.   Will you be alone, a river is alone, only in the sense of. Pleasure.
A river is alone. More. Than only. In the sense. Of pleasure. A river is not
alone. Only. Not. In any sense. Of pleasure. And a river flows like the
Rhone.
Mary River. May they mistake. A little river. For a swan.
May they mistake. All. That they take. As a meadow. For a little river.
With a. Swan. Andrew Dove. Will he be welcome. When they have no doubt.
Of their. Intervention. And always. Like that. Will they mention. That
they will. Never. Have any intervention. Nor. May they mention. That
they will never have any intervention.
     In liking it.
Mary River and General Thorne.   A pleasant place to choose, not to have.
Chosen. Nor in their amount. Nor even. As their circumstance. Do be amiably
careful.
Mary River.   A farther. Or a farther. Or aware. As farther. Or more.
Than farther. That they will. Not fail.
Mary River.   It should be always. Made very welcome.

Scene IV

Make it a pleasure.
To have it added.
That a. Carnation. Is tied up.
And a. Rose is likewise tied up.
And a. Piece of the wall.
Has fallen down. Without letting an opening.
     Without letting. An opening. Make it a. Pleasure. That a large amount.
Of wood. Not a. Very large amount of wood. Has been brought. Without it.

Needing. A cutting. But without. It not. Needing cutting. And it. Will be arranged that it will. Be cut. The water-fall. Is still in view. And so. Are you.

The anniversary of the College of France. Four Hundredth.

FINIS

THE FIVE GEORGES

George L.

George M.

George G.

George S and

George of England.

THE FIVE GEORGES

George L.

I know I sit and will
They know their care
For me.
She thinks it is
And better than they can
With wives be theirs.
Have had a ground.

George M.

Out likely in a minute
Leave it clear.
Let it be well enough alone to finish.
Theirs for abstraction.
As they will around.
He asked me would he come.

George G.

At a while in water
With their silk.
My father knew for money.
She was old and it is lost.
They may be came.
In all of it a chance
Made second for.
For me.
It is scarcely their older leading it to that owned wet to be a right for them
to have it held away. Thank you for politely reading notes.

George S.

A butter leaves Scotch butter or my hope.
Or my hope.
With them two to make prudence or my hope.
Love me for often.
I was theirs to be indicated with at once.
As to arrange
My thought.

George of England.

Was he one.
Two are one.
Three how are three two.
Two three carefully.
Ease is not eaves dropping.
In not
Eaves
Dropping.
The help of any one is leave leaves.
They make happiness exciting

George L.

But with by them with now
And wonder why a cow
Does relieve her.

George M.

Believe it or not as you please
She will tease
They may care for me
Or not
As they like
They must think alike
Without a hem
Because it is chosen
Or choose
With a cake that they mean
They eat when they come
I have felt welcome.
Do not bother them with ease
This is in an accounting.
Love and delight. They might.
Beneath Bequeath. Remain. Name.

George G.

A found and fountain.
They glance and vying
To have birds be five by name.
It is an and a just appointment
To come for them
On a stream
With having.
They will decide
Whether there is hope in their whether they will alter.
Water too.

George S.

He could be heard to hurry even
All the names can hurry
Even
Lain among the names
Without an adjustment in reams.
Could he pay for paper.

George of England.

How has Howard payed a place.
He has been loaning theirs in place
In with an all and in
More than announced
Should he pardon jealous and better yet permission
They thank relatively few.
Who can go where they ate.
Yes yesterday was yesterday too
It was not worthless
Will I always cause them
To come.
They will always come.

Books for butter.

George L.

Paved is as regular as layed.
She made pleasures do
As they liked
They were in distress of excellence
In their revision as they made amount
In her pleasure her perfection her reason.
It made relief to their annoyance concerning their around.
Annoyance should never be as likely

George M.

Have all a name
Sing me to sleep.
Ask wives to have been heard held Howard.
Do their thought bought with mature nature.

George G.

He was not even then invited yesterday.
To be awake to-day.
To be to always stay
To carry them away
To have a hope with which to stay
As they went singly on their way
Which may be may a day made day
They think it might be left and right in teasing.

George S and George of England.

How are Howards older than their mother. Mother how old are the chances of being with them there. Did George of England think well of on their account.

ACT II

George of England and George L. sit awhile.
Who ever made it partly habitable.

George M.

Do not do it.

George M.

With them.

George G.

Which they partly know.

All together.

To this in equal parts they will replace it now she must in any in all delight say so. Partly is more than they like as. Utterance for their place. There are three things to know. Place pleasure and acquaintance.

Scene II

The five Georges never made the nearness to likeness be amazing.

George L.

It is very reliable to be often apt to leave them to themselves.
Who do have them hold it.

It is remarkably theirs their learning.
That they have been with them
Enough.
Should it be wrong for them to be told that they were mainly to be told
with them.
It is in choice
Of which they change
Their mainly resolved for it
As a pastime.
Thank you.

George M.

Muse for them to pursue
Vaingloriously as a purchase
They will make their noise
As nobody knows with them
As avoiding add and adore and add in adding adroit in dovetail leaning,
Make it have narrowly their wishing,
They will amount to adding.
No one should do other than they do so
All which of it.
It is not particularly placed
They will enfold
This that they care
Do be without them
To be without them.
The in peace with consideration.
She made doors dance.
As never likely not.
So much in mean
That they mean it
How will they
They will call like them likeness
Which the first
They may with call be heard
Hard without it.
More in a hidden chance
That they will name their blaze.
Thank you for this time.

George G.

He will be asked to pass
And as they can contain

Theirs which make remedy
A please allow
For it to be theirs which as well as heard in offering.
This may be thank and you and offering.
She made it be as well as they might do
Which with without it.
All have to avoid lost because it is a frame in help and wish.
Too many to many thousand and their forty or their cause.
Saddle him with helping that he did it
It might have been that it was bought otherwise.
Very much better than they had it
Which they lost as they helped them.
Thank him for offering welcoming and a butter side to offering
Which made them seem
Hostile.
All of it for more.
How are How are parts made to crease in their expression
Very well for their thanks.
For all of many
For them
                              George S.
Harry has hold of having
And he has been and slain
Turtles
With or without selfish others
Who make hours without us.
How can they be in counting.
She likes him to sit
With them as well as ably
For more than without for their sake.
She must be thought about it
                              George of England.
For them frost and for them
They will for them
Have heard in the meantime for them
As illustration of individual separating all of it with them for them
As they like treasure for them
To have and manage
For them
As well as they do for them
As they must with them by them in amount for them.

Thank you for the Queen of England

Scene III

George L.

They have made a mistake in finish.

They will be without doubt in banish.

They have their minds filled with adding vanish

They must be requested to have to call out welcoming as willing adding a dish.

They must delight in their rival

They must also delight in their arrival

They will be felt to be filled with adding with to finish

They will be in the main not withstanding their arranging this as the way they had better finish with it.

The circumstances have been altered.

George M.

No one knows a cloud

Which they see

As a cloud.

They see a cloud as a cloud.

They are all bothered not at all as a cloud.

They are waiting as a cloud

They have been only told that they are not to be waiting.

As a cloud which will finish,

They are waiting

As a cloud.

It is by no means what they wanted whereas after once they made hearing be hats maybe.

George G.

Who knows goes.

They give goes to knows.

They have heard and waited.

They have been awfully early at a wedding.

Just why

Have they come to ask them.

They will be often caught which they mean as misses and chooses.

Do dictionaries always mean that they are and have been right.

George S.

May we be here.

George of England.

Be here while they last as they will be distributing better what she wants.
What she wants

George L.

Forget me as well as forget me not.

George M.

They pay or pair admirably compare.

George G.

He or she.
May be thoughtless.

George S.

Develop

George of England.

Their thoughts of their boats. Which they like as they will have to have
more in the place of must. She must go.

George L.

Who meant that they looked.

George M.

They were there in their search.

George G.

How do or can it be this.
Which they do or can it be which they did. They have done one with
done withdrawn with then then with then one.

George S.

One and one.

George of England.

Who knows that it is deliberate.

George L.

Herbert coughs.

George M.

And May carries them as they carry them hay where they or rather Carrie
will marry.

George G.

She thinks well of me

George S.

In distribution

George of England.

For as much as they prepare they will it.
Bequeath.

Scene IV

George L.

Made them be careful of their being here.
Which may be always what they will add.
They will be liking what they will think.
That they wish that they were to have had.

George L.

Has happiness in store
And he believes more than ever
That he will be restful and that he will be wanted at the time
In which he will repeat carelessness

George L.

They may be made plain to Mary.
She will marry and hurry,
And he will be thought beautiful
By them.

George L.

Have they changed their mind.

George M.

He will be large
He will have them enlarge
He will be without
Doubt.
Careful.
He will be with them as if they were unjust.

George G.

Carelessly and preferring
That they will awaken.
They will add will they hear of her
As they will talk often of soften
They soften it very often
They soften it for them
And they witness it for them
That they will trouble them
By giving it to them for them
As they will send it for them to them.
And so they think that they shall be blamed.

George S.

Forget forget me not
They will talk readily of more

Than they have
As for their harm
They will beg
That they have rejoicing
Which they might
In inclusion.
They must be held to be aware of fragrance.
They will have their wish with strove.
They will need them.
They must be often within touch of their liking.
Who makes theirs in turn.
Do be without
Which they have called
Reunite
Selfish
In turn.

George S.

A little dog looks for his chair by the door.

George of England.

Have indeed have have them come and whether without their being in trouble for this difficulty.

She made a gesture
Of distaste.

All the Georges.

They will sing as five Georges in memory.

George L.

Just when will I be unhappy.

George M.

It is never necessary to depend on any other

George G.

With me without them

George S.

For it for any reason

George of England.

As a pastime.

George L. and George M.

They came together and they were as much dissatisfied as satisfied.

George G. and George S. came together.

They were each occupied separately in entertainment and reflections.

George of England was alone as was necessary.

George L.

They fasten and I fasten.
They will change the credit.
So that I will have the benefit.
Of their desirability.
Which makes it precisely.
That they were inclined
To be mischievous
Which makes it readily
A commonplace
Just as it is.
They will be awfully well thought out
In leaving it
Just as it was
At any time they meant
To call.
If they like to call me.
They will be patient
Of being vain.
Not as they like
By which they mean them
Cautiously
Of course they do.
It is our chance.
For them
Just as it is
And in no way in carelessness
As in in division
Or much as it
Can mine be mine.
Fortune is made by fastening and fascinating and yet not
As they stretch.
I can go and see history.
Leave it for this.
I leave it for this and then.
They must be hurt by three.
They must be hurt by three readily
And just change
It for them
In time.

George   M.

How are how are hours stout
They are stout by their weeding covered and alone.
And a desirability
Of it.

George G.

She might sit and look at me
But I have been faithful
For this.
Because although it was best
I am not at all interested
In interest
And there would be that it would be willing that they worked.
Hours of all of it.
Finely so much.
Just when
And close.
Is it close to it.

George S.

It is of no interest to know that he went.

George of England.

Hours of eradication.
They mind.
And they do.
That clearly.

Scene V.

George L.

They were well.
I have no thought except to hear my hearing have been heard.
What does George say.
He says that she took this in that way more than within.
They were without.
Do be never without this yes.
They were without.
A halt.
She made them close.
As before
A circumstance.
Think well of me.

George L.

Do not be reproached.
Think well of how to preserve this intact.
Think well when a thorough sadly made is for and come.
Do relive pleases.
George L. had a name.
George L. had a name.
Please cry George L.
George L. comes in and loves.
He must be restrained.
They will placate them.
George L. was very well.
They may be awfully cautious.

George L.

How do you do George L.
Yes thank you.
George L. withstands.
Please spare for them this.
George L. undertakes to remain in an empty place.
They will hearken which is in no way favorable.

George L.

Who knew George L.

George M.

A politeness.
Who knew George M. with him.
They will marry for a mother.
George M. is alone one at a time.
Who can be arranged.
George M. does and in a way masterly is his name. I know. George M.
Who will hope to heat by the moon other than Joan.
George M. listens to a love alone.

George M.

Please seat George M.
They know.
That in the way forever believe me there is an error. In judgment. He was wrong. She was right. And he leaped from the chair so slowly that it was almost a fall.
Thank you for merriment.
And thank you for them.
And thank them.
They will be thanked and everything.

George M.

Field a field is a disappointment.

George G.

Love me.

George S.

They will have forty in their place.
All forty in their place.

George G.

Will you be.

George S.

Ready.

George G.

They need to be ready.

George G.

I knew I was inclined to to well and to be attended by not naming them.
I knew that they would like to be refreshing which they would be and they would like to be without naming them.

George G.

We would be
Readily.
Relieved as they would be.
They would as much as we would be
Able to be ready
To be left to have them
Be there without their naming them.
Naming them.

George S.

For what.
What and for.
This are two accountants.
They make glass blowers.
They fill houses.
They will favor treasures.
They might be cautious.
They have fortunately no real spoon.
She made him put a little in his ear.
This was not why they added him. He was a little dog and he was welcome with them.
How clever of you.

Thank you George of England.
Thank you and thank them for meddling.
Now think well of everything.

George G.

It is not with me.

George S.

All have dotting hoping.
Dotting is in enjoyment.
They will force them.
To refuse them.
They will blame them to have housing.
George of England is everything.

ACT III

Scene I

Quietly in their selection.
They made their leaving planned.
She knew that they would go.

George L.

He asked to say that no one who has praised will leave and for them
sing and dance formally in use of jurisdiction.
She made them thank well
For their delight
That they will make theirs there

George L.

Be tender not with alloy
Nor tenderness.
They will organise chance
And make blessings.
And have parts.
They will know another.
In carrying repetitions
As their fancy.
Fancy that I leave.
I love you.

George M.

Need be a queen.
Forget a city need be a queen.

Love delivery need be a queen.
They will be shrilly
Need be a queen.

George M.

Carelessly.
Need them to be named then with them
Leave them to have made them be for them
Should be with them.
As likely should and rest more of them than they turned as if they could
and with and like them.

George G.

Love to.
Go there
With them.

George S.

Coupled to regretting better than for them.
As a clause.
In their change.
Just more than allowance.
It is a revolt.
To have a boat.
Shelled by a better made
Than carried.
With cover
As sold
A boat
Should matter
That it is
Carload
In remounting
That is it is called so.

George S.

Goats and horses look like dogs when they are white.
They are carefully held.
And may be outwardly
But I doubt it
Craven.

George of England.

May you like me.

George L.

To this in my memory.

George M.

Just as you like.

George L.

Do fairly tower.

George S.

With plain in detail.

George of England.

They will see
That they will manage
It better.

Scene II

George L.

Ready for it yet.
Not yet.
Is he ready for it yet.
He is ready for it yet
As yet
Will he have it yet.
He will have it yet
As yet.
Will he keep it just yet.
He will make it do just yet
Then yet.
It may be better yet.
As well as ever yet
He must mistake yet for yes.

George L.

With them he went away to come away and it is a matter of course that he is away.

George L.

Finally he meant.
Will they give it as sent
Which they go to give them in partly their way.

George M.

Cordially
Do be apprised cordially of the distance which makes them determine resound as individual.

George M.

May be merciful.

He may be taught by known
And with it is a perusal.
It is a perusal that they alight.

     George M.

Made the most.
Of it.

     George G.

Just why may they die.

     George G.

Does better with it.

     George S.

Just made with intention that they barred their wishes it is of course known that they ring the bell at least very well highly.

     George S.

She expected the dog.

     George S.

Is there any difference between hearing them and seeing them.

    George of England.

He was anxious
Because he had seen them
And was waiting

Scene III

     George L.

Do be careful to have well known be partly their earnestness.

     George M.

To be a delight.

     George L.

In three.

     George S.

Ours
divided by Hours.

    George of England.

Happiness is a pastime.
Content is a quarrel
Joining is an incident
And remaining is to admire
They will be named accordingly
For them alone.

Scene III Part II

A doubt has been cast on a memory of their wildness they will be a bother that they come to them.
Does it make any difference to him that they come and go.

Scene IV

A long scene may be to double a division of a stream. Scene IV Who has hoped for more.

Scene IV

George L.

Should they put Herbert there.
They have
He is there
Ladies fair
Make their shade
In their lily
With their hair.

George M.

She makes a paper
Seem like a hyacinth clover
And a leaf
Without which mother
Makes double pansies shrink.
Double pansies how sweet for logs
If she closes the door
Without hurry but with a pleasure
In eating chicken fairly
George M. is made to marry.

George G.

Thou in thousands.

George S.

Butter in freshness.
He knows butter is fresh.

George of England.

He never knew his name was Francis.

ACT III   Scene V

A present little thought he bought.

George L.

Mamie think well.
Ink well
Shady dell
Love a bell
Have a medley
Just then
Just as well.

George L.

Very well.

George M.

Interim
They do not come in.
They hope that in the interim.
They have known them
As they have hoped for them
That they will bother them
If they come in.
Pretty poetry.
Come in.

George G.

How is it difficult a difficulty to have interrupted them lengthily.
But she will be if can burst
In.
Who has hyacinth taught.
Does does it blame them for their hearing them mean him.

George S.

What do you call it if you call it if you call it.
What does he or a hero or or just, loud is aloud and silk in tangle. He never knew only a color.
Just why opposition.

George of England.

Indeed in stream
All the Georges who have known English will now recite.
Aid and bright.
Shut it tight

Love alight
Made it rest and might.
Come to shore
Aided more
Sink and swim with women.
Love it as they can
Jump with all and fan.
A fan is a man made merry
By a cloak.
Who can always be
Just as they think.
As well
As he
With them alone.
To close.
It is without me which is George.

George L.

How are ours how are ours How are ours How are ours. To wade.

George L.

How are theirs to wade. It is mine. Edith which it is mine. Come. In define men and ten in define.

George M.

Ate is different from eight.

George G.

How are ours. Ask it.

George S.

Hurry a boat. I say ought or oat or oats or floats. I say ate oats. I say hurry oats or floats hurry boats and change the niceness of gone. Where have you gone.

George of England.

My dear.
All the Georges are here.
All the Georges who never see each other.
Five Georges make a difference. Not whether.
Weather.
Thank you for thinking of whether.
They gather
Together.
Thank you for thinking whether
They gather
Together

Thank you for thinking whether they are rather to gather
Together.
Whether
They are
To gather
Together.

FINIS

AT PRESENT

A Play

Nothing But Contemporaries Allowed

THEY BRING AND SOME.

George Hugnet.   It is felt wish which are they they might be wonderfully and a wish might men. A woman is wire or more.

Virgil T.   A spring like eye lashes which is released. They think their mother with mother.

Pierre de Massot.   Made is a vainly useful lowered with a repeal. He makes it. Made is why they wean herds.

Bébé B.   Five win baby.

Anita & Basket.   A train or pure purely with all.

Maurice G.   We hope to.

Scene II

They come in and they make it is in reason that make and wake made Mary seen.

Scene II

Charlotte comes in and makes women.

Eugene Berman.   Have hatters had a show.

Pablo Picasso.   So all dogs show their tail they mind a part of yesterday they lay.

Alice B.   When this you see remember me.
Ralph and Elizabeth. They are radicals to the core.

Scene III

Virgil T.   He makes a mistake in time.
   In time is reasonably meant let it left it for them to be accurate it is nicely whenever they are around.
George Hugnet.   Bewilder or fill there he filled it for Saturday in two.
   In the midst of this action two come in everybody keeps guessing they cannot guess. It takes patience to guess I guess yes.
   What is there needed in a dictionary this is a question they ask.
Henry Levinsky.   He comes in.
Bernard Fay.   They who are farther with them.
Mildred Sitwell.   It is well all well all very well. How are Howard to-night Howard and Ursuline.
   Tonny and Anita come in they are not welcome.

Scene II

   The door of the house is the same as part. Now when you say part you mean that it is very pleasant.
Tonny and Genia Berman. They repeat what they say.
                    Ours and ours.
   A wandering brook with them to look as well as with a bay.
   Andre Masson fastens a choice he makes day no delay.
   Andre Masson Eugene Berman and Kristians Tonny sing with a ribbon.
Virgil Thomson.   Buy or by a blind to put horses or a care.
   They will wish it for them for or to me.

Scene III

Avery Hopwood.   Is dead.

Scene IV

Pablo Picasso.   Has his hair made his hair has his hair on his head has his hair. So they or there.
Bravig Imbs.   May remain George as three men may remember George as three men.

ACT II

At present Bernard Fay.

Rene Crevel Pierre de Massot Yves de Longuevialle Herbert Milton and Eric Hauleville and George Neveux and Arthur Acton and William Cook and George Hugnet know Nelly apart.

Act I of a middle act.

At dinner Singria does not sing. After dinner Genia does not disturb a song. Afterwards they will welcome in a direction a correction of well and giving.

Ralph Church was a mother in singing.

Who has translated Ralph Church. Bravig Imbs.

Back to Act II as an ending.

Alice B. tenderly she asks is and are guessing and grading. Mrs. Hugnet makes it be indifferent.

Nobody leaves Maurice for me.

Now we can added Madame L.

Scene II

Bernard Fay and P. Picasso and Christian Berard and William Cook also Robert Graves.

Who has made it do will with them three times in singing.

Women as women.

Scene III

Genia Berman sends a message to George Hugnet.

George Hugnet sends a message to Pierre de Massot.

Pierre de Massot receives a message from me when this you see.

Scene IV

Shut the door.

Two and two make four.

Pablo Picasso mentions that he came.

Singria wakes them up as they go away. He is left a little.

Andreas Walzer is dead.

Scene V

I love my love with an l because she is little I love her with a p because she is pretty.

Scene VI

An antagonism is a flaw an antagonism made of shore a shore is a sea a sample of he with Lee Sherman. He was not invited because it was not certain that it was suitable.

Henry Horwood and McBride. They made speeches in English.

A blonde a blonde can be a Spaniard a blonde can be merrily a Spaniard.

Basket and Anita. He squeaks regularly so does Eugenia. Eugenia who married a postman.

P. Picasso.	I may go and stay.
P. Picasso.	I am younger.
P. Picasso.	I may go and be here.
B. Berard.	I am not acquainted with George who may although many are my cousin.
George Hugnet.	Met is meant and mistaken.

George Hugnet plans a festival.

George Gris could come if he wanted to say, Meyer is a name.

She is bathed in sunshine and flowers.

Scene VI

Will he break the basket. Or let it fall.

Henry Romeike.	Henry Romeike.
Virgil Thomson.	Virgil Thomson.
Pierre de Massot.	Pierre de Massot.
Alice Toklas.	Alice Toklas.
Jenny Chicken.	Jenny Chicken.
Pablo Picasso.	Marie Laurencin.
Helena Guggenheim.	
Humbert Griggs.	
Bravig Imbs and organisation.	

Scene VII

They pardoned the two.

Kristians Tonney and a tall Pole.

Polish who has a pretty manner.

Pavelik.	May be very well.
	But I doubt it.
Jenny Lind.	Sang a song.
Marthe Martine.	Singing.
Cliquet Pleyel.	Makes twenty five a woman.
Virgil Thomson.	By by fifty by.
George Hugnet.	Knows Juando.
George Hugnet.	Knows Maurice.
George Hugnet.	Knows me.

ACT III

Ralph Church and Bernard Fay and wealth and questions. There are no questions to answer. There are relatively no answers to questions.

It is frightfully in doubt not the dinner but back of it.

Bernard.	Will
Ralph.	Do
Edward Sept.	It.
Bernard and Ralph.	Will Edward Sept do it.

A very tall gentleman came in and said he was very good friends with his equally as tall sister who wrote a book about a general. These were Poles from Poland.

Pierre de Massot, Patrick McIver junior and Andre Masson were invited.

Andre Masson's sister.

Pierre de Massot's wife.

Patrick McIver's mother.

They were not the ones known first.

Scene II

Marguerite in case of all.

Scene III

They made weddings. It is all of it as any of it with a parallel.

All who can come can say parallel.

Busy as wooing.

Mr. William Bird has a shop a shop with canaries canaries are red Mr. William Bird has painted his shop a canary red.

Scene III

William Maciver is married to a woman. She is a woman who knows women.
Mrs. Maciver is a woman.

Scene III

P. Picasso.	Met a Pole. They invited him to an invitation.
Mr. Pierre Massot.	Came in and he asked.

Mr. William Virgil Thomson said let it by them.

Mr. Maurice Grosset.	Liked it as a wire.
Mrs. Emanuel Kant.	Needed to be certain that there is a bloom. To a rose.
Mr. George Hugnet.	Was not to blame. That Marguerite was displeased.
Tonney.	Has come.
Basket.	Has been painted.

Mr. William Erving has died of tuberculosis.

Scene IV

They may be measured for their hats but Basket needs a new collar. The
last one did more than wear his hair the last one tore out his hair.

Scene V

Picasso and Tonny.   Have no conversation.

Scene VI

It is very rare to have a scene six.

Scene VI

Harry H. enters and sings. Ellen does.

Scene VII

And what is your name.

T. Thoma.	I have no name in short have no name.
B. Barker.	What is the name of this I adore names.

Scene VII

P. Picasso.   Come and go.
G. Tonny.   Love her so
Henry McBride.   Leave matches be.
V. Thomson.   They are all to me.
V. Bernardine.   She will compel.
P. Tchelitcheff.   Very well after all it is what I like.
B. Berard.   They make classes.
    Baby windows resemble bay windows
    When you think of it.
    Mrs. Margaret and Mrs. Jacqueline.
    May end a scene.

Scene VIII

Pablo Picasso hears Alice talk to a dog.
Pierre de Massot has not come when invited.
Tristan Tzara has found that dogs foundered which is mentioned. He returns horses.
    Mrs. Tristan Tzara is very gracious.
    Mr. Guevara has married. His mother. Without them.
    William Charles Lamb. Have milk with their toast.
    Jacqueline is Jacqueline without hesitation. In spelling.
    May waltzes. Have sisters. In imitation. Of Hyacinths.

Act IV

Le Corbusier and Jeanneret
        and   Fasten it namely.
Maurice Darantiere
    Laura has a library.
    The play is to be now adagio. Will it be andante or adagio and save Laura.
    Save Laura they went there they all went there save Laura.
Me. This would never go into grammar.
Alice and Sarah. They would never go and save Laurie.
        A hymn of praise.

Scene II

Father who made a pleasure.

Tonny Basket and So.   How will they be an ally.
   Not by laying it as much there.
   It is difficult to make candy their fall.
   There believe it or not.

Scene III

Three Poles. One of them bought a picture that is gave it. It is a former.
   They went away.
   Two Russians and two a poles made a Russian pole, russian pole. We
said we did not like we prefer the Russian or the Pole.
   To come back to the present.

Scene IV

   It is awfully easy to not be thinking not at all awfully easy.
Virgin Ophelia.   She is a dog named Cleo.
A candle.   They will say. They have been successful for a protestant
named Ralph.
Bibliography.   They have been successful for a protestant named Jane.
Churches.   They have been successfully this is an effort.
   Jack always has difficulty.
   Lena always has always difficulty.
Birdie.   They made difficulty with them.
James Bush.   He was not dead.

Scene V

George Hugnet.   Can shave.
                  Beards.
George Hugnet.   Can kiss birds.
George Neveux.   Can love hers.
George Maratier. Can nestle.
George Prunet.   Can fish.

Scene VI

There is no doubt that I in believe names.

Scene VI

How many names are there in it.

ACT V

Predict pray so that they cross it out.

Herald Lean.   She made a cake.
Betty Jenny.   She is a mistress of a cook.
Helen Avocat.   Was an old looker on.
Jenny Chicken.   Was an individual.
Henry Thomson.   Was in his youth very short sighted and now is not a famous lawyer.

Scene II

In which they tell it to them.

Scene III

Bernard Fay.   Managed to close his ears.
William Cook.   Managed to doubt if any one had heard that he had an accident.
Why should she ring a bell three times. Why should she ring a bell three times. Because dinner was ready.
Continuation afterwards.
Herman and Elliot Paul. And Bravig Imbs. They came and stated.

Scene IV

It is very pretty to have wishes.
Maurice Darantiere have never seen Pierre de Massot.
With them.
Virgil Thomson has met Kristians Tonny and gone there with them.
George Hugnet has not neglected to attend to something that was missing with them.
And then it is lifeless.
P. Picasso is married and is made interesting with them.
All of it.
They have an allowance.
Geraldine Bonner is not the same as Grace Llwyllen Jones nor David William McIver with them.
They are sweet eaters with them.

Scene I

Bridget Gibb. Who is a wife of genius. She is a wife of genius.
Now realise a genius or genius.

Scene II

Virgil Thomson. Measures scenes in sitting. A sitting room is where they sit.

FINIS

PARLOR

A Play

between parlor of the sisters
and parlor of the Earls

There may be two ways to spell parlor parlor and parlour. Parlour is the old way still preferred by some and parlor is not a new way but a fairly old way preferred by any one. Most of them always spell parlor parlor.

This is a play that will be well as a way to make parlor a day in which they come and there is no way of telling beforehand that they were so and so.

The parlor of the Earles is one or was one parlor. The parlor of the sisters is one parlor. The Earles were sisters with a mother and a father. The sisters are sisters with any number of brothers and sisters and mothers and even fathers and none of them unknown.

Any one can remember anything.

A parlor is not a place to remember anything.

A memory is not the same as remembering anything.

She knows.

The Earles parlor in 1897.

How difficult it is to write 18 instead of 19 when it was difficult to write 19 instead of eighteen. It is difficult to remember anything oh how difficult.

There is no difficulty in remembering parlor. A parlor.

The sisters parlor.

The Earles parlor was a parlor in a house.

Their parlor. The sisters any sisters have as their parlor the room that is spelled parlor.

The Earles parlor was a parlor in a house in Lynn.

Mr. Earle has passed away. Mrs. Earle was very well when she was as one of four. If there are two daughters there are no more than four although they seem more. Why do they seem more.

Mrs. Earle is named Mrs. Earle.

Mr. Earle was named after his pleasure.

He was not placed there it was of no use as to privileges. He had been very useful and was very much maimed. They were both with him. How could they be very pretty as to color and also as to quality in their complexion. She well and very much as a place.

There is nothing untidy in a whole house.

ACT ONE

The Earles have prayers. They do if they pray. What do they say. It is necessary to have chairs unexpectedly. Unexpected is never yesterday. They pray to-day which is Sunday.

We may a name which is May.

The Earles were not named May Lidell.

Sisters are even when they have a cousin.

Two sisters Louise and Mabel. These have not a cousin.

Place that means forward and back.

Their cousin these have several one of them is a nun.

A parlor is where they sit if they wipe dishes.

A parlor is where they sit.

A hope if they own a painful with observation pension. A pension is when they might be a bookkeeper and are a carpenter.

Scene II

No no I knew.

A parlor which I have forgotten.
I have forgotten it so much.

Bring a hope to the fountain sing a song of the mountain.
A scene in the parlor at the Earles. It does not remind you.

Of having met the lot.
An empty lot.
For which they paid.
They were able to pay for it.
Which it is very nice for them to do.
They were not rich as they were poor.
The Mabel Earles which is really the name of one of the daughters were not rich she was not rich nor were her sister or had her father as they were poor.
Next example.
Parlor a play.
The Earles are a family of Parlor a play. They knelt to pray which was why they heard Sunday.
Why they heard Sunday with tries. If you went walking on Sunday.
Parlor with the sisters.
They knew they could not finish parts for me nobody knew what class of society until they saw their parents parents is here used in the sense of friends.
A parlor is where the sisters receive their parents and their parents friends.

Full of means to have friends.
There is a way to have friends.
There is a way. They have to have friends.
The Earles Parlor.
All the Earles are in the parlor. They are in the parlor some one is with them.
Two parlors.
No nobody.
Knows them.
They are used. To parlors.
A sister does not use cotton in a parlor.
The Earle's sisters did use what they pleased they did not have the intention of flourishing. Relinquishing is one word.
How are parlors exact. Exactly alike. They made. Without it.
There has never been any use for deplorably.

The Earles Parlor.
Who are there. That evening they were there and they also had a guest.
The sisters parlor.
In the evening no one was there.

It was later in the morning.
Now think of there being no difference.
          The parlor of the Earles. Mabel Pen Earle. Louise Jenny Earle.
Their friend.
They have never as much as seen the parlor of the sisters. They do not
connect the word parlor with sisters.

          A parlor acquaintance.

Mary Louise Earle it is rarely that she has three names.
Sister Peter.
They have often forgotten their names nor their language.
With them.
They are willing to be after they are there with them.
          An authority.

A parlor is very pleasant at home.
A parlor is just as pleasant as at home.

Easter. Who can tell the difference between Easter.

The word sister.
The seven sisters.
The sundered sisters.
The welcome sister.
The help of a sister.

There is suddenly very much observation of sleeping. The sleeping sisters.
They meant well with women.

What is an effective action.
They will help themselves with going.
The Earle sisters have now been forgotten just as a memory.
I see they observe they will feel well.
Louise Sabine Earle had not to change places but even so she guessed.

They knew that.

A Easter they ate eggs.
This made it as likely as won.

Louise Henry Earle was not born in Texas but in Lynn Massachusetts.

The Parlor of the Earles in Lynn Massachusetts.

They went to hear seasons wishes. They went at a time when they were to have greetings. Which is alone without them. They make it alone.

How can sisters have prayers.

The Earle sisters.

Other sisters.

Have prayers sisters.

I am grateful to the Uruguan. This is a saying.

The Earle parlor was for their mother and their father it is easy without a carpenter. To be without a building. It is different from the back.

The sisters Saint Vincent and Paul they make it. No they do not. They give it.

SAY IT WITH FLOWERS

A Play

George Henry, Henry Henry and Elisabeth Henry.
Subsidiary characters.
Elizabeth and William Long.

Time Louis XI.

Place Gisors.
Action in a cake shop and the sea shore.
Other interests.
The welcoming of a man and his dog and the wish that they would come back
sooner.
George Henry and Elizabeth Henry and Henry Henry ruminating.

Elizabeth and William Long.
Waiting.

Who has asked them to be amiable to me.
She said she was waiting.
George Henry and Elizabeth Henry and Henry Henry.
Who might be asleep if they were not waiting for me.
She.
Elizabeth Henry and Henry Henry and George Henry.
She might be waiting with me.
Henry Henry absolutely ready to be here with me.

Scenery.

The home where they were waiting for William Long to ask them to come along and ask them not to be waiting for them.

Will they be asleep while they are waiting.

They will be pleased with everything.

What is everything.

A hyacinth is everything.

Will they be sleeping while they are waiting for everything.

William Long and Elizabeth Long were so silent you might have heard an egg shell breaking. They were busy all day long with everything.

Elizabeth and William Long were very busy waiting for him to come and bring his dog alone.

Why did they not go with him.

Because they were busy waiting.

ACT I

Formerly they were married women.

They were having dinner as married women.

The cake shop in Gisors.

They did not open the door before.

Elizabeth Ernest and William Long.

Who makes threads pay.

Butter is used as much as hay.

So they will shoulder it in every way

To ask did they expect to come in the month of May.

Ernest and William Long and Elizabeth Long were not happy.

They will meet them and recover with them the afternoon which they were losing.

Elizabeth Long and Ernest Long.

They happen to like it themselves.

William Long.

I go to see if it is best left alone and after a little while they will like it it will not bother them they will not be careful to do it they will think as well as they can about it which is after all what they wish.

Ernest Long and Elizabeth Long are nervous when they hear about Louis the eleventh. They knew that they live in Gisors. They knew that they will not come home any more they know that William Long has gone to the sea shore.

Henry Henry and Elizabeth Henry come in and wish every one a merry Christmas they sing for money.

Who has been invited not to sell but to give away violets with a complaint.

George Henry walks away and in the distance he sees William Long. They need no one to like it noisily.

William Long.

They will be able to have it a hope that it will not rain.

George Henry. Rain is not happily what is to cloud our relation we are thoughtful we prepare to be often more than they disturb and finally it is no way more than their arrangement everybody can wait the arrival of a man and a dog.

Or whether they are serviceable.

William Long follows George Henry and they are thought to be very quiet.

George Henry.

If he heard if I heard mainly for that that if I heard often of it.

William Long.

They may be laying it where they will it is by the time that they are there for as often.

George Henry.

A noise is a pleasure if they come and go.

William Long.

It is never selfish of me to think easily.

Back to Gisors in the cake shop there is Elizabeth Henry and Henry Henry they are seated and the door can be open.

It is very likely that they make it matter. To them. That they are likely to go away. Farther. Than they went before. Because they like it as we have very well heard. Which they mean by what they say.

Elizabeth Long comes in and leaves them to think very well of it.

Elizabeth and Henry Henry.

Every one knows that Louis the eleventh is ill.

Elizabeth Long.

May be they do but I doubt it.

Henry Henry.

No advice is better than this come home easily and bring a hyacinth to your wife and make her happy by giving her this gift and she will be pleased with you and will say so and you will be pleased with her and equally will say so.

Scene II

The sea shore where they are near Gisors.

ACT II

The sea shore where they are near Gisors.

George Henry and William Long come in and see a ship in the distance they sing in unison.

I will be believed.

They make no mistake in their attachment.

George Henry and William Long save themselves for their pleasure. They may be thought to be welcome.

Elizabeth Long and Elizabeth Henry come to the seashore and gather roses. They say they will share their mother. All four of them look longingly and they see the ship and they know it is Louis the eleventh and they are slightly aware of the distances.

George Henry and Elizabeth Long.

Think they are waiting for the approach of their hope that they will be welcome welcomed by a dog and the hope that they will be very welcome when they come. They will be very welcome when they come. They do delight in being very welcome.

George Henry William Long and Christian William have many instances that they mention.

Will William come and will he be welcome.

Will he come and will Louis the Eleventh be willing to have been welcome when he has come.

Will Christian William be welcome.

Will Elizabeth Long be thought to be welcome. Will Elizabeth Henry come. Will George Henry be welcome.

They all stand and cover the happiness they feel as best they can.

It is a preparation for their hearing the preparation.

They all go away.

William Long and Elizabeth Long are waiting they have been discussing waiting.

Will we wait any longer for Henry Henry and Christian William. Will we wait for Elizabeth Henry. Will we wait for George Henry and Christian William. Will we wait for Henry Henry and Christian Henry and Elizabeth Henry and Christian William.

They wait patiently and they see Louis the Eleventh announced as coming and they go away disturbed and laughing.

Who has mentioned Christian William.

Scene II

Gisors and the baker's shop.

William Long and Elizabeth Long and Elizabeth Henry are sitting and they say they are waiting for Christian William and Henry Henry to come with him.

Who is pleased to see something. This is what they are saying.

George Henry and Christian William and Henry Henry come in they all like one another they are pleased that they are all helped by everything. Who can be seen as they are all leaving.

Elizabeth Long and William Long have been waiting.

She likes it.

ACT III

Ernest Long at Gisors.

Narrowly arrayed.
They have adjusted felt to names
They will be at last
With them.
Who does better it.
It is called careless
To think more than they are willing
Close at hand.

Ernest Long waits and Henry and George Henry come and ask him to wait.
They will be often present particularly if they think well of them.

All three of them are waiting and they they go away.
Who is called by the time they come they are called and they will wait for it themselves.

Elizabeth Long and William Long are seen covering the cakes with tissue paper they have to have the door closed at last.
Who may be always known as coming here.
They will be often able to save that.
They will think that Elizabeth is a name and also William.
They will wait while they are careful
They will hope that he is not nervous
They will delight in Louis the Eleventh so they say.
He has been heard to wait three times.
They will be careful to hear them preach

They need to be.
  William Long and Elizabeth Long add to it.
  George Henry and Elizabeth Henry are frequently seen together.
      George Henry and William Long.
Who likes to be near here.

Scene II

  The sea shore
  They all sit down as is natural.
  They may wait for the dog to swim.
  They may also go away.

Scene II

  William Long and Elizabeth Long have asked will they differ as to the matter of saying how do you do.
Be able to be careful.
They think very well of these things.
  George Henry is relieved that is to say he is waiting for a decision.
  Louis the Eleventh is expected at Gisors.
They will not allow them to interfere.
They will not allow them to interfere.
  William Long and Elizabeth Long may well not be a disappointment.
To them.
With them
In them.
They may then.
Will they hope to have her finish it.
Keep away from that door

Scene III

Why is milk good.
    Louis the Eleventh has come to Gisors.
They will ask him to be ready to marry.

Scene IV

  George Henry and William Long.
It is better.

To be most
Most and best
Finally
As it does happen
To matter enough to be that.
They will hope to eat slowly.
Always on account.
If they go
They will seem
To be mine.
In a way
All of it
Very well.
<blockquote>Elizabeth Henry and Elizabeth Long see each other.</blockquote>
Do not be very often thought to be held as they were equal to having it be felt.
A hyacinth is not awkward even in two.
All four meet and do not speak of whether they were there.
They will long to say more than they believe as if they were selfish.
<blockquote>Who made them leave me.</blockquote>
<blockquote>They all go away without Henry Henry and Ernest Long.</blockquote>
Better be with them.
It is better to be with them
And come with them
Because they will need to go there
As they have been waiting for it.
And it is not only that they will but they can be hurt by asking if they were waiting.
They will not come anxiously.

Scene IV

In pleasures they receive
Who has heard them believe
<blockquote>William Long and Elizabeth Henry think of these things.</blockquote>
<blockquote>George Henry and Elizabeth Long.</blockquote>
Follow fairly
They do better than without it
They think it of themselves
They will not be selfish

William Long and Elizabeth Henry and Henry Henry think well of it very
carefully
Who has been heard to give them names for themselves.
They will be very much more than they were with them.
It is is most of all a carriage.
                    Louis the Eleventh is exactly welcome.
Elizabeth Long and Ernest Long come alone to say how do you do singly.
They might be mistaken.
    George Henry and Elizabeth Henry are not made for them.
They will welcome women and then men.
                Louis the Eleventh is not patiently waiting.
        At Gisors Louis the Eleventh is to make his entry.
            Ernest Long and Genevieve Taylor are married.
They have meant to be gracious.

ACT IV

The Scene at Gisors.
Four men come in and two women.
They are not waiting to hear them say when they are coming they will not
presently go away they will be anxious to think this of them.
    George Henry and Ernest Long are waiting. They will be thinking present-
ly of leaving.
    Genevieve Taylor and Elizabeth Long know that they are leaving.
This is made pleasantly.
As if they were having
That they were without.
In its having been
Not carried further.

Scene II

Sixty-five if not seventy then.
They make it different then
When they come to wish them
To think of them
    Henry Henry and Elizabeth and William Long add to it.
They may be careful
Themselves and like to be

Mentioned separately.

Elizabeth Long thinks that she will accompany William Long and Henry Henry.

Elizabeth Henry comes with George Henry and they have to have rested. They were not standing.

Henry Henry.

Think well after carefully.

George Henry.

Be very well told affectionately.

Elizabeth Long.

They may be careful of treasure.

Elizabeth Henry.

They may not be long.

Ernest Long.

Away. They have meant more than they come to attach pleasures in amount. Who is curious as to why they attended.

Louis XI has hopes for France.

Scene III

There is no silence in their attention.
To please them.
They will be careful
To please them.
They will ask them
If it pleases them
That they like to know of it
As it is in a measure
A means of doing good.

Elizabeth Long and William Long stay away while Elizabeth Henry and George Henry put everything where they will be pleased to find that they may place it.

There is an opening of a door and most of the time they are very satisfied. George Henry and Henry Henry have liked Louis the Eleventh.

ACT V

Elizabeth Long asks them not to be made to have them ask them. She is obliged to them for having meant them.

They will be thought to think that they will give them what they would like to have in having had more than they had of them.

Genevieve Henry asks any one what they can do to think well of asking it of them.

George Henry.

Might they not be asked to have been having more than they had with them and so they will ask them to see them with them some of them as they have all of them with all of them as they will give it for them.

They will have if made by them.

They will without be asking it for them.

Elizabeth Henry thinking as she is walking.

They will then be having it for them.

George Henry adding something for nothing.

Thank you very much for asking for everything.

Scene II

Elizabeth Henry having been left to the encouragement of George Henry who said they are following they may be left to have it been heard or borne.

Elizabeth Long hears Elizabeth Henry repeating that she will be told that they were hearing it themselves.

George Henry and Elizabeth Long made it a part of their arrangement that they would wait for Monday.

The sea shore and they wished to remember that it had had a name as well as afterwards.

Who came to be left to have it helped as they were preparing to accustom them to their arrangement.

Scene III

Does dust make feathers they do and does give pleasure.

Leave Genevieve Long to never have pleasure in giving and gaining theirs as mine.

A mine makes a sea shore have a wealth of knowledge of better which they may be in aground.

Elizabeth Long and William Long.

They ought to be noisily in along.

Elizabeth and George Henry make it a return of a present of a melon. Which they have received. As well as chinese nuts. Which they have not. Undertaken to divide.

The tragedy of Louis the Eleventh and Louis the twelfth is that they will have the habit of hurrying.

Scene IV

They will please or they will not.
Which is why they are to originally distinguish between partly and why they have it.
The time that they were able to please is what reminded them of it at first.

Elizabeth Long and Elizabeth Henry come and see that they are without the habit of a purse in the middle. They will be advantageous mutually.
They think of it together.

William Long and Ernest Long and George Henry satisfy themselves as to their wonder.

Ernest Long saying that he has been without wishes.

William Long fairly well as puzzled.
Ernest Long.
They seize aloud in place of which they must they will be had around more than they caught. They will be joined in hurts and places which makes it for them whether they are felt to know now. In placing theirs around.

George Henry and Genevieve come in and please themselves.

Louis the eleventh is a king.
And he looks at anything.
They will think that they have explained this thing.

Scene

The inside of the cake shop.
Elizabeth Long and William Long are waiting and they are ready to sell to those who come in and wish to buy something.

All come in and give them what they are asking for everything that they are selling.

Elizabeth Henry and Ernest Long have made no difference in paying.
George Henry and Henry Henry have not hesitated about paying.
Scene on the sea shore.
Elizabeth Long and Ernest Long and Henry Henry and George Henry come along. They like to leave them as they were too exciting.
Who makes it do for them.
They will be having wealth of bettering which they may with enjoyment.

They all wait and as they wait they must be thought to like to have him be more to them than they were as they were coming.

Louis the eleventh might be reminded that everything is with them.

A scene in the place where they were standing.

How often do they mean to add more to add more to have theirs leave them with that.

William Long.

He was deceived.

He liked him because he was added before.

Before what.

Before they came.

And will willows have their leaves as they do.

They will have their leaves as they do.

They make for them.

They make it for them.

They will have theirs have their insistence that they will prepare theirs with them, which in allowance where theirs in theirs as in which they have in there not in with by the time with in their had with in their resting within the allowance.

She made changes in churches.

He made more than they combine with in a change.

They must be thought for them.   They will be welcomed with them.   It is in spite of quiet.

That they engage them.

In fortunate allowance.

For them.

They meant that they are taking the same as they mean as interruption.

Thank them in eddying.

Scene

Louis the Eleventh had been thought to be pleasant as a witness.

They will arrange more as they follow.

Scene

The sea shore.

William Long.

In welcome and they might.

Might remains as must they leave us.

They will go.

They will prepare whether.

It is falsely an alliance.

They manage to be used to it.
They kindle all of it.
For them shortly.
It is in amusement.
They may be prepared easily.
It is in their manner that they think.
They think that they thought them.
Very gracious.
To be not at all bothered.
In coming together.
To allow further
That they will
Have more of it.
Which is usual.
In the partly shown.
They will quit in hand.
By them By this.
They meant to be at once
Nicely.
Without them.
Could they do it.
Strangely
Not at all thank you.

FINIS

LOUIS XI
AND MADAME GIRAUD

The courtiers make witty remarks. Mike Sally Gabrielle and Danny.

Louis XI

They like to use oil as fuel.
Very well with bought.
They will use women as humming.
Humming is forbidden and why.
Because it means she has had to dry
Les Trompettes de la Mort,
Which is a fungus and edible
With skill.
With well
And as a bell
They will sing.
They need a song with whistling
Leaves are left to the Luxembourg.
And they will say that he did not say what they have to have as a flower
of May or a lady of May from Baltimore.
Now once again it has come to pass that there is a class
There are the rich and the poor.
Thank you for having been ready for anything and an attraction.

Louis XI and kisses

Misses misses kisses
Misses kisses most.
Misses misses kisses

Misses kisses most.

The time came when Louis XI was missing and she said.

I am determined to be king.

And she was obliging

And she admired Mike and the house.

                    Louis XI and Madame Giraud

Any William Johnson will do.

                              Louis XI

Any William Johnson will do

And little boys who follow

When a Jesuit runs too

They run before.

And leave it to look at a dog

Before the dog which is white

Could be discussed.

And they will be strange

Insofar as they are all different

                              Louis XI

She spoke to me.

She asked if she could bring me anything.

I answered no nothing

I did not tell her what I was doing.

Because that would have been a bother.

In the meantime the dog dreamed and what was it louder than ever before.

                    Louis XI and Madame Giraud

She knew the way to disperse the silk so that it covered will cover the
canvas.

                              Louis XI

That was a loud one

                    Louis XI Paulo and a dog

They have been afraid of thirteen as clean.

They make eight late.

They sing singing with I mean

They leave five more as they were

There is a chance that they will prepare water for them.

Which is it.

Made to be liked.

For them.

Will or has Virgil come or Henry or even Ralph with George or Elizabeth
or Georgia.

Not if they are asked

Louis XI thinks of things
Louis XI and Basket and Madame Giraud
She saw to it that he made no preparations for leaving.
Louis XI and Madame Giraud
They are as more than made with eight for them.
Who is Madame Giraud.

Scene II

Louis XI and Paulo
They ask her to have him to have her have and which is it for as they do
as it attaches.
Answer him.
They like to oblige.
Louis XI and the Seine
They may hope that it will seem to like his to subside.
They made a mistake.
Louis XI and Allan and Danny
If they build a house where it is high, it is apt to be dry.
Louis XI and Sarah
They change my family and that is all that they said.
I will soon follow their brother because they have a father.
I will never trouble them to like it.
They like them.
Louis XI and floods.
Hear them ring.
They mistook the number
27 is a number so is fifty
Fifty is a number so is twenty-seven.
They mistook the number.
Louis the eleventh and Michael
For them with them.
For theirs for them.
He knew the way to close them with and by them.
They will never change them for then.
Louis XI and Gabrielle
It was an excuse.
They will have hopes if they are different from being like them.
Louis XI and the sister
She was grateful for cake.

                          Louis XI
When this you see remember me singularly.

                         Scene III

                    Louis XI and a name.
We came to ask him to have it made for him.
He knows he likes a name all the same.
But they need weddings
And a present.
                    Louis XI and William the third
They will provide ears for birds. They may have radishes.
They forget wishes.
                    Louis XI and Jenny Pau
Believe that it was a mistake.
                Louis XI Sarah Gabrielle and Paulo
They think they are selfish they have a little dog that is called dear.
               Louis XI and Henry Richards
A name that adds s to tenderness.

                         Scene IV

    But it is alright.

                         ACT II

Who is through.
               Louis XI in the gardens of the Luxembourg
She made a change.
Once there were no fathers.
Now there are.
They may be taught.
Leave and Leaves.
               Louis XI and the gardens of the Tuileries
She may be taught.
That she thinks
Very well
Of them.
He may take a walk.
They like to leave it to them.

They must be prized.
Which is partly why they like it.
When they have it.
Do believe in who
They like.
They make with them.
A better home
For them
        Louis XI and the garden in which he goes
Do they like a stairway there.
          Louis XI and harmony
In Belley they make music.
We will invite Peter Revel.
          Louis XI and Peter Revel
Think very well
For yourself
And very well.
They think very well
When they have it as a kindness.
There is no disappointment in an assumption.

Scene III

          Louis XI and Peter Revel
He had a father
She made fun of a little girl
It was very carefully done.
I did not think you were in Paris.
          Louis XI and Peter Revel
They may be kind to them.

Scene IV

Four leaf clover makes a weight.
          Louis XI and the Queen of England
She was tardy to-day.
She had to stay
And do her mending.
Which had been forgotten
By some one who should have
Attended to it

This is no reproach it is a fact.

Louis XI

He understood English in english.

Louis XI and Lily Lehman

Who has been beforehand with her.

Louis XI

I knew I saw Madame Giraud.

I knew her when I saw her.

I knew she would like a republic

I knew it when I saw her.

Madame Giraud

I knew I would not like a republic

I knew it when I heard that I had liked it.

I do not like a republic.

But I prefer it.

I prefer a republic.

I knew it when I saw it.

Louis XI

Who has made a change in strings.

Louis XI and Pierre Revel

I knew it and we saw it.

We saw it.

Louis XI and Pierre Revel and his father

My father was a nice man.

He liked wood sawed for him.

He did not care to have it sawed for him.

He preferred that each one should be a long time living.

He was able to have it held for him

As it is often done by them.

Do not thank them

They will like it if you say it to them.

Louis XI and a cleaner

In the little place where they do it

It is often a pleasure to look for it

Because there is much conversation

While they are finding it.

Loius XI and his mother

We and they do not happen to be in comfortable circumstances because
they have moved from Belgium to England.

Was Belgium there.

Louis XI and his friends

He had many friends.

ACT III

Louis XI e and end

Opposed to the Luxembourg.

Which is a garden.

Louis the eleventh.

He was opposed to Paul.

Hs was not opposed to John

John was not opposed to Paul.

Who knows who details

Details provides prevails.

Does she speak

She does.

SCENE I

The gardens of the Luxembourg where priests play boys not romans formerly because they run.

Where dogs are led to smell at trees.

Where there are leaves which are leaves for which leaves are for which there are their trees.

They sit and leave two who are not through but they think they lean when one can does touch a little wheel as long as if it stopped it was not told not to so in as wet.

Madame Giraud is not there yet.

Louis XI and William

They will not name it William.

Louis XI makes pears precious she says she found them near the chateau in a valise.

Louis XI and plain doubling

Who made a double union in Westcot.

Do be changed.

Louis XI is doubtful whether she should do tapestry in the dark.

Scene II

Louis the XI loved a boat
A boat on the Seine
Sinks and leaves.
Leaves which have patterns
They with delight.
Make it be loaned
To administer their confinement
They will go away
Without which it will matter.

Louis XI

Has won gold for France
And in this way.
He has settled she and a girl
He and a wife
He and a friend
They and their mother
The mother and the son Percy.

Scene III

Shattered

Louis XI and an object which they have.
It is well to go and come
And come quicker.
She expected me.
But not so soon.
Which made her retire later
And be happy.

Louis XI and Madame Giraud

Butter.
Butter has long been known.

Louis XI and a home

Home where they are.
Louis XI and a home and their arrangement
Love a wife
And a home.
Go to the woods
Where they all roam

Have heard that they had
A home.

Scene IV

They did not shatter a home
Because they were able to come
And give them a home
To which to come.
                    George and Jane
Who has been heard to say
A name.
Louis XI and all the same.
They came to call for it
They call it by its name.
She will not go
He will not leave
They will not ask
She is resolved
To have the chance
That has been given
To them.

Scene V

Louis XI alone

When I finish a sketch I pass it to some one.
Who receives it.
Thank you for flattery.

One two three
All out but she.
                    Louis XI thinks melodiously
                    And he sits with women.

FINIS

MADAME RECAMIER

AN OPERA

Subsidiary Characters

Allen Pavelik and Cliquet Pleyel

Dependents

Georges Couleur Florence Descotes and Yvonne Marin

Monsieur Humbert and Louis Raynal

Scenes in

Paris Belley and Rome

MOTTO

Once when they were nearly ready they had
ordered it to close

MADAME RECAMIER

Grace is the name of a man yes.

Allen Pavelik and Georges Couleur take their places.

Whose place have they seen in their worry.
They made a calling leave an owl.
An owl is a little bird
It has a sound as if frightening.
And he he pays no attention.

Yvonne Marin
Why will they quarrel of a mother
And in vain if they contend further
And in remaining plainly gather
Which they mean fairly
Oh other other than their farther
They will be leaving mother and brother
They have never seen or felt whether
Leave or leaves and farther.

Allen
Bring bring they go away
Bring they come the way they go
Bring she often is not there
Bring she will be welcome

MADAME RECAMIER

She is reclining
They will prove the length of home
Here where they seated are
In duties which are doves
They will be noiseless
She will have distresses
It is as likely as that Naples is green.
      Madame Recamier has known a queen.

Pavelik

Leave melons and melody
And reaches and revery
Leave letters and let us
And be with them in a plain
In a little valley.

Monsieur Humbert

They will not wait to come to hear me
Leave it at a time as she is well
It must be that it is not pressed in any way
And she will like to have it
liking more than there will be held away from very well.
She is not without leaning nuns as well.
Who does make cake
And happiness with please
It is half of it that they will share with her.
It is by the device of a hat in blackness
She ate nothing.
     Yvonne Marin can go away from home the others cannot.

Scene II

MADAME RECAMIER

Do or did William
Pleasures have come
They must be either
Coming or have come

Janet Scudder

She changes her name

MADAME RECAMIER

By not leaving and in place
They must will they be increasing by grace.
Grace connects with treasure
Treasure is a pleasure
They make a manner
Harbors are through.

Yvonne Marin

It is perfectly a green
That they use in the sun
And here they will allow
That nobody needs a cow
As every one has had one

George Couleur

Has come
In will come
Do come
They do come
Where they are from I
As they may come
To have come
From.

Florence Descotes

Made mannish.

MADAME RECAMIER

It is very welcome to have length of banish
Very welcome to save them and banish
Very much what they want and they will banish
That they like the seed and they will banish
What is why they and why they will leave and vanish.
Thank you for all thought.

Monsieur Humbert

He made reels have fish

And barrels have water for hurting
And they have changes in a way
Because it is barely necessary to have it all
It is what is wanted.

MADAME RECAMIER

Needles are best known where they are
They are mending little thorns and given away
And they are a device for arranging
And she is in the reason why they are selfish
It is not at all grateful to have a home there
They will be often as much invisible
It is very kindly to hope for more
Do so
Do be careful of sparing them too much because employment and courtesy
and to say thank you and do be happily intelligent and make it for me.

Louis Raynal

He will thank you in time.
What is meant by thank you in time.
What is meant by I thank you.

Florence Descotes

The queen Elizabeth was a queen.

Scene II

Once when they were nearly ready they had ordered it to close

Georges Couleur

Obey oh say say she is there for me
It is as getting ready to come there
There where she was sitting
And there she had said
It would be better as much for me
As I liked it when I did see
That it was after said of me
That I was like it was for her
Which is in all they make
Which they will not add brokenly.
And so it was arranged

And we were married.

Florence Descotes
Ambition is made ready by their thanks.

MADAME RECAMIER

She was not better in a minute
With their song with sky so blue
She made hoping he was happier
In left to them to care to like it though
It was enough to come to grieve Saturday
And tapestry
She made a pleasant announcement
Of how many which is how often they were through
Yes he tries to look at you.

Madame Recamier and Monsieur Humbert
She will see through their name
That hiding the same
Is not their shame
No one being to blame
He will see to it that a sound
Is made in going around
Which is why they come
And leave aloud in time.
They will neglect something
Something which is for them
In replacing August with everything
And replacing theirs with none
She meant to be careful
And so did he

Scene III

Monsieur Humbert and Florence Descotes

Florence Descotes
They will imagine I am here
And learning it for me
And they will say
That I fulfilled honorably

Everything that I asked them to give me
And she said
I leave a little more
And I shall be very well pleased
And I will allow them to gather
And give me
Whatever they like.

Monsieur Humbert
There is no need of undertaking
More than that which they give them
Nor is there any arrangement made
To soften it with noise and practice
When they like it as it is spoken
Which may be an authority
For their arrangement
They are thoughtful
And they will be without delight
They must always have heard women
Ask them to come and pray and they will ask it about them.
    George Couleur announces that it has been a pleasure.
He is now to be ready to be anxious.
He has meant to call them to come
They will prepare the way for covering mountains with snow and more
than there was
They will also be certain that there is a connection with hovering and
feeling.
    And they will refuse companionship

Yvonne Marin and Louis Raynal
We will meet Madame Recamier and we will say we hope to be as many
times more thank you they say.

    Madame Recamier coming to be at home having left being older and
being younger.
    It is an incident that a grandson has a red head and left to them par-
ticularly.
    And a little more is appealing

Madame Recamier thinks of Yvonne Marin
Why will they be occasionally left and relish

Which they have.

Yvonnne Marin has come to Paris naturally
Louis Raynal had and left
Monsieur Humbert had also
George Couleur and Florence Descotes had not

Scene IV

MADAME RECAMIER

When they thought
That the worth
Of the hope
They will need
Which is made
For the sake
Of the use
Of the kind
They will share
With the thing
In the thought
They will have
They must attend
They will bequeath
They will disturb
They will correct
They shall with
They can better
They will alter
They do relate.
With extra bending
The most deserved
With all cost
To share hope

Monsieur Humbert

Land and renounce
Demand leaving planned
And adjoin renounce
They will give applause
To them.

Monsieur Humbert

He will be very unlikely
To have been cautious about suddenly
When this is seen by him
As he made Monday his king
Monday can be a king
And also Thursday which is a melody of a king.

MADAME RECAMIER

It is in amount that they are careless.

Florence Descotes

She thinks in wishes

Louis Raynal

In appetites and flourishes

George Couleur

Leave well enough alone
Is said and repeated by him alone
It is my plan to have it left to me
When this you think think well of me

Yvonne Marin

She makes it close
Do this for me
Place it for me
So that I see
That it is there
Where it is placed
In the way
I like it.

George Janvier

I will finish it at first
As they will when they leave most
Most and best.

MADAME RECAMIER

Entirely is a leaf
And letting which is more

They will and can arouse
Named this with all their chance
Of pleasing
The please me.

                              George Janvier
When this you see remember me.

                              Yvonne Marin
It is useless to discover
What they do in liking another

        The scene changes and they are once more in Paris

                    Monsieur Humbert
To practically leave me
With this as well as we
We can be meant reasonably
That they consider that they will leave them with me.
With more of them than they meant would deceive them
Which they will receive as in the presence of them
They will not better it in the way that they had them
In doing so in intending to call them
Which they were in relieving it with them
They must be settled to be separately with them
Which they have in leaving it in regretting for them
That they will allow it to be used with them.

        George Couleur neglects to be thought negligent
He will be careful to send every one that thing
The thing that means that he has undertaken something
That he will not be left with them
They know what they mean by being with him
He knows what they mean by having everything.
                    Yvonne Marin
Out loud is when the mother wishes
When the brother fishes
When the father considers wishes
When the sister supposes wishes
She will change to say to I say I say so.
Let her think of learning nothing.

Let her think of seeing everything
Let her think like that.

Florence Descotes

Never to be restless
Never to be afraid
Never to ask will they come
Never to have made
Never to like having had
Little that is left then
She made it do
One and two
Thank her for everything.

MADAME RECAMIER

It is not thoughtless to think well of them.

Louis Raynal

A place where she sits
Is a place where they were

George Janvier

Recall weddings by war time
And birds by dogs.
Who say so

MADAME RECAMIER

At least no one is careless

George Couleur

Who can be of any assistance

Louis Raynal

As they will think of taking
What they desire most
Most and best.

Scene V

Once when they were very happy they had happiness in store.

MADAME RECAMIER
Think of welcoming all those who are happy to be here.
Also of not neglecting that they will like it best
Nor of protesting that it is one pleasure more
Nor of dividing what is very well done
Nor of delaying in rapidly arranging
Which they do in welcoming
More than they can which is what should be a perpetuity
In leaving it more as it was.

Louis Raynal
It makes be a part of one two three.
She makes it very pleasantly presently
And they were willing to have it made at once
And they will like it when it is submitted
In a fashion of speaking they will like what they have

Yvonne Marin
It is of great use to be able to like to look at clouds.

George Couleur and Florence Descotes
They might like as a man as a man as a wife as a wife with them for in
addition. They will build with them where they will incline to receive it court-
eously just as it came to be about to be done.

George Couleur
The cause of their asking it of me.

Florence Descotes
Without them

George Couleur
With them

Together
They will go there with them.

MADAME RECAMIER
Needs no one

George Janvier

Plays as they like
They play as they like

Mlle Diane Descotes

She knew their brother.

ACT II

Belley

A scene and arrangement. They will have it valuable as a farm.

Monsieur Humbert and Christiane Degallay

We feel used to a sum
And they will shelter us
And they will like theirs
And they will be careful of all of it
They will do what they feel is the reason of letting it be theirs.

Madame Arthur Browne

I know why reasons are given
I know why I have left them there
I do not know what they are giving
I do not like it most of all.
She misses me.

MADAME RECAMIER

Madame Recamier has come and gone

Louis Raynal and Monsieur Humbert

It is a caress is it not
When I ask a dog and a wolf to be one
And a fox to be like a dog and dead
And all the land to be at home

Monsieur Humbert

It is at least not dangerous
And indeed it is not dangerous
Because they bleed it is not dangerous
Because they weed it is not dangerous

Because they succeed if they succeed they are pleased they have been well spoken to suddenly which is why they are careful of hoping for their care. They are not to be there at all any more.

Yvonne Marin
In learning hearing of it to them they who are not she and they are not tormented by being in doubt of their growth.

George Couleur Florence Descotes and Louise an orphan
It is a habit to change a name
And they will be obliging in acknowledging blame because it is steadily because of it that it might be that they could have been women they could have been men. In the meantime they call for them.

MADAME RECAMIER
Two are an authority three are perfectly dear to them they will arrange it that they are perfectly dear to them for them they will be left to have it made as often it is in leaving they were to be in having known obliging.

George Couleur
They think of me with gracefulness and liberty.

Florence Descotes
I can be fearful and not very brave because it is my hope to have to have and leave what they could like in their way careful

Louise an orphan
They are a great many who are often there.

MADAME RECAMIER
It has been a wish that I could know that it is not difficult to have it known that it is so in visiting.

Louis Raynal and Monsieur Humbert
It comes to be a habit
To have seen about how well
They will like me.
Thank you for all who think well of me.
Aria in which they sing Friendship's Flowers.

ACT II

MADAME RECAMIER
Receive hope as a wish.

Yvonne Marin
And receive hope as my wish.

Monsieur Humbert and Louis Raynal
Receive hope as their wish

George Couleur and Florence Descotes
We have hope as our wish

George Janvier
They receive hope as their wish

Christiane Degallay
To leave hope as their wish.

Mlle Descotes
They have hope as their wish

Janet Scudder
They will have their hope as their wish.

Mlle Descotes
It is in very much as they will feel
That it is made to have a hope
That theirs will be met by the hope that wishes are with them in theirs in place of that and to remember that it was their hope to have it with which it is all they like made to be thought that if it was to do she would be known to keep it as it was in not remembrance but in their return of leaving it as much as they could blame entirely in their entirety which is not hope make it a mention of what they could buy if they came but willingly to go and show what had been done to leave it last as any thing can be held hoping not for it but that it is caught in velvet. Velvet can be old in a way so can silk and black is always made a little better in leaving white alone and blue alone and where alone when it is not the hope of she must cherish there with what she had. They will not sell it. Possibly.

Louis Raynal and Monsieur Humbert
We like visiting very well.

MADAME RECAMIER

Having heard that it is a pleasure to be heard to read aloud
She knew that calls are coming to be made in a valley in a plain and on a hill and in a marsh and also in place that is not known as having a hill that arises out of a marsh and is at the same time cool in summer.

Christiane Degallay

It is nicely thought out
All of it.

Scene II

MADAME RECAMIER

In the playing with a ball
Which they like
They will please themselves in waiting
Which they do

Mme Descotes

She makes an arrangement once
In leaving him to have it once

Yvonne Marin and Louis Raynal

In giving it to them at once
They will be pleased to have it.
She will be asked to give it
So that they will like having it
It is best to have given it
And they will be very well able to receive it.
They must be careless in adding it
As they will add it in having had it
It must be partly theirs in have they it
In case that they will be robbed in receiving more than they have of all that there is of it.

Yvonne Marin

In the place of leaving them
A place where any and every one

Is made to have all of it for all of them
In the way they all like to leave it to them
They will add leaving it in adding to them
They will add more of it in having had it without them
They will give it to them after they leave without them
They will make more of it which they will very likely be of the rest of it for
them
And then they sigh.

George Couleur and Florence Descotes
We are married and we see that happiness is all for me which they see.

Louis Raynal
Actively in at a time
When it is best to see why they go whichever way that they do go there.

Christiane Degallay
I will entertain Madame Recamier.

MADAME RECAMIER
I will be pleased to have it known that they will like it as a perfume.
She will like raspberries
And all that is of benefit to those who like it.

Louis Raynal
She meant to be pleased with me

Yvonne Marin
In pleasing others softness is a pleasant pressure

George Janvier
In three there is no distress
In twelve there is no distress
There is no distress.

Louis Raynal
In three there is no distress

Yvonne Marin
In three there is no distress

George Couleur
In there being three there there is no distress.

Mlle Descotes
It is a pleasure to gather what there is there for them to gather

MADAME RECAMIER
In more than there has been to have them come.

Mlle Descotes
With pleasure

Scene III

Marketable space
Alliance of space
There measure of their enjoyment of their leaving it as they would.

MADAME RECAMIER
It is a pity that they see them there
A very great trouble that they do not share
In leaving it for them.
They will credit their liking all more than all of it.

George Couleur
Does he like to ask it to be better

MADAME RECAMIER
They will be there without doubt.

Mlle Descotes
They will have been left to like it better than that for which they were
welcome.
It is very foolish to look for it and yet in a way they will.
For them a naturally anxious moment
In the way of entrance.

George Couleur and Monsieur Humbert
To be displeased is as if asked to have have and to add in all they make
theirs be in an occasion of the wall.
Walls are not better although they have buds.

Walls and buds make it do.

MADAME RECAMIER
It is very often that they make a mention of letting it be and with and by
them.

Yvonne Marin
Should surely hinder nothing.

Louis Raynal
Matter that it does
They will relieve them all
They will be friendly for a time
And it is best for them
To have it.

Christiane Degallay
I need to plead that they will not succeed in giving it to them which they
will do for me surely and very nearly openly and very carefully and temperately
and never occasionally which is a reason for the noise.

Monsieur Humbert
Fragment and hopes and different ways of leaving and either more than
they had meant to give and it is as they have it in that way nearly.

George Couleur
It might be very much their wish and wishes.

Scene IV

Belley is not animated,
To-day the sky is grey,
Every one stays at home
They need all that they have
And they will presently be very pleased
Which is the reason
Which they give
In going there together.

MADAME RECAMIER
Never leave them to come here with them to object to the distribution
with them to arrange the regulation for them.

Louis Raynal and Monsieur Humbert
At this time
They will save
Themselves for them
Which they do
In the Happiness
Of their understanding.

Mlle Descotes

Very nearly
In intention
Not this
In hopes
Of appointment

Yvonne Marin

They leave the rain
They make the door
They have the land
They make the plan
They will be very likely to please
Which they must ask
As well as that
For instance
In the way that they have
Younger ones to leave
Where many go
Named as the place
In their coercion
Made reasonably well
For much of that
In hours of getting it
To have that hope
Much of it which they do
As usefully
It is prepared to have her here
That makes it
Be left to an announcement
Variously and prettily
She will have feathers in her hat
As they have heard it said

By little chains of their elaboration
Made candidly
In orange and in place
Of why they will be mostly in this use
He will come here
And stay.

MADAME RECAMIER renews her acquaintance with Monsieur Humbert
                        and Mlle Descotes
She is partly her own in their anticipation.
Which whenever they went.
They were without a burden
It is a variety in necessary extravagance
And also used in their appointment.
That she will be softly interrupted by their visit.

                        Monsieur Humbert
It is as well to be without in their reverberation in the meantime ways
which are in opening to their site do unexpectedly deliver it as in a tunnel and
they attend the opening and the exit of their voice.
And for it they have many do
This and that
Theirs as well
Without which they conclude
For it alone
By the time
They will abandon
And indeed.

                        Louis Raynal
In the country it is said that when the river Furon overflows

                        Mlle Descotes
Good weather comes and stays

                        George Couleur
With it a wish
May it be so
As they conclude
That they will vanish
In a flood

But then a flood
Can not come here
Where little mountains come to make them call a high mountain a mountain
which is seen and mentioned familiarly as wanting to be there which it is when
seen which it is.

Florence Descotes
I am married to George Couleur.

MADAME RECAMIER

In a very fairly arranged and thought it was kindly meant and wrought
so that in knowing thanks and lost they will be there to go away and not to
stay but to be often in the place of not away when they have made fairly
mention most it is in inclined that they like it for them instantly made surely
in exact in shutting it without theirs and they have found that it is named at
once like theirs in that ready to be eased in any place which makes understanding settled in theirs and entirety left as known to whenever it is caused as an
incense to our fires.

George Janvier
A wedding in a day
And birds are splendid for Sunday
And butter and melons are mellow for winter and Sunday
And theirs is mine for summer and winter and some day.

Monsieur Humbert
In repining with sun and left to adorn which they do by the aid and for
them.

Mlle Descotes
Makes it a by word.

Louis Raynal and Josephine Marin
Will they ever please by naming themselves Louise as she did and as they
do.

Christiane Degallay
I have been hoping hoping hoping every day

Monsieur Humbert
Makes it desirable and to discuss that she has of her a friend.

Madame Sainte Marie Perrin
It has not been my custom to be announced as having been without inquiry left to be thought that it would be mentioned by them more than once.

MADAME RECAMIER
A festivity is a common place to-day.

Mlle Descotes
Any day of being one without any hope of some being seen.
Any hope of being some without any day of being one without some being seen.

Louis and Louise Raynal
They will frighten a son and mother and a half of a wolf. Thank you.
They will say that it was done without any hope of some being some one who came to ask any one asking them to have it done as they would in the mean time for some one.

Louise Descotes
Having changed to being left to fortune they will neglect their affairs.
They will

Monsieur Humbert
In the midst of green they will ask them to place acres.

MADAME RECAMIER
It is a wish that they allow that it is thought that they will wish they will make theirs without their thought they must in this have all as well as bought and if in the mean time it is arranged as it will be that they will neglect doing it in the avoidance of their hope that in the way they can wish they will employ welding in the mixture of their allowance made ready and a bidding of in twice they will manage the matter better.
It is not by the chance of leaving that they will win whatever they could have as being with them and for them as if it meant messages and credit, they will pronounce in veiling hoping with their taste.

Monsieur Humbert
It is negligent

MADAME RECAMIER
Feeling in thought and their words in fancy and pleasures as allowance

and in gratitude they cannot say leaving or might but they will be very with what it is as weighed. She might in time. Leave readily for them. And make it be pronounced. On their account. With it as action.

Monsieur Humbert
Willingly remains reforesting. And theirs as plainly.

MADAME RECAMIER
Who makes a willow have been not sent by two but by one and then formally. It is left with a bitterness in their occasional casualty. It is hope with amusement. It is their tongue. They ask. They leave it with reknowing and renown and they establish chances. Will you please them with me. Will you please me

Monsieur Humbert
It is made restlessness with their deliberation. To say so.
Finally have no thought of their with them as there with me as will it be a ladder fortunately which makes gathering be meaning to be nearer to having.

MADAME RECAMIER
Left fortune to their cost.

Monsieur Humbert
Reserve is for them which is for them that they are measured in their frightening have it be with them that they could in their security be lost. As it is in mischief.

MADAME RECAMIER
Leaves what ever there has been with an appeal.

She leaves for a moment and Mlle Descotes comes in

Will it be best to see them.

They come in

Yes it has been best to see them.

George Janvier
In a pleasure
They will gather

With as rather
Made and whether
In as well
For as soon
When in shutters
Theirs in line
Made in tiling
Which is lost
In their progression
It is now in the room of their report.
Not as it was
Not with
Not for
And not indeed
In their recountal
Farther than they
Can
Should it in chance
They will be as alike
As that
Made nearly
With as plain
And as a motive
In relief
And further in the hope of it
Which is and will be taught
Them.
They can be my allowance.
In really and religion.
And difficultly with hopes of dwelling coming to be had as weighed.
In between time.
All of it shown
With them
With there and here
A joint and open thought of whether it is well to varied in and on account
of measure and a choice of treasure.

Monsieur Humbert

Felt very nearly it was time alone that made them leave what they did
with their shattering it by now.

Mlle Descotes

Finds no time that they should.
And will they call call it as well as often.

Louis Raynal Georges Couleur and Monsieur Humbert

They make it have what they like
When they leave very much to them
In their respect
That they will have plenty of it
As much as they call color
In variety of making it have pleasure
In their arrangement
Which is violently
Raised as a place
In place of plainly for them
In reality it is a measure
Of their contentment.

George Couleur

In place of why they wish it is with a great deal of their arrangement and
for them to make it for me an extra pleasure.

Louis Raynal

Dozens in more than ever without that that they do in partly leaving me.
Which makes it have their reasonableness in partly governing for themselves
more than they have constrained that after all is knowledge without thought
they will be actually attracted by relief and more than they can leave it there
with their own pleasure for which they care.

Monsieur Humbert

It is a relief to have mountains prepare to help the land be fertile a very
great relief.

MADAME RECAMIER Mlle Descotes Florence Descotes and Mlle Duvachat

Who knows how very nearly it is opposite to them who have thought very
well of obtaining in a happiness of their intermediate dwelling on which ever
they will unmistakably seize in the pleasure of an unlikeness to a wilderness
where there are trees. Who can please if not in mounting where they will
always all or gather in determination of determining why it is made without
which they will sing and lavish.

Christiane Degallay
It is partly made mine

Mlle Descotes
Shone without a splendid fact that they are with obliged to see and mounting a selection has been made which they know.

Florence Descotes
Of which they know which is the better.

Mlle Duvachat
In no case have they made it pleasanter to have them come and thereby leave it there.

Christiane Degallay
Not without wishes.

Monsieur Humbert
It is made for them that they will be resting.

George Couleur
Partly for me

Louis Raynal
In plenty of their own with their intention

Monsieur Humbert
Just as it was well just as it was.

Louis Raynal
They will be having it just as it was

George Couleur
Just as it was

Mlle Descotes
Made is the same as made for them they are as very well known.
In partly there.

George Janvier
Matter is more to them

For them it is their plan
With and without in little stretches.

Farther than with and that it can in their hope making it different that
it does and will and without blame can be their relief with a hope that it does
make it leave alone an opening without place which makes it caught having
heard left it to lay the matter before them.

MADAME RECAMIER

By the time that they will go
Who goes in joining places to their plainly adding theirs.
They will attribute in it as it calls
Who makes it better that they come away
From relief of what it is most to have
In little measures which they can belie
In liking they must have more to reunite
It is as well that they can call it for them
It is a better name than after all a very little will do now.
Do or do not in all of it a pleasure.
He will come and he will disturb those who know

That it is always well to think that it is taught as readily by them as if they
were undertaken to go away every day fairly as if when about which they need
to think it is not by the time that they are willing leave it in rapidly shown
finally made as it were a finely readily as well as there. They will have made it
singularly real to have it be theirs which it is more in case of that it is what
does it differ wherein and more leaves are without a pleasure they are poplar
leaves they are the leaves that are without that measure made in and with
namely their better hope of never with and without pause able to relatively wait
in their adjoining just as many have a better than their own in names which
can be often after any all in written. They will think well of many that is
plainly all that this is why to go away and this is why to stay do better what this
is for me.

When this they see they can as well as will remember me.

ACT III

ROME
THEY ARE INDIFFERENT WHETHER THE WIND BLOWS NOT INDIFFERENT TO THE WIND BUT INDIFFERENT WHETHER THE WIND BLOWS.

Scene I

Monsieur Humbert Cliquet Pleyel and Mlle Descotes
In this instance they will manage arrangements for the pleasure of acknowledging that they came there to have it known that it is best to be reminded of their agreeable reason for being separated in the middle of their exchange of the fashion of being without aid in the opportunity which is accomplished as they interested in not neglecting may be in an alteration of their meaning which they had as they were present in no sense with carelessness nor best allowed for them to challenge in their change made ready in a chance that they will blossom as they call it hers for them made more in all and on account of their preparation to go with them as it was on account of a requital which they furnished in hoping for it as it was managed in the pretty way of sailing from to-day and yesterday where they went as it is mine.

Pavelik and Mlle Descotes
It is in no sense their chance
That they will yield
And place it there
Where they will like
Which hopes for that
Where they will make it do
For them.

Cliquet Pleyel wandering meets them
How do you do
Very well I thank you
And where have you been
We have been very pleased with what we were doing.

MADAME RECAMIER
In making Rome be selfish

Who has been wonderful with them
They are an appreciation
Of all who can be heard
They will allow whatever
They will care to have
And they will oblige them
To come and be pleased
They will not neglect
Nor do they adventure
To have announcements
Made for them
They will be evidently attentive
They will attach ribbons for many reasons
And they will all like that.

Cliquet Pleyel comes in
Who has been heard to laugh at women. They do and they can be con-
tradicted

Pavelik and Mlle Descotes come in and stay
Madame Recamier speaks to all of them
It is not a very ingenuous task to find that they walk as they stand well
and vigorously nor is it at all a doubtful thing to have it be a temptation they
will arouse more of them than they might of if they had been with one of them
as a beginning which they consider that it could be best to ask it of them as
they are women. Who are women. They are women.

Pavelik and Mlle Descotes and Allen
It is time that they no longer stayed out in the sunshine

Monsieur Humbert and Christiane Degallay
Once every day and in almost that way they could think of everything.
They will be remarkable they will coincide they will account for it and they will
be in distress they will have it as an advantage and they will like it clouded they
will be perfect and they will change water on flowers and they will put back not
put back what has been put away and in this way they will enjoy September.

MADAME RECAMIER

In lingering longer
And leaving them
They will think

That it is fortunate
That they will gather
What they like
Which they have
And will do.

Scene II

Monsieur Humbert and Pavelik

It was about that that they thought
They will value that in this way
It is necessary that they should like
What it is wisely that they manage
To have theirs.
They will originate that finally
In precisely the fashion that they like
They must in their variation believe
That it is as well that they are attentive
They will have it made in the fashion of their being
With which they will welcome theirs

As they have managed principally that they are in that way effective for their result

In and leaving they will change this with windows and that that which they will resign.

They will finally distribute what with in case of their injustice it is for this for them

When they will think readily

When they will be foremost

In the having it which is needed for that that which they like in rapidly indubitably ran. It is not only for it that they can in their hope just as when it is rapidly left to inaugurate made in a plan their in place which is truly a necessity.

When they can be hurried they can be made as if they wish

When they must use this they do not feel it to have made it through their usage which they mean to measure. They do mean to have both

They may in the meantime leave it suddenly. They may for the reason that praise is praise be after in the meantime should it be with them. They must account for this. They will be known as if they were more than they were established. Who has praised whom. In effect it is made theirs as fervently as it is mine.

Mlle Descotes

She may be readily for it in the meaning of made with and more than they care.

Monsieur Humbert and Pavelik

It is never rudely to remind them that they will have hopes and hope to favorably leave with the hope of theirs. They will leave it to the bettering of theirs with mine.

They will not be all of it in politely and as a strain of reference to make all of it uncloud in their report.

And do they wish me to go.

Mlle Descotes

It is partly for a time that praises which do color their information loses for itself all of it.

Monsieur Humbert and Pavelik

It is not often that they are willing to come.

They are very readily searched to find many have a plan of pressure and they will mind. They mind us very well they do as we say.

Mlle Descotes

There is no mischief meant in their withdrawal.

Allen and Monsieur Humbert

They will mind what has been heard but not at once and not readily they will also interest themselves.

Cliquet Pleyel

Just as to be generous

MADAME RECAMIER

In and appoint
Which they do
They must think
And with thoughts
So that leaves
Have meant rights
And let falling
Makes it be
What they relieve

In their account
On that refusal
To be thought
By their share
Of which pleases
Made necessarily accustomed
In an allowance
Of ineffective joining
Of their detachment
To their use
Which is meant
By appointing them
In their abundance
Usefully in choice
In added repetition
To their amusement
As they like.

Monsieur Humbert and Pavelik

Leave it be mentioned that theirs is their gain. They know nervously that they will belie it in their case by the time that it is wished that they will be requited by finery.

Allen and Cliquet Pleyel

Do often go together.

Christiane Degallay

Makes a time to cry.

Mlle Descotes

In their reunion there is a preference.
In their reunion they must be their own.

Allen and Cliquet Pleyel

Feel that it is no hindrance

Monsieur Humbert and Pavelik

Are very well pleased with the result.

Mlle Descotes visiting Christiane Degallay

And who has any hope of their failing in having many see the plain from which they can see that.

They will be a little more than pleased that they have been faithful to their permission that all of it is dependable as when no one is disappointed. They will have a pleasure in their relief that is they will leave more than they have liked. They will ask for it in and by an intermediate they will be calm and they will have preferred their intention.

Mlle Descotes and Monsieur Humbert

They will astonish and wish.

They will prepare and they will prefer to care as they do for that which they have been able to have left to their partly in relief of precision. It is not at all taught.

Monsieur Humbert and Pavelik

They will manage to hurry and they will be greatly exhausted by their detention.

Monsieur Humbert makes it be his own by his place

How many thousands make how many hundreds.

Allen

Four and twenty thousands make four hundreds and twenty thousands

Allen and Christiane Degallay

It is not by blindness that they separate money from money.

Pavelik

There is an appointment in intermittance
Which they share

Allen and Mlle Descotes and Monsieur Humbert

It is not that they manage not to have an opportunity to plainly arouse them from their relation to following their mother.

Who knows how many fancies there are in their despatch.

Mlle Descotes

There is plenty of hope agreeably.

Monsieur Humbert

Finally all cases are presented in isolation they will languish

Pavelik and Christian Degallay
Formerly two meant when three went and now how often are there doors
in selfish doors in selfish and places where they will call them for me.
Monsieur Humbert
Next time and very much it is an interest in advantage.

George Janvier
Name them.

Madame Recamier comes to be here
It is on account of their meaning
Which is it that they will have heard her voice.
It is by their naming pointing that they will color their house.
They will be wealthy in their choosing they will adorn water with houses
They will pass the winter in their measure and they will be by themselves
in their strangely choosing the rest of the weather. It is pleasant weather.
She would be very much pleased with a return of plains.
Plains is where Rome is meant.
It is an opening with and for them.

Pavelik and Mlle Descotes
Do be careful and patient in summer.

MADAME RECAMIER
For them fortunately
With them
They will like a feeling
Of the inference
Of how they manage
To have all of it
Be worthy of their ease
Which makes it variedly
A chosen site
For voyaging.
They will be meant plainly
If it is feasible
Which they entertain
As parlors have glass
They will not buy it without it.
They like it to be loyal
They will be and prejudice

Of their betrothal
Which is why many come
And very often
It is always alike
In a seam.
They know
That it is so
That they will learn
That they announce
That they gather better
That rounds are lent
That merely very well
She will go there
It is in an amount
And they will carry it away
In their determination
To surround
Them with it.
It is not by their announcement
That they gather pleasure
They will do that badly
And they will leave all theirs
In the habit of winning
Which is by relief
In the case of care
It is very careful in the hope of Louise.

Monsieur Humbert and Allen

They made many of them train them with them in the same intention of leaving them with them they have been with them they will manage to have it known that they are allowed to have any one of them mingle dislike of them with their arrangement of their announcing that they will not go there without them at all neither ever for them.

Pavelik and Madame Recamier

Who knows how often it has been carried away.
Not far away.
Yes as they will have it made
And they leave a choice of their said. They said.

Pavelik and George Janvier

But politely.
Firmly
Lamely
Namely.
How many houses are there there.

George Janvier

Fortunately three.

Pavelik

Four

Allen

Four more is never said

Christiane

To me.

Mlle Descotes

Why do they wish to finish

Allen

Because they need to be sure to be there on their return.

Monsieur Humbert

It is not as they have it to be known that he tries.

Mlle Descotes

She must be able to reverse the better known relief that it is they that they
hope when they attach them.

Monsieur Humbert and Mlle Descotes

Fortunately two are felt.

Last Scene

Monsieur Humbert comes to be sent and they know that he is here.

MADAME RECAMIER

For which they thank him.
He will be ready to thank me.

He will not be careful of a boat.
He will be in doubt of why they are likely to fish
They must be all of them nearly finished
They will all of them like what they see.
When they see them they will furnish them with reproaches.
They will have no objection to their liking what is known as well.
They will second what they can see presently
They will allow what they know as his.
They will see that they like what they will finish
They will come when they fasten better
Than it is in their share of choice.
Which makes gain of their letting it be ready
It is not with it that they must manage
They will account for it by their choice
They will know they will name reasons
They will do what they can lead the way
They will like which it is and they are lining
What they know for them which is what they will like as they will say
They will not say.

Monsieur Humbert enters and says that he does not wish to intrude.

MADAME RECAMIER
You do not intrude neither do they. They do not intrude neither will they.
They will not intrude.
Who knows when they go out.
They go out as if they had been about.
They will stand and call. Many are one at a time

Pavelik and Allen
We come to say so.

George Janvier and Cliquet Pleyel
Very well.

Monsieur Humbert and Mlle Descotes
Very well.

Cliquet Pleyel and Monsieur Humbert and Christiane Degallay and Mlle Descotes
Very well.

A MOVIE

Eyes are a surprise
Printzess a dream
Buzz is spelled with z
Fuss is spelled with s
So is business.
The UNITED STATES is comical.
Now I want to tell you about the Monroe doctrine. We think very nicely we think very well of the Monroe doctrine.

American painter painting in French country near railroad track. Mobilisation locomotive passes with notification for villages.

Where are American tourists to buy my pictures sacre nom d'un pipe says the american painter.

American painter sits in cafe and contemplates empty pocket book as taxi cabs file through Paris carrying French soldiers to battle of the Marne. I guess I'll be a taxi driver here in gay Paree says the american painter.

Painter sits in studio trying to learn names of streets with help of Bretonne peasant femme de menage. He becomes taxi driver. Ordinary street scene in war time Paris.

Being lazy about getting up in the mornings he spends some of his dark nights in teaching Bretonne femme de menage peasant girl how to drive the taxi so she can replace him when he wants to sleep.

America comes into the war american painter wants to be american soldier. Personnel officer interviews him. What have you been doing, taxiing. You know Paris, Secret Service for you go on taxiing.

He goes on taxiing and he teaches Bretonne f. m. english so she can take his place if need be.

One night he reads his paper under the light. Policeman tells him to move up, don't want to wants to read.

Man comes up wants to go to the station.

Painter has to take him. Gets back, reading again.

Another man comes wants to go to the station. Painter takes him.

Comes back to read again. Two american officers come up. Want to go to the station.

Painter says Tired of the station take you to Berlin if you like. No station.

Officers say give you a lot if you take us outside town on way to the south, first big town.

He says alright got to stop at home first to get his coat.

Stops at home calls out to Bretonne f. m. Get busy telegraph to all your relations, you have them all over, ask have you any american officers staying forever. Be back to-morrow.

Back to-morrow. Called up by chief secret service. Goes to see him. Money has been disappearing out of quartermaster's department in chunks. You've got a free hand. Find out something.

Goes home. Finds f. m. Bretonne surrounded with telegrams and letters from relatives. Americans everywhere but everywhere. She groans. Funny Americans everywhere but everywhere they all said. Many funny Americans everywhere. Two Americans not so funny here my fifth cousin says, she is helping in the hospital in Avignon. Such a sweet american soldier. So young so tall so tender. Not very badly hurt but will stay a long long time. He has been visited by american officers who live in a villa. Two such nice ladies live there too and they spend and they spend, they buy all the good sweet food in Avignon. "Is that something William Sir," says the Bretonne f. m.

Its snowing but no matter we will get there in the taxi. Take us two days and two nights you inside and me out. Hurry. They start, the funny little taxi goes over the mountains with and without assistance, all tired out he is inside, she driving when they turn down the hill into Avignon. Just then two Americans on motor cycles come on and Bretonne f. m. losing her head grand smash. American painter wakes up burned, he sees the two and says by God and makes believe he is dead. The two are very helpful. A team comes along and takes american painter and all to hospital. Two Americans ride off on motor cycles direction of Nimes and Pont du Gard.

Arrival at hospital, interview with the wounded American who described two american officers who had been like brothers to him, didn't think any officers could be so chummy with a soldier. Took me out treated me, cigarettes everything fine.

Where have they gone on to, to Nimes.

Yes Pont du Gard.

American painter in bed in charge of french nursing nun but manages to escape and leave for Pont du Gard in mended taxi. There under the shadow of that imperishable monument of the might and industry of ancient Rome exciting duel. French gendarme american painter, taxi, f. m. Bretonne, two american crooks with motor cycles on which they try to escape over the top of the Pont du Gard, great stunt, they are finally captured. They have been the receivers of the stolen money.

After many other adventures so famous has become the american painter, Bretonne femme de menage and taxi that in the march under the arch at the final triumph of the allies the taxi at the special request of General Pershing brings up the rear of the procession after the tanks, the Bretonne driving and the american painter inside waving the american flag Old Glory and the tricolor

CURTAIN.

FILM

DEUX SŒURS QUI NE SONT PAS SŒURS

Au coin d'une rue d'un boulevard extérieur de Paris une blanchisseuse d'un certain âge avec son paquet de linge qu'elle était en train de livrer, s'arrête pour prendre dans ses mains et regarder la photo de deux caniches blancs et elle la regarde avec ardeur. Une automobile de deux places stationnait le long du trottoir. Tout à coup, deux dames en descendent et se précipitent sur la blanchisseuse en demandant à voir la photo. Elle la fait voir et les deux dames sont pleines d'admiration jusqu'au moment où une jeune femme qui est coiffée comme si elle venait d'avoir un prix au concours de beauté et après s'être égarée dans la rue, passe et à ce moment voit l'auto vide, se dépêche d'entrer et se met à pleurer. A ce moment, les deux dames entrent dans l'auto et jettent la jeune femme dehors. Elle tombe contre la blanchisseuse qui commence à la questionner, et l'auto, conduite par les deux dames part, et tout à coup la blanchisseuse voit qu'elle n'a plus sa photo. Elle voit un jeune homme et elle lui raconte tout de suite l'histoire.

Quelques heures plus tard, devant un bureau de placement, rue du Dragon, il y a une autre blanchisseuse plus jeune avec son paquet de linge. La voiture des deux dames approche, s'arrête, et les deux dames descendent et font voir à la blanchisseuse la photo des deux caniches blancs. Elle regarde avec plaisir et excitation, mais c'est tout. Juste à ce moment la jeune femme du prix de beauté approche pousse un cri de joie et se précipite vers la voiture. Les deux dames entrent dans leur auto et, en entrant, laissent tomber un petit paquet, mais toujours elles sont en possession de la photo et elles partent précipitamment.

Le surlendemain la première blanchisseuse est encore dans sa rue avec son paquet de linge et elle voit la jeune femme du prix de beauté approcher avec un petit paquet à la main. Et en même temps elle voit le jeune homme. Ils sont tous les trois alors ensemble et tout à coup elle passe, l'auto, avec les deux dames et il y a avec elles un vrai caniche blanc et dans la bouche du caniche est un petit paquet. Les trois sur le trottoir le regarde passer et n'y comprennent rien.